HOMEBUILDING & RENOVATING MAGAZINE

BOOK OF

contemporary Homes

39 INSPIRATIONAL INDIVIDUALLY DESIGNED HOMES

344 PAGES ■ 351 COLOUR PHOTOS ■ 59 COLOUR ILLUSTRATIONS

OVOLO

HOMEBUILDING & RENOVATING MAGAZINE
BOOK OF
contemporary Homes

SECOND EDITION

OVOLO

Ovolo Publishing
1 The Granary, Brook Farm,
Ellington, Huntingdon,
Cambridgeshire
PE28 0AE

This edition © 2006 Ovolo Publishing Ltd,
1 The Granary, Brook Farm, Ellington, Cambridgeshire PE28 0AE.
Original text and illustrations © 2003-2006 Ascent Publishing Ltd,
2 Sugarbrook Court, Aston Road, Bromsgrove B60 3EX

ISBN: 0 9548674 6 7
(ISBN13: 9780954867461)

**The material in this book previously appeared in Homebuilding & Renovating magazine –
Britain's best selling monthly for self-builders and renovators (www.homebuilding.co.uk).
Some of the homes featured in this edition previously appeared in the first edition.**

Book Design: Gill Lockhart

This edition published by Ovolo Publishing Ltd, November 2006
Printed in China

**For more information on books about property
visit: www.ovolopublishing.co.uk
email: info@ovolopublishing.co.uk
or call: 01480 891595 (24 hours)**

CONTENTS

➤

■ CONTENTS

FOREWORD

THIS BOOK SHOULD sit on every planning officer's desk as a timely reminder that contemporary design can add terrific visual value to almost any location. The houses in this book form an extraordinary testament to the skill and artistry of home designers and architects working in Britain today and the vision and passion of their self-builder clients who are commissioning buildings that are both beautiful to look at and practical to live in.

The 39 houses in this second edition of *The Homebuilding & Renovating Book of Contemporary Homes* are just a proportion of the self-build projects featured every month in *Homebuilding & Renovating* magazine. It is only when you see them grouped like this that you can fully grasp the importance for housing innovation of the self-build community.

While speculative housebuilders large and small concentrate on repeating a relatively limited repertoire of designs – largely based on a tired reworking of vernacular themes – self-builders are striking out to produce homes which are not only the envy of buyers today but are the classics of tomorrow.

But the innovation isn't just in external design. There is innovation too in the use of materials and building techniques, from structural insulated panels through to insulated concrete forms and in the many ways of utilising timber. Self-builders are using prefabrication techniques, basements, extraordinary levels of insulation as well as green technology such as rainwater harvesting and grey water recycling.

This book is, first and foremost, a celebration of great homes, great buildings and great self-buildings! Enjoy leafing through the hundreds of superb photographs and dream. But remember that all of these buildings began as dreams and it was the determination and vision of these self-builders which have lead to such fantastic results.

There's no reason why we should not be featuring a home you have created in a future edition of this book. And to help you we have included details of architects, builders, contractors and suppliers with every one of the 39 homes featured in these pages.

Finally, I salute every one of the self-builders whose labours appear in these pages.

'THESE HOUSES FORM AN EXTRAORDINARY TESTAMENT TO THE SKILL AND ARTISTRY OF BRITISH ARCHITECTS AND THE VISION AND PASSION OF THEIR SELF-BUILDER CLIENTS'

Michael Holmes, Editor-in-Chief, Homebuilding & Renovating magazine

COOL CUBED

BUILDING A CONTEMPORARY-STYLE MINIMALIST HOME

Daniel and Angela Mok's new home in Surrey took three years on site and countless reworkings before completion; the result is a triumph of minimal design and refined engineering.

WORDS: ANGELA PERTUSINI   PHOTOGRAPHY: PHILIP BIER

THE FIRST THING you notice when arriving at Daniel and Angela Mok's home is how uninteresting it is — different from its neighbours, admittedly, but so blank-faced and underwhelming that you wonder if you've got the address right. The Moks' house could be said to lack kerb appeal if the deluxe, drive-everywhere Surrey estate on which they live had a pavement from which to view it.

Whereas the other houses on this titivated private road have opted for pillars, porticoes, complex webs of Tudorbethan beaming, feature windows and all round architectural bling, the Mok house offers a short, plain, two storey elevation with a run of garage doors and a large window above. It's a slightly disconcerting moment as the judges scratch their heads, exchange nervous glances and wonder if they have got the details mixed up with another entrant.

But, in what amounts to an abracadabra moment, all is revealed the moment the (rather plain, unostentatious) gate slides back with expensive smoothness and we walk around to the side of the house. Daniel, obviously used to this reaction, grins as our eyes open wide and the clichéd but inevitable "wows" and gushings start. For he has built the most magnificent, most extraordinarily precise and beautifully engineered contemporary house.

It is vast: stretching for what seems like forever from its front to its back walls, but the long runs of glass on the ground floor achieve the impossible – giving the impression that this huge rectangular structure appears to float above its manicured lawn surroundings. It is some feat to have created a house this large and this, well, monolithic, which still feels so delicate and crisp.

Daniel and Angela had bought the house on the site their new home stands in the late 1990s. It was a 1970s effort and, even if they had wanted to keep living in its dark and cramped interior, it had outgrown the narrow confines of this triangular plot and could not be reasonably extended any further. They approached a local developer about building a replacement but he could only offer them a neo-Georgian mini-mansion (and then, according to Daniel, only a choice from six different patterns). "We wanted something that wasn't like our neighbours," says Angela firmly. "This is the only house of its kind in Esher," says Daniel, perhaps somewhat unnecessarily.

A stunning glass staircase provides the focal point for the ground floor space ➤

"WE WANTED SOMETHING THAT WASN'T LIKE OUR NEIGHBOURS… THIS IS THE ONLY HOUSE OF ITS KIND IN ESHER."

The first floor is designed to have the effect of floating above the ground floor structure. A fireplace services the informal sitting area and master suite upstairs.

Planar structural glazing provides the walls for the ground floor structure. Limestone flooring is used both inside and out.

THEY FINALLY MOVED IN APRIL ONLY TO HAVE TO MOVE STRAIGHT OUT AGAIN AFTER ONE OF THE ENORMOUS ROOFLIGHTS SHATTERED AND FELL INTO THE HOUSE.

Having lived in Hong Kong, they had little fear of the modern, and commissioned Julian King of Wilkinson King to draw up plans for their contemporary dream house. Although the new house was not allowed to exceed the volume of the old one, Julian cleverly gave them extra space by using a flat roof and reallocating the unused volume from their original steeply pitched roof into the accommodation. With five bedrooms, 440m2 of living space and a swimming pool leading from one end of the ground floor (which adds to the feeling of floatiness), it is not just the sense of scale which overawes but the incredible attention to detail and technical proficiency of the builders: the overhanging upper storey; the massive amount of glass which, because of the site's privacy, feels entirely suitable and unexposing; the small, frameless glass entrance hall that juts out from the main glass structure and whose transparency seems, like Daniel's collection of perspective-confounding art, a visual trick.

Inevitably, such high standards of design and finish took time and the construction of the house lasted almost three years. Julian did in fact use two teams of contractors: one set to build the structure and another that could fit it out to the the highest levels of excellence. "A lot of contractors talk the talk," he says, "but when you get them on site, they're not really up to the job." Nevertheless, even the builders who won the £1.6 million contract must have wondered, at times, whether it was a prize or penance: Julian had no qualms about making them repeat jobs two, even three times if he did not feel that the finish reached his exacting pass rate. The piling alone took almost a year as there were concerns about movement on the steeply sloping garden (so vertiginous that the lawns have to be cut using a Flymo on a piece of rope) at the rear of the site.

During this time, Daniel, Angela and, during school and university holidays, their three children, lived in a two bedroom flat nearby. They finally moved in in April this year only to have to move out almost immediately after "teething troubles" saw one of the enormous rooflights shatter and fall into the house. But now, safely installed, the glass obediently remaining in place, they are just beginning to furnish and get to grips with their home.

Decorated throughout the ground floor in pale

The exceedingly spacious first floor landing/ corridor features reinforced glass balustrading. ➤

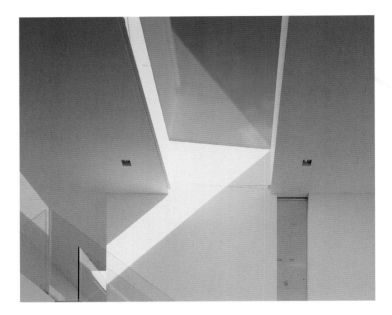

DOORS SLIDE AND GLIDE, BLINDS
PURR INTO POSITION, CUPBOARDS
OPEN AND THEN DISAPPEAR AGAIN
WITH A BARELY AUDIBLE CLICK

grey — one of the few colours that wouldn't clash with the in-your-face verdancy of the lawns and mature trees that surround the house and edge the plot — the house, it has to be said, must take no small amount of discipline to inhabit. The pale grey limestone floors have been untouched by outdoor shoes, the glass walls and (slightly scary) glass staircase betray not a smear nor a smudge, the Bulthaup kitchen is clean enough for Daniel, an orthopaedic surgeon, to use to carry out the odd shoulder operation. It is the sort of house where a carelessly discarded paperback or, heaven forfend, a stray cat hair, would look as shocking as an abandoned fridge or rusting shopping trolley.

Likewise, the mechanics of the house are equally unobtrusive and serene: doors slide and glide, blinds purr into position, cupboards open and then disappear again with a barely audible click.

The ground floor is completely open plan with just a small study, half hidden from sight: the kitchen opens onto the dining area, one end of the room is dominated by a large piano and enormous sofas and the other by a more informal seating area. The space above the dining room and the glass staircase is double height and effectively cuts off the Moks' master bedroom suite from the four ancillary bedrooms. Each bedroom contains a glazed — but thankfully frosted — bathroom cubicle and, whether out of a sense of design purity or to stop sibling rivalry, all the smaller bedrooms have been finished and furnished virtually identically. Visual motifs from the rest of the house have been repeated upstairs such as the glass splashbacks which crop up again in the bathrooms; the solid but discreet use of joinery; the glass tops on the bedroom desks. The glass staircase has been echoed in equally unreassuring — but, Daniel swears perfectly safe, as he leans heavily upon them — glass balustrades. The corridor which connects all the bedrooms has been kept unusually wide and is drenched with sunshine from the rooflights in order to display Daniel's paintings.

Asked what their neighbours think of their extraordinary house and the couple looks slightly shifty. On an estate such as this one — where the only people you see are gardeners and security staff — finding out your neighbours' names, let alone their architectural preferences, must be an uphill struggle. Yet, as the Moks cheerfully confess to having joined a waiting list in order to buy their rather unattractive former home within this enclave, at least they will not have to worry about potential problems selling the house on. The postcode alone will cover their costs and, if a buyer isn't keen on their particular style, on the evidence of the other homes nearby, there is a local builder only too willing to add on a some Ionic columns and a portico. ■

The triangular plot now boasts a huge rectangular structure that appears to float above its manicured lawn surroundings

Daniel and Angela have – with the help of talented architect Julian King – created a modern classic. The couple's joyous indulgence in the fineries of architectural design – and consideration in places of the art above the practical – should be applauded as a continuation of the fine tradition of creating new houses. While the house draws on fairly obvious modernist influences, the startling result is a truly contemporary house that is packed with subtle design beauty and attention to engineering perfection — but is also incredibly tranquil.

FACT FILE

Names: Daniel and Angela Mok
Professions: Consultant surgeon and homemaker
Area: Surrey
House type: Five bedroom, two storeys

House size: 440m²
Construction: Masonry with piled foundations, flat roof, expansive glass
Build route: Architect and subcontractors
Warranty: Architect's certificate
Finance: Private
Build time: August '02 – April '05
Land cost: £1,000,000
Build cost: £1,600,000
Total cost: £2,600,000
House value: £3,000,000
Cost/m²: £3,636

14%
COST SAVING

FLOORPLAN

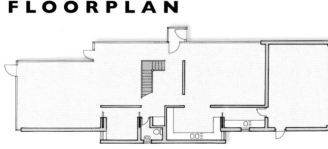

GROUND FLOOR

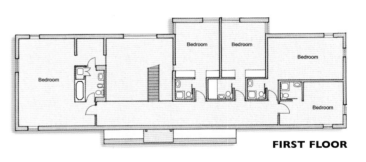

FIRST FLOOR

The open plan ground floor layout is largely overlooked by a substantial galleried landing. The master bedroom is to the left of the plan, with additional bedrooms all enjoying en suites.

USEFUL CONTACTS

Architect Wilkinson King Architects: 020 7284 1975; **Main contractor for phase 1** Swift Southern Ltd: 01737 362571; **Main contractor for the internal fit out and pool** ODB Contracts Ltd: 01252 704400; **Landscaping contractor (phase 3)** North Hants Construction: 01252 540584; **Frameless double glazed units and internal glass cladding** Birchdale Glass: 01895 259111; **Swimming pool** London Swimming Pools Ltd: 020 8874 0414; **Brick slips** Epsicon Epsiwall Brick Slip Cladding: 01942 717100; **Opening windows** Velfac: 01223 897100; **House roof membrane** Sarna installed by Southern Membranes: 01634 869800; **Opening rooflights** Velux: www.velux.co.uk; **Pool roof Sarna Installed by** Delomac:

01234 851222; **Copings** Delomac Roofing Ltd: 01234 851222; **Kitchen** Bulthaup: 020 7317 6000; **Furniture** Viaduct: 020 7278 8456, **Pool cover** Ocea: www.ocea.be; **Limestone floors** Stonell Ltd: 020 7738 0606; **Beam and block floor** Techspan Flooring Systems: 01285 862344; **Staircase** Murphy Stanwix Partnership: 020 8960 8882; **Blinds** Waverly Contract and Supply: 01252 737973; **Concrete hearths** Kayode Lipede: 020 7916 8290; **Flue and fan** Exhausto Ltd: 07841 613095; **Mechanical installation** MPL: 01252 792002; **Electrical** Richard Bell Electrical services Ltd: 020 8287 0500; **Lighting** Lumino: 01279 635411; **Security systems** MR Security: 020 8336 4080; **Joinery** Willowbridge: 01233 643883; **Garage door** Crawford Amber:

01226 351135; **Gate** Venturer Security: 01435 873087; **Underfloor heating** Kestrin: 01403 711772; **Specialist grilles** Euroslot: 01483 421199; **Gutters** Marley Alutec: 01234 359438; **Sanitaryware** Durante Bathrooms: 020 7589 9990, **Carpet** John Lewis: www.johnlewis.co.uk; **Gas Fires** Platonic Fireplaces: 020 8891 5904, **Trench radiators** Sill line Perimeter Heating Ltd: 01327 301922; **Ironmongery** Dorplan, Allgood and Hafele: 01707 647647; **Swimming pool glass doors and partitions** Cantifix of London: 020 8203 6203; **Pool render** Wetherby Building Systems: 01942 717100; **Pool tiles** Tilco: 020 8481 9500; **Pool ladder and grab rail** Astral pool www.astralpool.com; **Land drains** Aco: 01462 816666

BUILDING AN INNOVATIVE OAK-FRAMED HOME WITH A LIVING ROOF

CURVE APPEAL

Alex and Debra Barnes overcame a planning nightmare to build a new contemporary-style oak-frame home.

WORDS: CLIVE FEWINS   PHOTOGRAPHY: ROB JUDGES

SELF-BUILD CAN HAVE its ups and downs, as nearly all who partake in the activity are well aware. Alex and Debra Barnes were two weeks away from completing their 316m² oak framed self-build on a glorious site in open countryside near Banbury, Oxfordshire, when their marriage failed and Debra left. Unfortunately, divorce proceedings are now under way.

Alex, who is living in the new four bedroom house with their two daughters, is not prepared to attribute the blame to their long and arduous self-build experience, although he does advise prospective self-builders to think very hard before committing a family of four with two dogs to 18 months in an on-site mobile home. However, he has not ruled out another self-build in the future.

The property is to be sold, which is an enormous shame because the house, which has a very complex ➤

"WE FELT THAT A FULL COURTYARD WOULD PROBABLY NOT BE ACCEPTABLE TO PLANNERS, BUT A SLIGHT CURVE IN THE REAR OF THE HOUSE WOULD PROVIDE AN INTERESTING SHAPE AND SOME SLIGHT ENCLOSURE FOR A PATIO."

and attractive planted roof that covers the main two-storey wing and curves on plan as well as in section, had been planned as a long term investment.

It has also been a very individual project, for which they sacrificed a great deal. "We lived in a nearby village for 12 years, heard of the plot, made a bid at auction and failed to gain it first time. 18 months later when it came on the market again, with planning permission for a dormer bungalow, we got it for £200,000 and then fought for many months to gain permission for the style of house we wanted,"says Alex.

After the sale of their previous house in December 1999, the Barnes calculated they had a budget of £350,000 for the build if they took on a mortgage of £170,000. They had been discussing a self-build for at least two years and decided they liked the oak framed barn style houses of architect Roderick James, who has been a pioneering figure in the rebirth of oak frames over the past 20 years.

"We found Roderick excellent to deal with and very receptive to ideas," says Alex. "We were keen to build a south facing house that turned its back on the road – it is a country lane but carries quite a lot of traffic at certain times of the day – and make the most of the south facing views over fields and a wood.

"We felt that a full courtyard would probably not be acceptable to planners, but a slight curve in the rear of the house would provide an interesting shape and some slight enclosure for a patio."

Roderick came up with the idea of a house with two single storey limbs, with a round tower at the centre housing the upstairs bedrooms.

The exposed post and beam structure is very much the defining feature of the house's character.

Alex and Debra particularly liked the idea of a glazed lantern at the apex and the round clerestory glazing beneath the eaves. However, planning officials ➤

23

"WE HAD PRODUCED SOMETHING INNOVATIVE THAT WAS NOT TOO MASSIVE AND KEPT LOW, THAT LOOKED AS THOUGH IT HAD EVOLVED WITH THE LANDSCAPE."

The cantilevered oak staircase is given a contemporary twist with the use of full-height steel balustrading.

at Cherwell District Council were emphatic that there was no way it would conform to local guidelines.

All this took the best part of 12 months and cost them several thousand pounds. The design they resubmitted had a curved rear and a curved, barrel- shaped planted sedum roof. The object of the curved roof was to enable them to raise the eaves and so gain two full storeys on a planning permission for a one-and-a-half storey dormer bungalow. The curved roof achieved this with the minimum roof height thanks to its low pitch.

As with all Roderick James' designs, there are large expanses of glass between the oak posts that form the exterior of the frame, especially on the southern side. There are also some innovative features, such as the staircase, built by main contractor, John Varney. It comprises slabs of solid oak, hung from a stud interior wall but supported by cables from

a section of the first floor timber frame. At the south facing rear this is cantilevered out to avoid the use of posts and so give a clear space in the curved conservatory area. At first floor level, below the windows, there is a clear space with an open guarding, formed by taut wires to encourage the movement of air through the building.

Despite these innovative features, plus the single storey oak framed 'barn room' — lit by six roof lights and joined by a glazed link which serves as the main relaxation area — the house design proved only marginally more acceptable to the planners than the first. "We were rather dispirited as we had really taken on board the objections first time round," Alex says. "We thought we had produced something innovative that was not too massive and kept low, that looked ➤

Freestanding kitchen
furniture has simple
shaker-style panelled
doors and a painted
finish. The floors are
from Classical Flagstones,
warmed by underfloor
heating from Wirsbo.

■ CURVE APPEAL

"I HAVE BUILT MANY RODERICK JAMES HOUSES AND THIS IS ONE OF MY FAVOURITES BECAUSE OF THE CURVED STRUCTURE AT THE REAR AND THE GLORIOUS VIEW IT AFFORDS ACROSS OPEN COUNTRYSIDE."

as though it had evolved and blended in with the landscape. We also used local stone in the walls and Welsh slate on the roofs of the single storey sections."

The single-storey oak-framed 'barn room' is lit by six roof lights and joined by a glazed link which serves as the main relaxation area.

Alex and Debra argued that all of these factors conformed with local guidelines and reduced the impact of the design. They also pointed out that the curved main roof section mirrored the roofs of Dutch barns in the locality, and submitted photographs of examples. They also submitted shots of local stone buildings with curved walls — one in the adjoining village — and, with the aid of Roderick, produced a set of detailed notes, plus a model. With this they lobbied local councillors on the planning committee.

It paid off: the elected members overturned the views of the officers and the plan was passed by the full planning committee. "It took a long time and we could not quite understand why," Alex says.

At this stage Roderick introduced them to builder, John Varney, and handed the detailed design over to one of his partners, Hugh Wray-

McCann, who acted as project architect. Together with Alex and Debra, Hugh refined the scheme, adding a small boot room to a single storey lean-to section to the right of the main entrance. At the same time the garden room was made smaller to try and ease the design through the planning process. The curved sections of the roof are constructed using glulams. The rest is oak, though much of it, in typical Roderick James fashion, rests on a ground floor of double skinned blockwork.

As you drive past you see very little — just a glimpse of the curved stone elevation, the small windows on that side and the planted roof. "The full glory of the house is on the far side — the south facing elevation," says John Varney. "I have built many Roderick James houses and this is one of my favourites because of the curved structure at the rear and the glorious view it affords across open countryside."

The planted sedum roof has two high performance membranes beneath it that cover 120mm insulation placed above a vapour barrier. It is guaranteed for 20 years. "It should last a great deal longer because of the planting," says Alex. "Sadly, like many other aspects of the house, that will be one more factor for someone else to enjoy." ■

FACT FILE

Names: Alex and Debra Barnes
Professions: Health service manager and community educator
Area: Oxfordshire
House type: Four bed detached
House size: 316m²
Build route: Main contractor
Construction: Oak frame and dual skin blockwork with local stone cladding
Finance: Private plus Skipton BS mortgage
SAP rating: 81
Build time: July '02 - May '03
Land cost: £200,000
Build cost: £292,500
Total cost: £492,500
House value: £850,000
Cost/m²: £925

Cost Breakdown:

Groundwork	£20,700
Block and stonework	£35,000
Oak frame inc erection	£71,700
Sedum roof	£28,500
Slate roof	£9,000
Glazing	£14,000
Plumbing and heating	£19,000
Electrics	£9,500
Doors and windows	£17,400
First fix joinery	£10,400
Second fix joinery	£15,500
Kitchen	£6,500
Architect's fees	£26,500
Misc	£8,800
TOTAL	**£292,500**

GROUND FLOOR

Hall · Utility · Bedroom · Kitchen · Conservatory · Study · Library · Barnroom

FIRST FLOOR

Bedroom · Bedroom · Bath · Landing · Bedroom · Balcony

FLOORPLAN

The house has two single storey limbs, with a round tower at the centre housing the upstairs bedrooms. A glazed lantern at the apex and the round clerestory glazing beneath the eaves lets the light flood in. The design also has a curved rear and a curved, barrel-shaped planted sedum roof.

USEFUL CONTACTS

Design — Hugh Wray-McCann, Roderick James Architects 01803 868000; **Structural engineer** — Mark Lovell: 01380 724213; **Main contractor** — J D Varney: 01869 343422; **Joinery, including windows** — Neil Wilkins: 01865 331036; **Electrics** — John Gibb: 01869 278269; **Plumber** — Cliff Stoneman: 07774 137990; **Underfloor Heating** — Uponor: 01455 550355; **Glazing** — Chipping Norton Glass: 01608 643261; **Downstairs flooring** — Classical Flagstones: 0117 937 1960; **Oak frame and glulams** — Carpenter Oak Ltd.: 01803 732900; **Welsh slate roofing** — Bicester Roofing: 0870 264 6454; **Reclaimed stone** — Jakeman's Reclaim: 01295 710739; **Sedum planted roof system** — Bauder: 01473 257671; **Contractor for planted roof** — Julian Tyrrell: 01865 371329; **Galvanised steel guttering** — Lindab: 0121 550 5115

The wooden house, part of which is built onto poles, was tailored to suit Mike and Lizzie's love of the East and yet fit into the English countryside.

21st CENTURY LIVING

BUILDING A NEW HI-TECH CONTEMPORARY HOME

Mike Thrasher and Lizzie Vann have built a cutting-edge home packed with the latest hi-tech features.

WORDS: DEBBIE JEFFERY
PHOTOGRAPHY: NIGEL RIGDEN

"LIZZIE AND I discussed the idea of building our own house soon after we first met," explains Mike Thrasher. "We both love imaginative, unconventional properties and gathered ideas from our travels, but were unable to find a suitable plot of land. Eventually, we viewed Hillside Farm, situated a short distance from where we were living, and made a sealed bid for what was essentially a converted chicken shed!"

Set in 55 acres of organic farmland in the heart of the New Forest, the property is extremely remote with no near neighbours and views across open countryside. Lizzie and Mike discovered that they needed to gain retrospective planning permission for the chicken shed conversion, which they spruced up and painted to resemble a New England house. They lived in the property, which had virtually no insulation, and planned to replace it with an altogether more adventurous structure.

Gaining planning permission for this replacement took approximately three years because the planners insisted that no dwelling should ever have been built on the site in the first place. "It wasn't our design they opposed but the whole concept of building a new house," Mike explains. "Originally, we had started out with a five year plan, but ended up living in the chicken shed for a total of seven years."

The couple had found a US company marketing an updated version of traditional wooden Haiku houses, which were originally built in 14th century Japan. Raised on wooden poles to promote air circulation within the building, the houses seemed to blend into the landscape – a factor which led Lizzie and Mike to investigate importing a kit.

"We discovered that building regulations are so different in the UK that the structure would need to be completely adapted, so we decided to build something similar from scratch," says Mike, a graphic designer, who was keen to combine the Haiku form with more contemporary architecture which would offer bold interiors with large expanses of glazing.

With help from their concept architect, David Underhill, permission was eventually granted for the radical design, which resembles a group of zinc-roofed farm buildings rather than a single structure; with three timber ➤

Additional gadgetry has been included in the open plan kitchen, which was designed by Mike and Lizzie. A periscope-like Gaggenau extractor rises from the kitchen unit and extracts air from the hob, while a wine fridge has preset temperature zones and the waste management system emits clean water from the house waste.

"I DO FEEL ANNOYED THAT WE HAD TO COMPROMISE, BUT WE WERE STRICTLY LIMITED TO BUILD NO MORE THAN 30 PER CENT LARGER THAN THE CHICKEN SHED."

clad buildings joined by glazed corridors. A dark brown single storey living wing stands on poles beside the separate green bedroom block – made up of the master bedroom, dressing room and en suite bathroom – and a purple three storey tower contains a basement laundry with a guest bedroom above and a top floor office. In the corridor that divides the living and bedroom wings is a home library, with racks of books, DVDs and CDs, a work station and a specially built AV cupboard, which houses equipment such as the CD changer and power amplifier.

The planners were keen that the house should be predominantly low level, and so rooms have been left full-height right up into the roof space to increase the impression of space. Restrictions on the overall footprint have meant that the master bedroom needed to be relatively compact in order to achieve a comparatively spacious living area. At 6' 4" Mike requires a large bed, which further shrinks this room. "I do feel annoyed that we had to compromise," he admits. "No neighbours overlook our house, it is completely hidden, and a few extra feet would have made all the difference but we were strictly limited to build a property no more than 30% larger than the chicken shed."

Mike and Lizzie decided to employ a project manager to co-ordinate the 38 specialist subcontractors required for their build. The new house was built right next door to the chicken shed and, as the couple planned to continue living there until it was eventually demolished, part of this needed to be taken down to make way for the concrete pillars and plinth foundations.

Ten poles of locally grown Douglas fir were turned on lathes off site and support the huge roof trusses – forming an important element of the interior design. These poles were bolted into position, protected from the damp earth by the concrete plinth, and the trusses winched on to create the load-bearing structure.

Mike had meticulously researched the internal fixtures and fittings, as well as the latest home automation options, and felt that building a house from scratch offered the perfect opportunity to install some hi-tech gadgets. He wanted the home entertainment system, lighting and heating to be custom-made, and approached Bournemouth based ➤

Hidden technology
The centrepiece of the living room is a 50" plasma screen with speaker system. The screen is hidden behind an oil painting and the flat panel speakers merge into the neutral wall.

HI-TECH HOMEBUILDING

Homes at the forefront of design need also these days to incorporate the very latest in home technology – recognised by industry insiders as the biggest development in housing for decades. Features such as controlled lighting, multi-room audio, home cinemas and automated heating and security should all be considered. For more information visit www.smarthomeshow.co.uk.

USEFUL CONTACTS

Concept architect DUA Architecture LLP: 01425 278252; **Working architect** QED: 01962 842042; **Structural engineers** Andrew Waring Associates Ltd: 01794 524447; **Project manager** Graham Davies: 01590 675900; **Waste treatment plant** Clearwater Polcon Ltd: 01278 433443; **Piling and substructure** Able Piling & Construction Ltd: 01489 797600; **Roofing** Pace Roofing Ltd: 01794 515155; **Window and door frames** TK Joinery (Blandford) Ltd: 01258 455521; **Window furniture** Spiller Architectural Ironmongery: 01935 432929; **Steel** Allfab Southern: 01794 518911; **Sliding door gear** Hillaldam Coburn Ltd: 020 8336 1515; **Plumbing and water systems** Clinton Foakes: 07712 645568; **Skylight** Polar Plastics: 02380 899611; **Bathroom fittings** Aston Matthews Ltd: 020 7226 7220; **Underfloor heating** Warmafloor: 01489 581787; **Column turning** Spindlewood Woodturning: 01278 453665; **Flooring** Kahrs UK Ltd: 01243 778747; **Tiles** Fired Earth Interiors: 01295 812088; **Deck** All Decked Out Ltd: 07789 206240; **Plasma TV** Dawsons: 01202 764965; **Kitchen units** – Rational Built-In Kitchens (UK) Ltd: 01543 459459; **Lighting control** Lutron EA Ltd: 020 7702 0657; **Lighting supply** Contract Lighting and Design: 01202 520266; **Paint and stain finishes** Sikkens Ltd: 01480 496868

FACT FILE

Names: Mike Thrasher and Lizzie Vann
Professions: Graphic designer and MD of organic food business
Area: Dorset
House type: Two bedroom house
House size: 165m²

Build route: Self-managed subcontractors
Construction: Douglas fir posts, timber frame, zinc roof
Warranty: Architect's Certificate
Finance: Private and Portman Building Society self-build mortgage
Build time: June '03 - Feb '04
Land cost: £250,000
Build cost: £350,000
Total cost: £600,000
House value: £850,000
Cost/m²: £2,121

29%
COST SAVING

FLOORPLAN

FLOORPLAN: three distinct zones linked by glazed corridors: an open plan living/kitchen wing, a master bedroom suite and the three storey control tower with a laundry, guest room and top floor home office.

GROUND FLOOR

FIRST FLOOR

SECOND FLOOR

THEY AMAZED EVERYONE BY TOUCHING A BUTTON ON THEIR REMOTE CONTROL WHICH RAISED THE PICTURE UPWARDS ON MOTORISED RAILS – BRINGING THE PLASMA SCREEN INTO VIEW.

custom installer Dawsons. "I was aware of different companies who could do this," he explains, "but it was important to have someone local who would be flexible. We were so single-minded in our plans and we needed a company that could find ways to help us achieve them."

The Dawsons team went through the plans for the house in the early stages of building and worked to incorporate the technology within the structure. With no loft voids the cables have been laid in special floor ducting, alongside the underfloor heating, to act as the veins that power the lighting and audio-visual systems from a central computer.

Once the house was completed the couple invited around 40 guests, and amazed everyone by touching a button on their remote control which raised the picture upwards on motorised rails – bringing the huge recessed plasma screen into view. Lighting also plays an important role both inside and outside the house, with a Lutron Homeworks system that can be operated by remote control or from a six bank switch system in each room – which can set the mood for activities such as watching films or reading. LED lighting was added to the floor of the glass walkway which leads to the bedroom wing of the house, and provides a soft light to guide the way without the need to switch on overhead lights.

"Keeping everything free of clutter is a major occupation," says Mike. "We have no loft space, and so storage is at a premium. The house doesn't really need any further embellishment, because we have used strong, natural materials, and the setting and views are the main focus. We never get bored of looking out across the farmland and countryside. It has taken a long time to finally build this house, but it has proved to be worth all the waiting." ∎

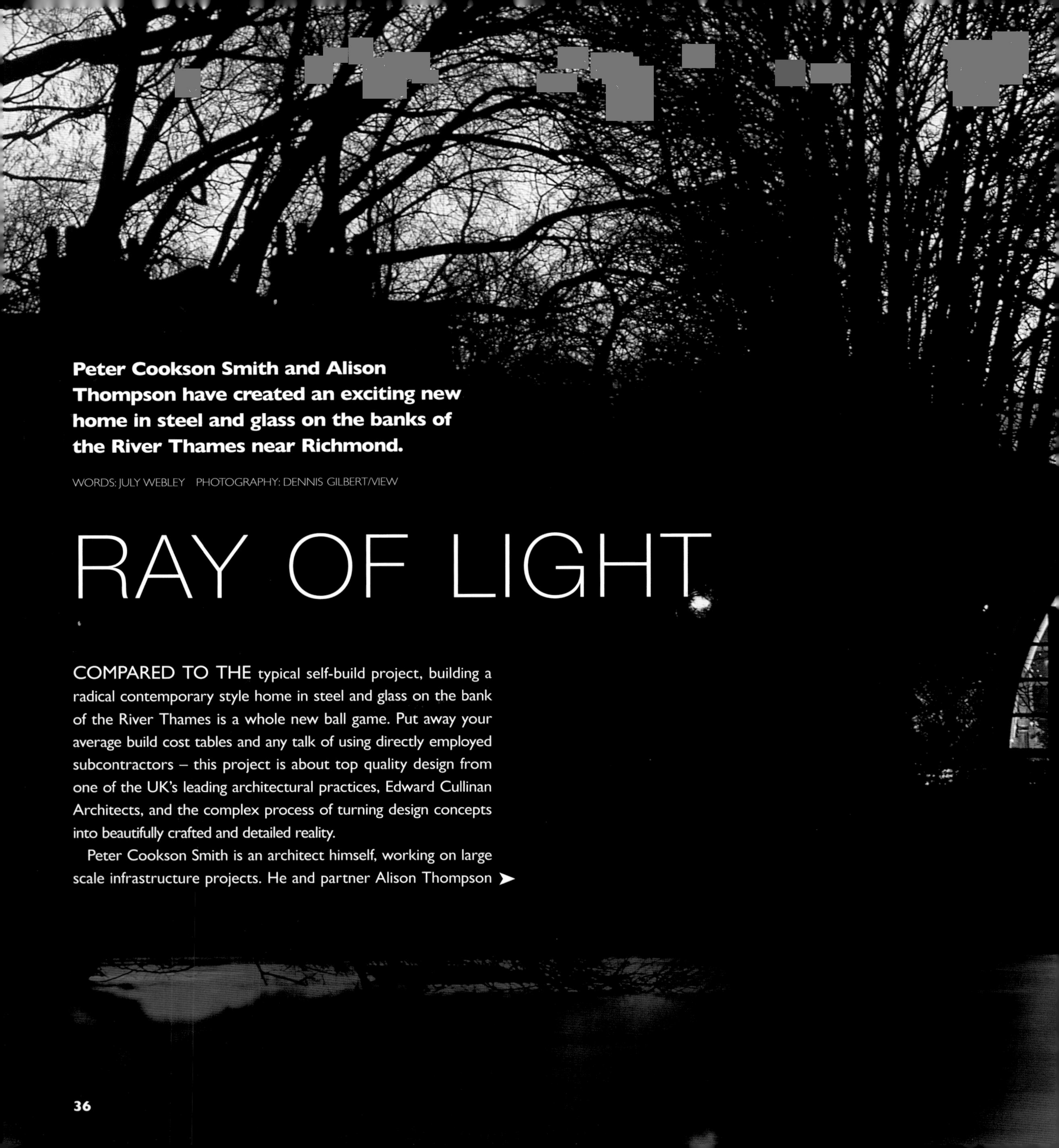

Peter Cookson Smith and Alison Thompson have created an exciting new home in steel and glass on the banks of the River Thames near Richmond.

WORDS: JULY WEBLEY   PHOTOGRAPHY: DENNIS GILBERT/VIEW

RAY OF LIGHT

COMPARED TO THE typical self-build project, building a radical contemporary style home in steel and glass on the bank of the River Thames is a whole new ball game. Put away your average build cost tables and any talk of using directly employed subcontractors – this project is about top quality design from one of the UK's leading architectural practices, Edward Cullinan Architects, and the complex process of turning design concepts into beautifully crafted and detailed reality.

Peter Cookson Smith is an architect himself, working on large scale infrastructure projects. He and partner Alison Thompson ➤

"WE CAN ADVISE PEOPLE HOW TO ACHIEVE THE SHAPE OF THE BUILDING THEY WANT FOR THE MONEY THEY HAVE…"

had been living and working overseas in Hong Kong but planned to return to the UK. Peter had snapped up the fantastic plot overlooking the Thames some years before. Following the erection of a new flood wall, some plots of land adjacent to the riverbank that previously flooded became suitable for development. Peter and Alison wanted to build something special and contemporary that would require the inspiration of not just an architect, but an artist.

The couple commissioned the Cullinan practice to come up with a design study. The brief called for a house containing a variety of spaces for quiet study, relaxation, entertainment and all of the other normal domestic requirements. They wanted a design that would make best use of the fantastic river views and allow in as much light as possible but without sacrificing privacy.

The initial design study met with client approval but, predictably, failed to win planning consent. It subsequently took a great deal of determination and a refusal to admit defeat to get this proposal accepted.

"The original consent on the plot was for a small cottage," recalls project architect Peter Inglis. "This consent had lapsed but the planners did not seem that keen to discuss new proposals for the site. Our application was refused, principally on the grounds that it was detrimental to a line of sycamore trees.

"Fortunately the client, who had previously worked in planning himself, decided to appeal. He hired a firm of planning consultants who produced a lengthy document showing, amongst other things, that the trees would be able to survive and prosper alongside the proposed house." In March 1998, two years after work started on the design, the planning inspector accepted the appeal and work could start in earnest.

"A lot of people lie down and wiggle their legs in the air when the planners turn down their proposal," comments the contractor, Paul Gilby of Gilby Construction. "If you want to build something unusual and challenging in this country my advice is to put a great deal of effort into choosing the right architect and then keep faith with him. You have to be prepared, as in this case, to appeal against planning decisions and let the planners know you will go all

Because of the large expanse of glazing the solid structural walls were super-insulated to 0.18W/m2K. ➤

"YOU HAVE TO BE PREPARED, AS IN THIS CASE, TO APPEAL… OTHERWISE YOU'LL END UP LISTENING TO WHAT THEY SAY THEY WANT AND END UP WITH A HOUSE LIKE EVERYONE ELSE'S."

the way. Otherwise you'll end up listening to what they say they want and end up with a house like everyone else's."

The design of both house and garden, starting at the roadside and going right through to the riverside, was based on a grid of multiples of 1200mm. A great deal of care was taken with the setting out of the project on site to ensure that each element of the design related correctly to the rest. The buildings, composed of London stock brick, western red cedar, and zinc cladding, are set back from the road to provide an open area for two car parking spaces together with an entrance drive. An elevated entrance extends through the internal entrance hall and beyond as an external timber deck. This is set back from the edge of the site in order to retain the existing trees along the boundary (in tune with the planners' wishes) but gives a clear and uninterrupted view of the river from the entrance itself. On the river side of the house is a private garden. This includes the raised timber deck which steps up to "oversail" the existing floodwall leading to a (yet to be constructed) river mooring.

The internal planning of the main house is ordered around a curving wall, which incorporates stairs, storage and display cases and provides vantage points throughout the house from which to enjoy framed views across the river. The large expanse of glazing can be shaded when required by external timber blinds which are operated by an electric motor. This system of environmental control was partially developed for the project.

Heating is provided by warm water underfloor heating from Thermoboard and cooling can be assisted by natural ventilation provided by high and low level opening windows which are again motorised. The building services engineer who designed the heating system ran a computer modelling programme to predict the effect of solar gain (natural warming from the sun) on the house. Because of the large expanse of glazing the solid structural walls were super-insulated to a far better than building regs U-value of $0.18W/m^2K$ as a trade off so that the structure as a whole attained an acceptable SAP rating.

Gilby Construction had been brought in at an early stage at the suggestion of the quantity surveyor. "In the practice generally we've not been happy with the standard ways of procuring buildings," comments Peter Inglis. "Instead of operating in what often turns out to be an adversarial way with the contractor we wanted to partner with him and use his expertise.

"Paul Gilby's firm had special expertise in piling, steelwork and waterproof concrete techniques. We wanted to get him involved in the detailed design stage and with implementing our rolling cost plan along with the QS." Paul Gilby takes up the story. "We're very rarely on tender lists since we normally refuse to tender. On this job we were presented with 1:100 planning drawings and a cost plan from the QS with a series of budgets to work to. It's important that there are realistic expectations. We also have to check that the skill base required for a particular job is available at the right time as we will only work with subcontractors whose work we know and trust.

On the river side of the house is a private garden. This includes the raised timber deck which steps up to "oversail" the existing floodwall leading to a (yet to be constructed) river mooring.

➤

The internal planning of the main house is ordered around a curving wall, which incorporates stairs, storage and display cases, and provides vantage points throughout the house from which to enjoy framed views across the river.

41

"INSTEAD OF OPERATING IN WHAT OFTEN TURNS OUT TO BE AN ADVERSARIAL WAY WITH THE CONTRACTOR WE WANTED TO PARTNER WITH HIM AND USE HIS EXPERTISE."

"Cost planning is everything. If we're involved early we can advise against overspecification in some areas if it's going to mean the budget won't work. We can advise people how to achieve the shape of the building they want for the money they have. We came up with a method statement of how the house was going to be built, in a lot of detail, and then provided fixed prices for every element and a fixed contract period. On this job we were able to advise on how best to achieve the brief for the available budget. Really this was a pretty straightforward project making sensible use of available technologies."

The structural frame of the house is formed in cold rolled steel, infilled with Metsec stud partitioning with 9mm OSB board, Rockwool roll insulation, Tyvec membrane and vapour check, plywood clad on the exterior with western red cedar and London stock brick. Once the steel frame had gone up the project was weathertight in

a week. The only slow part was the brick wall (the planners insisted on some "wattle and daub," says Gilby sarcastically).

On the roof rolled steel T-sections followed the roll of the roof and were fixed to the primary cross steels. Timber joists were then fitted from left to right, again following the curve of the roof, overlaid with planks of pine, two layers of Rockwool Rainscreen Duo (as well as thermal insulation this product provided acoustic shielding from the sound of rain drumming on the roof), a Tyvek membrane and a RheinZink roof.

According to the contractor, the most challenging part of the job was in the ground. Due to the ground conditions, piled foundations were necessary, plus Peter and Alison wanted a full basement for storage and to house the boiler and so on. There was only 30mm of clearance on one pile from a neighbour's fence.

Since the plot is so close to the Thames the water table rises and falls by 2ft according to the tide. Being experienced in waterproof concrete technology Gilby took responsibility for the waterproofing of the basement. No tanking was used. The walls were formed from in situ poured concrete using a special formula concrete vibrated in a particular way with chemical water bars. "Because of the tide we had to be really careful with the timing of concrete deliveries," explains Paul.

How did this all work with the client thousands of miles away in Hong Kong? "The detail design stage was all done by fax," says Peter Inglis. "The client responded very quickly and it all went very smoothly, in spite of the distance.

"When it came to selecting the materials we used to get samples of everything in the office and the client would come and inspect a batch on one of his trips to London. On site, as always, there were plenty of decisions that needed taking and the client was always fully involved."

The project was run on a standard JCT IFC98 contract for intermediate value projects administered by the architect. ■

FACT FILE

Costs as of Dec 2001
Name: Peter Cookson Smith and Alison Thompson
Professions: Architect and Coroner
Area: West London
House type: Contemporary
House size: 377m²
Build route: Architect/Quantity Surveyor/Main Contractor
Construction: Steel frame + in-situ cast waterproof concrete basement
Warranty: Architect's Certificates
SAP rating: Not known
Finance: Private
Build time: Two years
Land cost: Undisclosed
Build cost: £900,000
Current value: £3-4m

Cost/m²: £2,387

Cost Breakdown:

Enabling work:	£25,000
Substructure/Basement:	£155,333
Steel Frame:	£34,998
External Walls & Joinery	£29,646
Windows/Blinds/	
External Doors	£63,602
Upper floors:	£20,022
Roofs:	£47,882
Internal Walls:	£49,093
Staircases:	£53,900
Internal Doors:	£4,675
Wall, Ceiling, Floor Finishes:	
	£26,814
Sanitary/Kitchen/	
Built-in Fittings:	£110,482
M&E, Plumbing, Electrics:	£72,984
Landscape/External :	£43,300
TOTAL	**£900,000**

FLOORPLAN

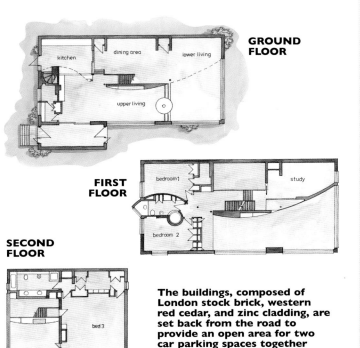

The buildings, composed of London stock brick, western red cedar, and zinc cladding, are set back from the road to provide an open area for two car parking spaces together with an entrance drive.

HIDDEN DEPTHS

Joan and Roland Witton's travels inspired them to build a large open plan home on the site of a former bungalow.

WORDS: ANGELA PERTUSINI PHOTOGRAPHY: NIGEL RIGDEN

YOU KNOW HOW it is. You get back from holiday to a grey, British winter and everything seems dreary and dull and you need something to give you a bit of a lift. A new haircut perhaps. Feeling a bit more ambitious? You could start planning your next trip. Or you could build a house.

"We'd been skiing and everything felt so flat when we got home," explains Joan Witton, savouring a cigarette as only a woman who has spent several years living in Singapore can. "We had an old Arts & Crafts house in Sevenoaks and I'd been vaguely looking in estate agents' windows when the details for the bungalow came through."

Joan went to see it, convinced that if it had any potential, it would have already been snaffled up by the local developer mafia, and ended up buying it for £340,000 "on the hope factor". Without hope, all she and her husband, Roland, had was an extremely shabby and run-down wooden Victorian bungalow without heating, nicknamed 'the scout hut' by their children. What the ever-hopeful Joan could see, however, was a beautiful Georgian farmhouse standing in a two-acre plot. She didn't know at that stage that the seller had already had his plans to develop the land turned down.

So, full of enthusiasm and with ideas for a perfectly symmetrical house at the centre of her land – "dead simple, the sort of thing a child draws" – she set about finding an architect who

The double-height informal living/dining room to the rear of the property looks over the large two-acre garden. ➤

would be able to steer her through the formalities of acquiring planning consent, then she could join her husband back in Singapore while the house got built and avoid all the dust and flimflam about drains and fire escapes and roof insulation. It really would be that simple. But it wasn't. The local authority, as you might have predicted, turned her plans down.

"Because we were abroad we thought it would all be done while we were away. But the council knocked it back: too tall, out of keeping – although the place is surrounded by Georgian farmhouses. We kept altering the drawings and negotiating to see what we could get away with. We agreed to everything: we lowered the roof, took away the outhouses, it took two years of backwards and forwards."

With the help of planning consultants the house went through four redrafts before it was finally accepted in 2003. Although it is broadly traditional from the outside, there is little, if anything, of the Georgian farmhouse left. A purely symmetrical exterior has also been broken up by a series of delicate overhangs as well as a small balcony at the rear. The bricks are new although they look much older and have been laid to include a simple dentil course which runs the entire circumference of the

house. "I really wanted symmetry but John, our architect, kept saying, "It's a bit boring… how about we try this?"

Unfortunately for Joan and her husband, Roland, their plans for mud-free living several thousand miles away from the build also took a battering. The years of negotiations meant that the couple were just being stationed back in England as work was about to begin – in fact they were to spend the next eight months living in the much-derided scout hut. "We came back from a wonderful house in Singapore to that," grimaces Joan. "Cooking over a Baby Belling in a lean-to. My daughter almost died when she came and saw it."

Still, it could have been worse – they might have been living in the scout hut with no prospect of building their dream house next to it. Within a couple of weeks, in early October 2003, work had started on the couple's home which was to be influenced by the many homes they had lived in overseas due to Roland's work in the oil industry.

"We had a jumbo house in Vietnam with great big rooms and we loved ➤

The ground floor has mainly been given over to Joan's desire for a large kitchen-breakfast room with an informal living area. A beautiful, double-height living space is situated at the other end.

"EVEN THOUGH IT'S JUST THE TWO OF US, WE COULDN'T SEE OURSELVES IN A COSY COTTAGE."

"WE WEREN'T AWARE THAT IT WAS TO BE THIS MODERN. [THE ARCHITECT] NUDGED ME INTO IT."

it, and even though our kids are grown up and it's just the two of us, we couldn't see ourselves in a cosy cottage," says Joan. "We wanted a great big kitchen-diner family room and a big bedroom. And a big sitting room if we could. I wanted a dressing room and an en suite. Roland wanted open space and a multi-media room – we used to visit Australia quite often and everyone there has a media room and we loved that. And we had lived in Canada and liked that open plan feel where there are arches between rooms rather than doors."

That the couple achieved this on an impressive but not an epic footprint is in part due to their cunning use of a basement – although the "b" word can only be whispered quietly. "It's not, it's a cellar," reiterates Joan. "We

called it a cellar and the planners never picked up on it although it was in all the plans." This "cellar" now houses a large bedroom and bathroom, a smaller bedroom, a gym, a utility and the longed-for media room. Despite being semi-underground on a site that slopes up away from the house, it feels neither stuffy nor dark, in large part due to the unusually high ceilings.

The bedroom has an internal window with a balcony that looks over the rear atrium space.

The ground floor has mainly been given over to Joan's desire for a large kitchen-diner family room: and it is vast, easily bigger than some one bedroom flats, and with a beautiful, double height lounging area at one end – "the planners didn't go on volume and the voids saved on floor space," explains Joan. Huge glass doors open out onto the patio and then the full length of the garden – currently unlandscaped except for the family's two bounding labradors. When the garden work is complete it will be spectacular but, even in its raw state, it is unlike most London gardens. Because, although this house and its surrounds have no gas connection,

The extensive basement, which mixes bedroom and non-habitable space, has no impact on the external view but transforms the amount of accommodation the house provides.

FIRST FLOOR

GROUND FLOOR

BASEMENT

FACT FILE

Names: Roland and Joan Witton
Professions: Works in oil industry, homemaker
Area: Kent
House type: Four bed detached
House size: 360m²
Build route: Architect and main contractor
Construction: Masonry
Finance: Private
Build time: Oct '03 – Sept '04
Land cost: £450,000
Build cost: £450,000
Total cost: £900,000
House value: £1,200,000
Cost/m²: £1,250

68%
COST SAVING

no sewage connection and there are cattle lowing in the next field, it is on the outskirts of the borough of Bromley and therefore technically a part of Greater London, albeit as remote and unlikely a spot as you could come across in the capital.

The costs have come in at £450,000 – the couple had planned on spending about £900/ft2 but have probably spent closer to £1,250. It's not an extortionate amount for a house of this size or this quality – they have not stinted on modern comforts such as underfloor heating and multiple bathrooms. At a very conservative guess, the house would fetch well over £1million. Still, does Joan have any regrets that her Georgian farmhouse never materialised? "We weren't aware that it was to be this modern. We lived in Copenhagan and so we were used to Scandinavian modernism but it wasn't what we envisaged. John nudged me into it – he would say: 'You'll like that' – and I did." ∎

A large living room leads off the other side of the hall which is dominated by a handsome staircase, made all the more impressive by vast windows that look out into the garden.

REPLACING A BUNGALOW

Canny plothunters tend to see bungalows as temporary inhabitants of desirable building plots. So-called 'bungalow gobbling' can be a risky process, however, with policies on replacement changing from council to council. Generally, however, self-builders can expect to replace a bungalow with a new home of around 30% extra volume (or floor area, depending on the council). Call the planners before you buy!

USEFUL CONTACTS

Architect – Jon Hughes Designs: 01732 451947; **Main contractor** – Exel Construction Ltd: 020 8947 8858; **Landscaping** – Regent Landscapes: 01959 562120

Jacob's Ladder has been built on the footprint of a dilapidated house which was constructed by the Dean of Windsor for his family.

DOWN IN THE WOODS

Architectural experiment or practical modern house? Whatever your view, David and Shelley Grey's new self-built home certainly gives visitors to its hideaway location a surprise.

WORDS: DEBBIE JEFFERY PHOTOGRAPHY: DAVID GREY

WITHOUT EXCEPTION EVERYONE who visits Jacob's Ladder, nestled in its woodland setting, is in awe of this fantastic modern structure. Building the house proved far from easy, however, and its owners, David and Shelley Grey, are only now beginning to relax after the stressful process. "We never set out to own an award-winning house," laughs David, "and, although we find it incredible to live in, we were rather naive when it came to the build process itself."

Their project started when, becoming concerned about the increasing traffic passing outside their previous home – a beautiful Georgian vicarage – the couple decided to self-build. "We loved the house but, after five years, knew it was time to move on," says Shelley. "It had become almost impossible to sit out in the garden due to the noise from the traffic, and we decided that what we needed was space."

Nine and a half acres of private beech woodland is about as much space as any two people could require and, when a chance comment from a friend led to the Greys viewing the plot, they knew they had found the answer. Complete with a derelict 1950s house and full planning permission for a traditional replacement dwelling, the woods offered a peace and privacy most of us can only dream of. "For a long time we had thought it would be quite good fun to build a house – although 'fun' isn't a word I'd use any more!" says David.

A sealed bid won them the site, which is

Right: The double height living space is overlooked by the master bedroom ➤

"WE LOOKED THROUGH THE ARCHITECTURE FOUNDATION'S NEW ARCHITECTS BOOK AND APPROACHED TWELVE PRACTICES. NIALL MCLAUGHLIN ARCHITECTS WAS NUMBER THIRTEEN."

within a conservation area, and the option to build the "heavy-looking" property the planners had approved. "What the woodland needed was a light house, which acknowledged its surroundings rather than dominating them," says Shelley. "We looked through The Architecture Foundation's New Architects book and approached twelve practices. Niall McLaughlin Architects was number thirteen."

David spent a great deal of time visiting the various architects, but found it extraordinary that only two actually wanted to come to the site. "When Niall walked into the room we had instant rapport. The question that we asked ourselves was: 'would we trust this man with all our worldly wealth?' Niall has a lot of gravitas and credibility. He brought a pile of books and we sat on the floor showing him the things that we liked – it was very exciting to see ideas evolving."

Although they admit that their knowledge

David and Shelley requested a single lane exercise pool, which extends out over the hill and into the view itself – becoming one of the main features of the house.

"FOR A LONG TIME WE HAD THOUGHT IT WOULD BE QUITE GOOD FUN TO BUILD A HOUSE – ALTHOUGH 'FUN' ISN'T A WORD I'D USE ANY MORE!"

of architecture and design was minimal, when the Greys picked out houses by the likes of Mies van der Rohe and Corbusier, Niall knew that the house would be drawn from early Modernist essays. He began with the Tugendhat villa, built by Mies van der Rohe in Czechoslovakia – which has a strong visual relationship with the landscape, distinct areas of accommodation linked by a flat roof, and a curved glass wall around the inner stairs.

"David and Shelley gave me a wonderful brief," recalls Niall, who was selected as the Young Architect of the Year in 1998. "Coming from a compartmentalised Georgian house, where they only ate in the dining room four times in five years, they wanted a more open building — with rooms that could be used even when they were empty." His partially open plan response frames the views, with glazing on all sides and internal windows ensuring that several areas of the house may be seen at once. A single storey swimming pool wing, with glass walls, shoots off from the simple rectangle of the main structure to create an eye-catching feature.

Although the local planning officer preferred the concept of a traditional house, with a pitched tiled roof, she accepted that the new property would not be overlooked in any way – permitting an altogether more contemporary glazed steel framed design.

"I told Niall that the two ways of getting himself fired would be to give us a red pitched tiled roof or a blue swimming pool!" laughs David.

The nature of the setting ensures total privacy, which made the

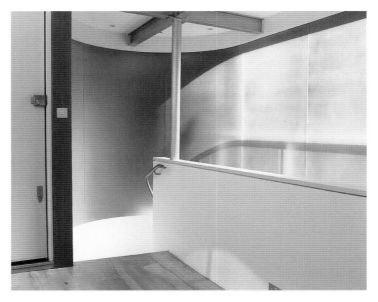

concept of a glass house a practical consideration. "We have no curtains in the house at all – even in the bathroom," says Shelley. "Our driveway is 200 metres long, with an electric entrance gate and CCTV security cameras – so we don't worry about unexpected guests dropping by!"

Work began on site in January 2000, with a completion date scheduled for nine months later. Concrete pads support the structural steel frame, which was erected in under two days and then clad in glass and warm coloured Douglas fir. After a year had passed the Greys grew concerned that something was amiss, and their fears were confirmed when the builder's company went into liquidation – leaving the building unfinished.

"I actually gave up work for a year to protect our investment and complete the house, whilst we continued living in rented accommodation," says David. "It wasn't

The timber staircase is enclosed within an opaque glass wall, inspired by the Tugendhat villa built by Mies van der Rohe in Czechoslovakia. ➤

"I STILL GET A BUZZ
EVERY TIME I COME
HOME. IT REALLY IS
THE MOST FANTASTIC
PLACE TO LIVE."

what we had planned, and various other people let us down so that a lot of the work needed to be redone at our expense. It was far more difficult than we had expected, but we soon took off our rose-tinted spectacles."

One piece of advice concerns the builder's insurance. "We found out that our contractor was under-insured for our project — which meant that the insurance company would only pay a percentage of our losses," he says.

Living in a woodland setting brings its own benefits and ensures that the log fire is always well stocked. Additionally, underfloor heating has been laid throughout the building, with trench heaters sited beneath ground floor windows to prevent condensation. David cut his own beech trees from around the house, which were kiln dried and machined to create floorboards for the interiors, and wild cherry trees were also felled — some of which have been used to build a wood and steel framed dining table.

With the house completed after almost two years the Greys have finally moved in. Jacob's Ladder, which received an RIBA 2002 Award, is perched on the steeply sloping hillside, with its glass walls built close to the surrounding beech trees. Niall McLaughlin designed a single gap in the dense enclosure of trees which gives a view into the valley below.

Views from the first floor entrance deck out over the internal pool and flooded swimming pool roof to the west.

Water plays an important part in the design, with the black tiled exercise pool actually giving you the impression of swimming out into the landscape. The silver ceiling of the pool house reflects the light, and Shelley suggested that this wing should have a flooded roof — which adds a further glassy, reflective element to this extraordinary new house.

"I still get a buzz every time I come home," David Grey remarks. "You arrive through the woodland and are greeted by the back of the house — which appears very strange. A gangplank bridge leads onto the first floor entrance deck and from here there are views out over the internal pool and flooded swimming pool roof to the west. It really is the most fantastic place to live." ▪

FACT FILE

Costs as of Dec 2002
Names: David and Shelley Grey
Professions: Photographer/
Film Director and Lawyer
Area: West Country
House type: Detached
contemporary
House size: 260m²
Build route: Contractor and
subcontractor
Construction: Steel frame
clad in glass and Douglas fir
Build time: Jan 00 - Dec 01

Land cost: £250,000
Build cost: £412,000
Total cost: £662,000
House value: £1 million+
Cost/m²: £1,585

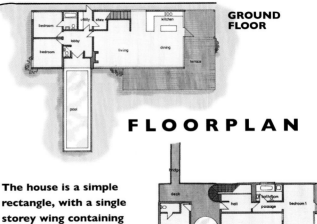

GROUND FLOOR

FLOORPLAN

The house is a simple
rectangle, with a single
storey wing containing
a glass walled
swimming pool. To the
north side is a first
floor office with guest
rooms below, whilst
larger living spaces
occupy the south side.

FIRST FLOOR

USEFUL CONTACTS

Architect - Niall McLaughlin Architects: 0207 4859170; **Quantity Surveyor** - Sworn King and Partners: 01865 241159; **Electrician** - Darke & Taylor: 01865 290000; **Sanitaryware** - C P Hart (Starke): 0207 9021010; **Glazing** - McLeans Glass: 01865 715165; **Plumbing (boiler room)** - Carfield Heating Ltd: 01372 722277; **Underfloor heating** - Uponor: 01455 550355; **Septic tank** - P V Construction: 0118 987 6493; **Glass** - Pilkington: 0121 3265300

WHITE LIGHT

Kevin and Catherine Cooper have designed and built a contemporary-style house in Scotland which also works effectively as a stylish family home.

WORDS: CAROLINE EDNIE
PHOTOGRAPHY: ANDREW LEE

KEVIN AND CATHERINE Cooper have achieved a rather rare double whammy with the design of their new home Mayar Bhan. For not only have they created something of a domestic tour de force in terms of the house's unique form and impeccably modern-minimalist interior spaces, but they have also managed to simultaneously pull off a real living and breathing family home. Indeed, the couple's seven year old twin sons Calum and Jack certainly seem to have endless fun in the house — which is a refreshing change from the clinical and often untouchable spaces that characterise so many of the new generation of cool, contemporary homes.

➤

The rectangular
house, built using
traditional masonry
construction,
was welcomed by
the planners as
a contemporary
take on traditional
Scottish architecture.

"IF YOU'RE GOING TO SPEND MONEY, I BELIEVE IT'S WORTH SPENDING IT ON THE ROOF AND ON THE GLAZING…"

"When we set out to design the house we had certain things in mind, but the priority was as much flexibility as possible. So, in the main living area, we've had everything from a mad kid's party, to a pensioners' dinner dance," explains Kevin. "We had contrasts in mind when we were designing the house," he adds: "We wanted a big, extrovert, light and airy space upstairs, and a cosy and intimate, more introvert area downstairs. There are lots of other contrasts too – for example it's glazed at the front and solid at the back."

Although the modern form of Mayar Bhan does look fairly unorthodox, flanked as it is between two traditional Victorian villas on a wooded site, it apparently posed few dilemmas for the local planning department. "We did talk to the planners first," explain Kevin and Catherine, who both work for Glasgow based architectural firm, The Parr Partnership, as well as their own practice.

"The house is very contextual, and sits back and respects the integrity of the buildings on either side," claims Kevin. "The building line is directly aligned with the houses on either side, so it's not highly visible. We thought the monopitch roof might have been a problem, but because it doesn't rise too high, it seemed to go through planning easily. We've dug the house into the ground in order to get the height down, and due to the fact that the ground level at the back is higher, we've built a massive retaining wall. So, it's now set in against the contours of the sloping site. In that respect the planners were happy that we had worked with the site, and I believe that the materials we used, such as the slate roof, are in keeping with traditional Scottish materials."

"If you look at the house in terms of its final cost, I think the budget worked out well," states Kevin. "Timescale-wise it took around 11 months from digging the first hole to moving in, and although developing the site was expensive – as it has a big retaining wall at the back – generally I think to do something really good you're realistically looking at £1,000/m². " Mayar Bhan has come in at around £1,325/m².

"The extra steelwork was probably the only thing we hadn't anticipated. Because of the wind loading there are four steel portals in the living room just so that we can avoid having any trusses in it. And to put them in we had to hire a 300 tonne crane – and that was extra. The boys loved it though – it was like an episode of Thunderbirds for them," laughs Kevin. ➤

Making the most of the Scottish light was a priority in the design, particularly on the first floor, which houses the main living spaces.

Although an impressive recessed solid fuel fireplace is one of the dominating features in the living area, the solar gain from the extensive external glazing, as well as the effective central heating makes it only a backup.

"IF WE HAD BUILT THE HOUSE AS A TIMBER KIT, IT WOULD DEFINITELY HAVE BEEN DONE CHEAPER…"

"If we had built the house as a timber kit, it could definitely have been done cheaper. And with the doors, windows and timber cladding, we thought it was important architecturally that it was the same material, so we haven't scrimped there. But the windows are bespoke and handmade – so this was a huge cost. If you're going to spend money though, I believe it's worth spending it on the roof and on the glazing," argues Kevin.

Kevin and Catherine assumed responsibility for supervision of the site – and since they were handily based in a house adjoining the site during construction, this didn't prove too troublesome. "Construction involved separate trades all taking part. It would have been nice to have one contractor, but there wasn't a local joiner who could cope with the work, for example," claims Kevin. So, according to Catherine "we looked at things every night, and often the only way we could get instructions to the contractors was to leave plastic bags with notes in, tied to the front door!"

The external appearance of Mayer Bhan is simple and unfussy. Essentially, it is a rectangle with a monopitch roof, and two top lit bays – one is a study and the other is a staircase. Kevin and Catherine were keen to try and minimise the cost, which is why there are no fancy details, such as dormers and the like. The house is constructed by means of masonry lateral walls, supporting timber beams, a flitch beam and four portal frames, which provide wind bracing to the main living space. Classic stone white polymer render and a type of mahogany called 'serayah' characterise the external cladding.

"We had a contemporary Scottish house in mind. 'Scottishness' is quite an elusive thing to describe, but I think it evokes a certain austerity and the way the massing works, to create a sculptural yet solid effect. And this is what we've tried to achieve," explains Kevin. "It's more open at the front, and we designed the clerestorey glazing so that we get ➤

The kitchen units are simple and low-cost, with Kevin and Catherine prioritising budget on creating high quality spaces rather than on fittings which could easily be replaced later.

The impressive six foot wide door from the kitchen/dining area onto the porch means that Kevin and Catherine can enjoy al fresco dining in the summer.

"THE PRIORITY WAS AS MUCH FLEXIBILITY AS POSSIBLE. SO, IN THE MAIN LIVING AREA, WE'VE HAD EVERYTHING FROM A MAD KIDS' PARTY, TO A PENSIONERS' DINNER DANCE"

all the warming sun. Scotland has got a lovely quality of light, which is the single most important quality in any building, and we've attempted to harness this in the interior spaces. The house feels airy and, being orientated west south west towards views of the island of Arran, on a crisp winter's day the views are fantastic. There is also a lot of privacy for us and the neighbours.

Internally, Mayar Bhan takes the form of an upside down house built over two levels. The entrance is met by a staircase which is expressed as a top lit volume, where the roof lights pull you upstairs to the main living spaces from ground level. The ground level itself comprises four "simple and functional" bedrooms (one en suite), a hall, bathroom and a study. The study, which occupies a niche to the right of the entrance, is Kevin's haven. "It's a fantastic place for concentrating in, because when the sun comes out it's flooded with light but you can't really see out to get distracted, as the windows are high up. It's in the quiet end of the house, so I spend a lot of time in it," says Kevin.

The upper level of Mayar Bhan is characterised by a great swathe of dramatic wide open, airy and expansive spaces. Dominated by a vast living and dining area, a bridge then links through to the kitchen/dining area which extends to an exterior timber deck. According to Kevin "people like big sexy kitchens, but we couldn't really afford a bespoke kitchen

with real granite and such details. We took the view that the kitchen can be replaced any time, and that the important thing is the quality of the space and the way it relates to the outside. As long as that's right you can change the kitchen any time. So, for now, our kitchen is very simple and small, but it's adequate for us."

Catherine was particularly keen for the kitchen to extend to the porch. "The six foot wide door in the kitchen means that you can totally open the kitchen to the back space, so you can sit outside in the summer. The sun rises in this area, which faces east, so you can get the best of the sun in the morning."

The flooring, which comprises of composite timber with a solid beech wearing layer, was laid by Kevin himself, as was the majority of the tiling and shelving, and some joinery work, not to mention laying the turf and gravel in the surrounding landscape garden.

The Coopers wouldn't change a thing about their new home. "We aimed to make a good piece of architecture but also a comfortable family home. And I think the house is not only conceptually what we really want, as it's sculptural, geometric and crisp, but it also has a happy atmosphere. The old walls and trees also create a lovely context for the house. So, although it's a contemporary house, it's also a well mannered house," concludes Kevin. ■

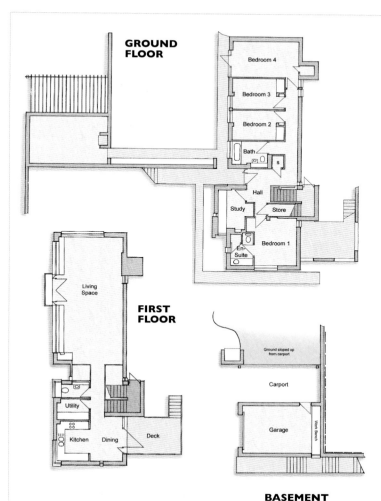

GROUND FLOOR

Bedroom 4
Bedroom 3
Bedroom 2
Bath
s
Hall
Study
Store
En-Suite
Bedroom 1

FIRST FLOOR

Living Space
Utility
Kitchen
Dining
Deck

BASEMENT

Ground sloped up from carport
Carport
Garage
Work Bench

FLOORPLAN

The main living spaces are all situated on the first floor, with four bedrooms, a master suite and study below. A carport and basement were introduced to the design to make the most of the sloping site.

FACT FILE

Names: Kevin and Catherine Cooper
Professions: Architects
Area: Ayrshire
House type: Contemporary four bed detached
house size: 166m²
Build route: Selves as main contractors
Construction: Masonry
Warranty: Architect's certificate
SAP rating: 71
Finance: Halifax
Build time: Apr '00 – Apr '02
Land cost: Value £40k
Build cost: £220,000
Total cost: £260,000
House value: £270,000
cost/m²: £773

4%
COST SAVING

Cost Breakdown:

Enabling work	£6,500
Substructure/basement	£30,000
Frame/external walls	£54,000
Joinery (1st/2nd fix)/ windows and doors	£81,500
Roof and rooflights	£13,500
Internal doors	£2,600
Wall/ceiling/floor finishes	£7,500
Sanitary/kitchen/built-in fittings	£11,200
M&E/plumbing/electrics	£11,800
Landscape and all external works	£1,500
TOTAL	**£220,100**

A NEW CONTEMPORARY-STYLE HOME BUILT FOR JUST £110,000

PERFECTLY
COMPOSED

**Musicians Graham Fitkin and Ruth Wall have created a
unique contemporary home on a remarkably low budget.**

WORDS: DEBBIE JEFFERY PHOTOGRAPHY: NIGEL RIGDEN

"FOR YEARS RUTH and I lived in a small, dark Cornish cottage which made rehearsing our music very difficult," explains Graham Fitkin. "We are both musicians, and trying to work at home was cramped and extremely noisy!" The couple had been house hunting for some time, but found that property prices always outstripped their means. "We had absolutely no desire to build our own house, but someone alerted us that a plot might be available and we decided to take a look out of desperation," Graham continues.

The site had previously contained a 1950s Dutch barn, and is set on the edge of a Cornish village in an Area of Outstanding Natural Beauty, near the coastal footpath and a Site of Special Scientific Interest. With no new houses built in the village for over 50 years, the planning history was long. Permission had been granted for a large two storey dwelling to replace the barn, but these plans were not suitable for Ruth and Graham – who gambled on producing a design that could be distinctly their own. ➤

"WITH AN EXTREMELY TIGHT INITIAL BUDGET OF JUST £95,000 WE DECIDED TO PROJECT MANAGE THE BUILD OURSELVES…"

The site itself, although in the highest part of the village, is also lower than the surrounding fields, so a distant view could only be achieved by having an upper storey – the height of which was limited by the previous application. "We approached the local planners for advice even Ruth and Graham decided to take the plunge, and purchased the plot for £80,000. They then contacted a number of local architects to discuss design options. "Barrie Briscoe happened to be the last architect we approached, and he was the only one who suggested a meeting on the site," Graham recalls. "We had seen examples of his work and liked the fact he designed each building to be site specific – he seemed to understand our requirements and worked hard to fulfil our brief."

Barrie Briscoe's practice takes on only a few carefully chosen projects each year and sees them through personally from the first feasibility study to the last interior detail. This philosophy has resulted in him winning the RIBA National Architecture Award as well as Cornish Building Group and Civic Trust Awards.

Graham and Ruth gave Barrie a detailed list of their needs. They both spend a great deal of time working from home, and wanted the domestic and work elements of the house to be separated in some way. "We love anything Italian and, although the house has a light, minimal feel, there are also elements which are distinctly Mediterranean," says Ruth. "We wanted to incorporate interesting shaped rooms with alcoves and nooks rather than straightforward rectangles, with as much sunlight entering these rooms as possible."

Barrie Briscoe took the couple's brief and, incorporating the required materials, designed the house as two wings – set at right angles to one another – with an octagonal, timber framed living room and balcony on the first floor and the master bedroom and en suite bathroom tucked into the eaves. Music studios have been positioned to either end of the ground floor, with a spacious kitchen/ diner set at the heart of the house.

The enveloping ground floor walls are insulated cavity blockwork, with recycled granite quoins and fieldstone facing. The southerly aspect on the ground floor is a system of timber columns and edge beams with steel connectors, accommodating large panels of K-glass. Whilst the main roof is covered in slate, the octagonal roof consists of principal rafters with steel connectors and tongue and groove sarking, which forms a warm roof construction.

An octagonal sitting room on the first floor provides a cosy retreat, with views across the surrounding Cornish countryside.

➤

Graham and Ruth now have their own music studios at opposite ends of the house, with enough space to store all of their instruments and equipment.

PERFECTLY COMPOSED

The bespoke kitchen units have been made from birch ply, with slate worktops and a French ceramic sink.

The central kitchen/dining room combines practical work areas with comfortable seating, book shelves and a grand piano.

"We loved Barrie's design, and the planners approved," says Graham. "With an extremely tight initial budget of just £95,000 we decided to project manage the build ourselves, using local subcontractors and DIY labour to keep costs down. Barrie offered help and advice throughout – including lists of local tradesmen." Ruth and Graham engaged an experienced mason and carpenter, set themselves eight months to build the house and began excavating into the bedrock in May 2001.

"We sold our cottage to help fund the build, and moved into rented accommodation nearby," says Graham. "When the project overran we decided to move into the unfinished house, and lived there for six months without a front door or glass in the windows. With no kitchen or heating we made do with a single extension lead, a camping gas stove and an outdoor hosepipe."

Each morning Graham and Ruth would get up at 6am to work on their music for two or three hours before the builders arrived, and would continue working until midnight. Graham performs as a soloist on piano and in duet with Ruth, composes music and has conducted groups such as the New York City Ballet and The Royal Liverpool Philharmonic Orchestra. He and Ruth mainly perform on digital sampling keyboards and they are currently working together on a music and visuals project called Kaplan.

"Deadlines are crucial in my business," says Graham, "and I have

"WHEN THE PROJECT OVERRAN WE DECIDED TO MOVE INTO THE UNFINISHED HOUSE, AND LIVED THERE FOR SIX MONTHS WITHOUT A FRONT DOOR OR GLASS IN THE WINDOWS."

never missed one in my life. It was certainly interesting working in a different world, with builders' merchants and suppliers for whom time is more elastic!"

Although camping out in the house was fun, both Ruth and Graham were exhausted by the process, and began to grow weary of sleeping in a freezing bed coated with cement dust. Meanwhile they both worked alongside the tradesmen on virtually every aspect of the build, including most of the decorating.

"My father built his own house, and always joked that I was the least practical person he knew," laughs Graham. "It's true – but I have learnt a huge amount from watching other people. The one aspect of the whole project I didn't enjoy was haggling over prices, but we managed to drastically cut costs by phoning around and using the internet."

Considering that the final build cost totalled just £110,000, nothing about the 160m² house indicates that this was a low budget self-build. ➤

One of the couple's best buys was the granite used for facing much of the house which had been reclaimed from an barn and cost them just £1300.

The site itself, although in the highest part of the village, is also lower than the surrounding fields, so a distant view could only be achieved by having an upper storey

One of the couple's best buys was the granite used for facing much of the house, which had already been purchased by the previous owner of the site and was lying in a neighbouring field. This had been reclaimed from an old barn and cost just £1,300.

Pilkington K glass was specified, the building is massively insulated and an oil fired boiler provides underfloor heating for the whole house – with the studios floored in birch ply panels and the kitchen/diner in riven slate slab on screed at a cost of just £19/m².

The kitchen units were designed by the architectural practice and made by a friend in birch ply, with Chinese slate worktops and a French-style ceramic sink. Unusual touches are evident throughout

"IT WAS CERTAINLY INTERESTING WORKING WITH BUILDERS' MERCHANTS AND SUPPLIERS FOR WHOM TIME IS ELASTIC!"

the house, and include a heavy wall of mobile shelves, which may be pushed back to open up the dining area.

With so many glazed walls, storage was a vital consideration, and discreet cupboards, drawers and shelving create features in every room. "It is fantastic to finally have enough space for all of our stuff," says Ruth. "We could never have found a house which suits our needs so perfectly. It really is made to measure." ■

FLOORPLAN

The ground floor accommodates the majority of rooms, with two music studios set at opposite ends of the building and a central kitchen/diner. There is also an office, cloakroom, utility room and guest bedroom on this level. Upstairs, the living room provides views of the surrounding countryside, with the master bedroom and en suite tucked into the eaves.

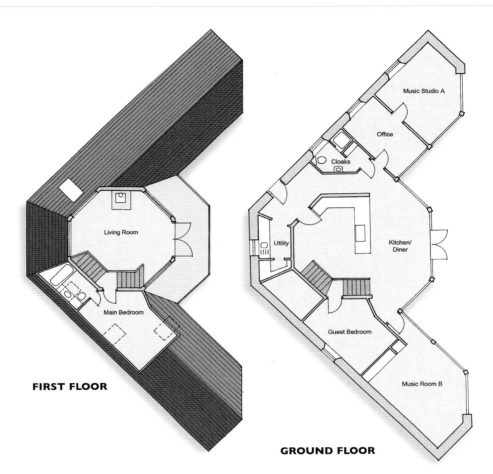

FIRST FLOOR

Living Room

Main Bedroom

GROUND FLOOR

Music Studio A

Office

Cloaks

Utility

Kitchen/ Diner

Guest Bedroom

Music Room B

FACT FILE

Names: Graham Fitkin & Ruth Wall
Professions: Musicians
Area: Cornwall
House type: Two bedroom, two studio detached house
House size: 160m²

Build route: Self-managed subcontractors and DIY
Construction: Cavity blockwork with stone facing, timber framed first floor, slate roof
Warranty: Architect's Certificate
SAP rating: 97
Finance: Cheltenham and Gloucester Building Society
build time: May '01 – Aug '02
Land cost: £80,000
Build cost: £110,000
Total cost: £190,000
House value: £375,000
cost/m²: £687

49%
COST SAVING

Cost Breakdown:

Granite	£1,300
Underfloor heating	£4,000
Pilkington K glass	£5,000
Window joinery	£8,000
Guttering	£800
Electrician	£2,900
Kitchen units	£1,000
Slate worktops	£260
Kitchen sink	£230
Other materials and labour	£86,510
TOTAL	**£110,000**

USEFUL CONTACTS

Graham Fitkin - www.fitkin.com; **Architect** - Barrie Briscoe: 01736 350999; **Interior design consultant** - Petra Elkan: 01736 350999; **Structural engineer** - Richard Holbrook: 01872 580170; **Services engineer** - Mike Crook: 01872 274312; **Carpenter and joiner** - Richard Boekee: 01736 787465; **Underfloor heating** - Osma: 01392 444122; **Steel bath** - Bette: 01789 262262; **Slate floors** - MC Slate: 01363 82598

LOOKING FORWARD

BUILDING A REMARKABLE CONTEMPORARY HOME

Lightweight timber framed 'boxes' clad in untreated western red cedar are supported on a masonry ground floor construction.

Matt and Linda Fox – with help from H&R Award-winning architect, Stan Bolt – have built a remarkable new family home.

WORDS: DEBBIE JEFFERY   PHOTOGRAPHY: NIGEL RIGDEN

"MATT AND I can be rather impulsive and, once we had met architect Stan Bolt and seen his work, we decided not to approach any-one else," explains Linda Fox. "The strange thing is that my taste is quite traditional – country cottages and barn conversions – but Stan designs such incredible contemporary houses that we both loved the idea of being adventurous and trying something completely different. Now we have lived here, I don't think we could go back to living in a conventional house because it would seem so dark in comparison."

Matthew and Linda Fox are both GPs and have two young sons –

Harry, aged four, and Oliver, two. They bought their first home together in a tucked away location near Torquay in Devon for £95,000. The couple lived in this modest bungalow for six years, and planned to extend the property, which overlooks a rural landscape to the south west and has distant coastal views.

"We knew we wanted something out of the ordinary, and had been looking for ideas in magazines," Linda continues. "Stan was the first architect we approached, and we gave him an open brief to substantially extend, alter and modernise the existing bungalow, which had restricted views and no real access to the garden. We wanted to be able to throw open the doors and get outside really easily, and Stan came up with a radical design that replaced the pitched roof and sat two projecting timber clad bays on the existing walls, transforming the bungalow beyond ➤

Delabole slate flooring has been used in the kitchen, bathrooms and hallway, with ash flooring in the living areas and bedrooms.

"WE COULDN'T POSSIBLY HAVE AFFORDED TO BUY A BUILDING PLOT IN SUCH A GOOD LOCATION, SO IT MADE SENSE TO BITE THE BULLET AND KNOCK IT DOWN."

"Not only were the bungalow's foundations not particularly sound, but there would be the added bonus of being able to reclaim the VAT on a new build," says Stan. "We decided to develop the project as an entirely new construction, honouring the height of the bungalow and retaining established building lines to avoid blocking views for the neighbouring properties. The house grew naturally from the site constraints – in many respects it designed itself."

Stan created a detailed scale model of the proposed new dwelling, which enabled the planners and neighbours to better visualise the building. Its layout centres around a ground floor entrance/circulation area and two storey interconnecting living spaces formed by a glazed atrium and the curved rendered masonry stair tower, with more cellular and private spaces subservient to these core areas.

A planning application was submitted in August 2001 and received the full support of the Local Authority, Teignbridge District Council. Construction commenced in November 2002 on a Minor Works Contract to the value of £300,000, following a formal tendering process.

"It was hard watching our old home being demolished," says Linda, "but we were aware that we couldn't possibly have afforded to buy a building plot in such a good location, so it made sense to bite the bullet and knock it down."

The Fox family moved in with Linda's parents, who lived just two doors away, and continued working throughout the build. With a young family and demanding jobs, they were relieved that Stan Bolt could oversee the contract on their behalf. "We did absolutely nothing – although the boys did get to drive the diggers," says Linda. "We would have had no idea where to start. Choosing the paint colour for the wardrobes was about as far as our involvement went!"

recognition using large amounts of glazing and a curved stair tower."

Matthew and Linda immediately loved the scheme, but Stan grew concerned that upgrading and altering the existing structure to meet current building regulation standards would prove expensive, and suggested that the couple could consider totally demolishing and rebuilding their home instead.

The ground floor has been constructed in rendered cavity blockwork with beam and block flooring, and the lightweight timber framed first floor is packed with insulation. "A certain amount of steel framing was

A bridge with glass balustrades crosses from the upstairs sitting room to the balcony, enabling contact with the dining room below (left). ➤

required to achieve the cantilevers, which gives the building its sense of abstraction," Stan Bolt explains.

These dramatic boxes have been clad in untreated cedar, with Roofkrete used to cover the flat roof. This is a waterproofing membrane which solves the problems usually associated with flat roofing materials and consists of natural minerals which do not decay. The stair tower has been built in brick to achieve the curved walls and finished in render. "Although the house is unconventional, it is quite low-tech and was very logical to build," says Stan, who paid great attention to every detail.

The staircase is suffused with light from a rooflight in the top of the curved tower. Right: Matthew and Linda with their two sons two young sons – Harry, aged four, and Oliver, two.

The couple's faith in, and commitment to, Stan's design saw him making almost every decision regarding the internal fixtures and fittings, from lights to door handles – a process which he considers to be part and parcel of his overall role. "Everything that's fixed is our remit," he says. In return, he has included generous storage areas in the hall and bedrooms which help to conceal the usual clutter associated with a young family.

The children have their own ground floor wing, behind a sliding door – a shared bedroom, bathroom and playroom, with comfortingly low ceilings, filled with toys and brightly painted furniture. A small guest room in this part of the house doubles as a retreat where Linda may paint and read. "I tend to use this room for relaxing, as we have a separate study area in the family room," she explains. "Having a partially open plan ➤

"HAVING A PARTIALLY OPEN PLAN LAYOUT WORKS WELL BECAUSE WE CAN BE IN THE STUDY OR KITCHEN AND ARE STILL ABLE TO KEEP AN EYE ON THE CHILDREN."

layout works well because we can be in the study or kitchen and are still able to keep an eye on the children."

Upstairs, the spacious adult living room is a truly contemporary space, with a high ceiling and large sections of virtually frameless glazing. Corner windows with glass to glass junctions erode the definition between inside and out, while panels of birch-faced plywood may be lit from behind — creating a glowing border of light.

"Stan had very firm ideas on everything, and we changed only a couple of minor details – such as repositioning a toilet door and adding a strip of

pink to the wall in the en suite bathroom," says Linda. "We were also responsible for choosing the kitchen units, which were fitted by a friend, but virtually everything else was suggested by our architect. It means that the end result works extremely well as a whole."

In order to meet planning approval the new design needed to keep the same ridge height as the bungalow it replaced, as well as its neighbours.

Matthew and Linda have purchased new items of furniture for the house, including the understated sofas in the sitting room which complement the sleek lines, white walls and modern fireplace.

"Fortunately, we didn't have much furniture to begin with," Linda continues. "We gave away some things and others were burnt because they were so horrible. It was a completely fresh start for us, and the house has proved very practical for family life. With no carpets the children can ride their bikes on the slate and ash floors and have made a den in the space under the stairs. Although the design is most definitely a Stan Bolt house, it works for us, and we feel very proud of our new home." ■

FLOORPLAN

The majority of the accommodation is on the ground floor, where the kitchen, utility, WC, family room and study area are located. There is a children's wing with a bedroom, playroom and bathroom in addition to a guest bedroom/ studio. Upstairs, the spacious living room and master bedroom suite lead out onto a decked balcony.

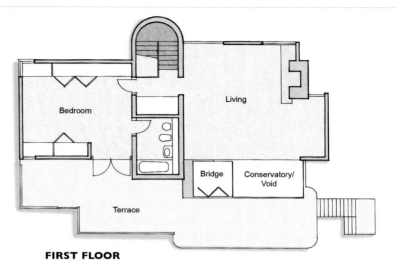

FIRST FLOOR

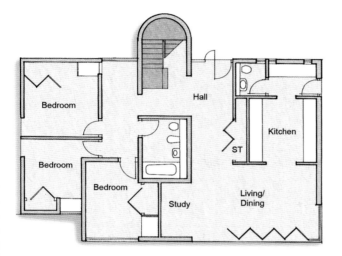

GROUND FLOOR

USEFUL CONTACTS

Architect Stan Bolt: 01803 852588; **Structural engineers** Nicholls Basker Partners: 01626 776121; **Services engineer** Dodd, Cumming and Love: 01752 253559; **Main contractor** Hannon Young Ltd: 01626 770099; **Ironmongery** Allgoods PLC: 0870 609 0009; **Catches/fittings** Häfele UK: 01788 542020; **Stains** Akzo Nobel Wood Care: 01480 496868; **Paints** Ameron Coatings: 01623 511000, Farrow & Ball: 01202 876141; **Internal doors** Premdor: 01226 383434; **Fireplace** Jetmaster Fires Ltd: 0870 727 0105; **Floor beams, pre-cast concrete cills and copings** Mexboro: 01803 558025; **Pivot gear** Dorma Entrance System: 01462 480544; **Insulation** Kingspan Insulation Ltd: 0870 850 8555, Rockwool Ltd: 01656 862621; **Waterproofing** Ruberoid Building Products: 01707 822222, Vandex (UK) Ltd: 01372 363040; **Slate flooring** Delabole Slate: 01840 212242; **Light fittings** Zumtobel Staff Lighting Ltd: 020 8589 1800, Marlin Lighting Ltd: 020 8894 5522, Amos Lighting: 01392 677030; **Sanitary ware** Armitage Shanks: 01543 490253; **Shower fittings** Hansgrohe: 01372 465655, CP Hart: 020 7902 1000; **Shower tray** Neaco: 01653 695721; **Taps** Vola UK Ltd: 01525 841155; **Sliding/folding doors** I-D-Systems: 01603 408804; **Timber floors** Atkins & Cripps: 01752 841333; **Flat roofing** Roofkrete Ltd: 01647 277475; **Underfloor heating** Uponor Plumbing and Heating Systems: 01455 550355

FACT FILE

Names: Linda and Matthew Fox
Professions: GPs
Area: Devon
House type: Four bedroom detached
House size: 223m²
Build route: Main contractor
Construction: Rendered blockwork, timber and steel frame, flat roofing
Warranty: Architect's Certificate
Finance: NatWest stage payment mortgage
Build time: Nov '02 – Aug '03
Land cost: £95,000
Build cost: £300,000
Total cost: £395,000
House value: £650,000
Cost/m²: £1,345

39%
COST SAVING

Cost Breakdown:

Prelims, insurances, scaffolding, site set-up	£35,000
Demolition, form site access	£15,000
Carport, workshop and stores	£12,000
Drainage, service trenching	£9,000
Foundations and below ground blockwork	£8,000
Ground floor beam and block flooring	£7,000
Ground floor walling	£30,000
First floor beam and block and joists	£7,000
First floor walling	£30,000
Roof structure, terrace, balustrade	£8,000
Roof covering	£13,000
Carpentry incl. doors and windows	£45,000
Mechanical incl. fitting	£18,000
Electrical incl. fitting	£13,000
Plaster and render	£12,000
Floor finishes	£11,000
Decoration	£8,000
Glazing	£5,000
External works, driveway and pond	£13,000
TOTAL	**£300,000**

A NEW HOME BUILT ON A SMALL SITE

URBAN OASIS

**Tessa Ashley-Miller and Clive Evans
have built a new house in North London
which combines a deliberately aged
exterior with contemporary interiors.**

WORDS: DEBBIE JEFFERY   PHOTOGRAPHY: PHILIP BIER

"VISITORS ARE SHOCKED when they first walk inside our house,"
says Tessa Ashley-Miller. "They expect traditional interiors and are
surprised when they see just how modern everything is."

With its soft edges, uneven rendering and traditional detailing, most
people mistake the secluded three bedroom house in London's Highgate
– which is set within its own tropical oasis-style garden – for a period
original. In contrast, however, the interiors
of the property are a showcase for
modern living, with uncluttered open plan
spaces, clean lines, creative lighting and
home automation.

**The curved staircase
was produced by a local
metalworker and clad
in limestone, forming
a centrepiece for the
open plan ground floor
arrangement.** ➤

"INTERNALLY, I TOOK MY INSPIRATION FROM HOLIDAYS SPENT IN ASIA AND CHOSE SIMPLE, NATURAL MATERIALS."

"Internally, I took my inspiration from holidays spent in Asia and chose simple, natural materials," says Tessa, an interior designer. "We live in a Conservation Area and so the exterior needed to be sympathetic to the surrounding buildings. I asked for the rendering to be uneven and used non-uniform grey slate tiles and traditional lead rolls for the roof. The main windows are arched with Gothic detailing, and we have grown plants up against the walls of the house to help create the impression that it has stood here for many years."

Tessa and her partner, Clive Evans, had been searching for a home when they discovered a property which already had planning permission for a new house to replace the existing garage. The couple decided to

The kitchen was ergonomically designed, with a large island unit acting as a breakfast bar and containing the hob.

purchase the house, which they developed into flats, eventually demolishing the garage in order to build The Coach House.

"As an interior designer I'm used to planning rooms, but this was the first time I'd built anything from scratch," says Tessa. She and Clive decided to radically change the layout of the plans and incorporated a conservatory in the compact 145m² design.

"We were limited by the height and footprint of the original garage and the size of the plot, but in some ways these restrictions helped us to refine our ideas and focus on what we really needed," she states.

The accommodation is predominantly on the ground floor, where an open plan kitchen leads directly into the sitting room and the conservatory beyond. Two bedrooms, a bathroom and utility room are positioned to the other end of the ground floor and a sculptural curved staircase, clad in limestone,

The Coach House sits within a walled tropical garden oasis, tucked away in North London. ➤

"ENCLOSING THE GARDEN WITH A WALL HAS GIVEN US REAL SECLUSION AND SECURITY."

wardrobes have been built into the eaves in the master bedroom. Ivory walls and pale limestone flooring increase the impression of space, with sheer fabric panels, glass balustrades and split levels designed to zone the various open plan areas.

Tessa and Clive lived next door in one of their flats during the build, and found being so close to the site a real bonus. Tessa decided to reduce her workload in order to act as project manager, purchasing materials and co-ordinating the various trades. "We employed a local builder who had previously converted our flats, and then used specialist subcontractors," she explains. "There was a great deal of excavation involved on site and we needed expensive piled foundations which added to the final build cost.

"I would have liked to use Welsh slate for the roof but it was just too costly, so we ended up compromising with Spanish slates and some lovely lead roll detailing around the dormers. The conservatory has a glazed lantern roof like an orangery, with a deep lead lip which allows us to walk around the edge and clean the glass."

Underfloor heating has been laid throughout the house, and an advanced heating control system divides The Coach House into nine fully independent heating zones, with thimble-sized temperature sensors discreetly located in each area which provide accurate temperature readings, allowing the system to determine precisely when the heating should be activated.

Lutron lighting allows Tessa and Clive to set lighting scenes using a remote control, which also activates the television and integrated music system. "We can choose different light settings for watching a film or having a dinner party," Tessa explains.

"The blinds in our bedroom are electronically operated and the television is concealed and pops up at the end of the bed. I'm not particularly good with gadgets, and setting the various controls has taken a while to get used to. When Clive went away for a week I read a lot because I couldn't work out how to turn on the TV!"

Tessa was responsible for designing every detail in the house, from the windows, fireplace, bespoke sofas and bed to the TV stand in the living room, which may be swivelled to face the

leads up from the sitting room to a galleried study area and the master bedroom suite.

"I work from home and wanted a study where I could enjoy some privacy without feeling cut off from the rest of the house. The garage that was here had two different roof levels, and theoretically we didn't have the double height for a gallery, so we had to work out every last centimetre of space," says Tessa, who drew her ideas to scale and used an architect to produce the final plans.

The couple were allowed to extend the overall size of the building by 10 per cent, which enabled them to have slightly larger bedrooms on the ground floor and a balcony off the master bedroom.

In order to achieve clean, uncluttered spaces it was vital to incorporate adequate storage, which has been concealed throughout the house. Cupboards are cleverly hidden behind mirrors in the bathrooms and

The en suite bathroom is clad in travertine and has a square sink, inset bath and walk-in shower.

The glazed lantern roof has a deep lead lip around the edge which can be walked on to clean the glass. ➤

"THE ENGINEER SAID 'I DON'T DO CURVES,' BUT I CONVINCED HIM THAT IT WAS POSSIBLE AND SPENT HOURS DRAWING UP EVERYTHING IN GREAT DETAIL."

kitchen when required and forms a partial partition between these open plan areas. The kitchen was ergonomically designed, with a large island unit acting as a breakfast bar and containing the hob – creating a sociable space for cooking and eating.

"I had to think about items such as the staircase very carefully," says Tessa. "The engineer said 'I don't do curves,' but I convinced him that it was possible and spent hours drawing up everything in great detail – although we were held up for several months while the metalworker finished making the stairs. The wall of the first floor shower room bends around in the opposite direction, and these are the only curves in the entire house.

"Designing the garden was just as important as the interiors," she continues. "Clive suggested a tropical theme, and I undertook an enormous amount of research into plants which have the right shaped leaves and can survive the English climate.

The nature of the site dictated the solution: different levels with decked areas and steps to soften the effect. We bought a hot tub which we were told could be sunk into the ground, but discovered that this wasn't the case, so I had to quickly redesign the entire layout at the last minute.

Enclosing the garden with a wall has given us real seclusion and security; it's lovely to be able to relax in the hot tub listening to music through the garden speakers, and easy to forget that we're actually living in London." ■

Tessa, an interior designer, also designed the sofas and chose simple, natural materials

FLOORPLAN

A gallery level is used as a study, with double doors leading to the master bedroom suite and balcony. Downstairs, the kitchen and living room are open plan with a separate conservatory/dining room, two guest bedrooms, a bathroom and utility room.

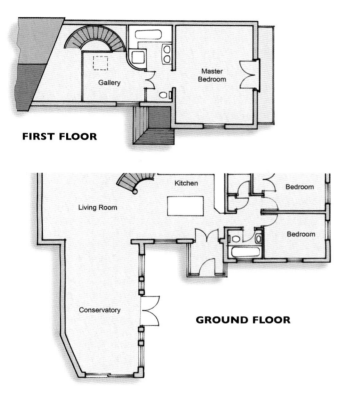

FIRST FLOOR

GROUND FLOOR

USEFUL CONTACTS

Interior design – Maison des Arts: 020 8348 9990; **Intelligent heating controls** – Smartkontrols Ltd: 01825 769812; **Bespoke TV cabinet and joinery** – Wooden it be Nice: 01707 644224; **Bespoke sofas and ottoman** – Sofabed Shop: 020 8444 7463; **Sanitaryware** – Original Bathrooms: 020 8940 7554; **Stone, fireplace** – JR Marble: 020 8539 6471; **Handles** – Architectural Fittings: 020 8883 3980; **Carpets, wood flooring, laying limestone** – The Essential Flooring Co: 020 7688 2019; **Lantern roof** – Hi-Glaze: 01440 762014; **Kitchen units** – Plain and Simple: 020 7731 2530; **Fire burner** – Platonic Fireplace Co: 020 8891 5904; **Electronic blinds and panel system** – Ace Contracts: 020 8801 9011; **Sliding doors** – Californian Closets: 020 8208 4544; **Music, security, lighting** – Rococo Systems: 020 7454 1234; **Tropical plants** – Mulu: 01386 833171; **Piled foundations and beams** – Select Pile: 01985 840977; **Bed** – De La Espada: 020 7581 4474; **Roofing and building contractors** – SW Gill: 07961 114482

MAKING MAXIMUM USE OF SPACE

The most restricted sites often bring out the most interesting and innovative of all individual home designs. Clever techniques that help to make the most of the space include eliminating the traditional entrance hall in favour of a dining hall, and large open plan spaces that further cut down on circulation space.

FACT FILE

Names: Tessa Ashley-Miller and Clive Evans
Professions: Interior designer and chartered surveyor
Area: London
House type: Three bedroom detached
House size: 145m^2
Build route: Builder and subcontractors
Construction: Rendered blockwork, Spanish roof slates
Finance: Private
Build time: June '01 – Dec '02
Land cost: £150,000
Build cost: £400,000
Total cost: £550,000
House value: £1,200,000
Cost/m^2: £2,758

54%
COST SAVING

Cost Breakdown:

Fees	£3,500
Piling	£13,000
Earthworks	£14,500
Builder	£100,000
Roofs and gutters	£29,000
Windows and doors	£8,000
Electrics	£8,000
Underfloor heating and controls	£12,500
Flooring (labour)	£4,000
Video/music automation	£23,000
Staircase	£6,000
Bathrooms	£6,000
Plaster/render/screed	£11,500
Decoration	£5,000
Marble	£20,000
Floor tiles	£8,500
Plumbing	£6,500
Kitchen	£16,000
Wardrobes	£7,000
Internal doors and cabinets	£3,500
Automated blinds	£3,500
Fireplace and burner	£14,300
Glass balustrade	£6,000
Metalwork	£800
Black limestone driveway	£4,500
Landscaping	£5,000
Sliding gate	£5,000
Bespoke carpentry	£3,500
Pool	£12,000
External walling	£13,000
Exterior lighting, water irrigation system	£8,000
Decking	£1,500
Hot tub	£6,400
Tropical plants	£5,000
Miscellaneous	£6,000
TOTAL	**£400,000**

PREFABULOUS

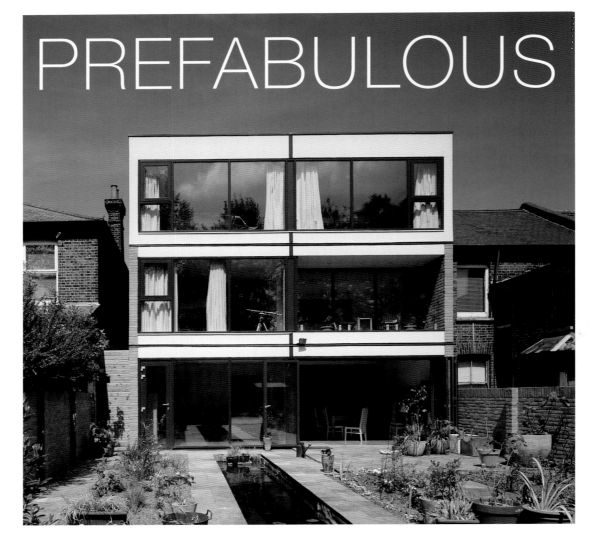

John Lock and Jan Tallis have replaced their tired 1930s house with a new prefabricated home which took just five days to erect on site.

WORDS: DEBBIE JEFFERY PHOTOGRAPHY: PHILIP BIER

FOR MOST SELF-BUILDERS the concept of watching their new home being delivered as complete prefabricated pods would be a dream come true, but for John Lock it proved to be the most nerve-wracking experience of his life. "Although it was exciting to see the six pods which make up our house being craned into position, I did wonder whether everything would fit together and how it would look once it was built," he admits. "We had invested a great deal of money in what was essentially a prototype, and watching our home swinging overhead on the end of a crane was quite a worrying sight. Thankfully all the units fitted together perfectly and the installation went exactly as planned."

John and his wife, Jan Tallis, had been living in a four-bedroom Victorian property with their sons, Nathaniel, now 11, and eight-year-old Cato, when they decided to move. The family needed more space and, after discussing the possibility of building a rear extension and converting the loft, they decided that it would prove less expensive to find another house altogether.

"We like this part of East London and I had always wanted to live in Capel Road, about half a mile from our previous house," Jan explains. "It overlooks a large Victorian cemetery with mature trees and is close to the southern tip of Epping Forest, which makes it relatively easy to access open ➤

"THE 1930S HOUSE WAS A TWO STOREY CONSTRUCTION, BUT ITS HUGE MANSARD ROOF CREATED ENOUGH HEIGHT… FOR THREE STOREYS."

countryside. Large houses rarely come onto the market there as it is such a sought-after area so, when we discovered a detached three-bedroom 1930s house was for sale in a road we really had liked for a long time, we were keen to try and buy it."

The brick property was shabby and needed rewiring, replacement windows and re-plumbing. The stairs up to the small attic space were a death trap, and John and Jan realised that they would need to spend a great deal of money on extending and renovating the building. Despite this fact they agreed to pay the rather inflated purchase price and moved into their new home in September 2001.

"By this time we had concluded that it really would be more economical to knock down the house and build a new one from scratch," says John, "and we approached an architect to try and come up with a low-cost design for a modern town house which would suit the site. Unfortunately, quotes were coming in at around £400,000 for a conventionally built house, which was significantly more than we could afford."

John and Jan contacted the Royal Institute of British Architects (RIBA), who suggested three local practices, and the couple selected Bryden

Wood Associates who specialise in industrial design and prefabrication. "To put it crudely we wanted to get the maximum amount of bang for our buck," John continues, "and our architects, Martin Wood and Paul O'Neill, came up with an ingenious scheme which involved prefabricating 'pods' off site and then craning them into position. All of the work was to be completed for a fixed price of £300,000, including £40,000 for groundworks and landscaping, which would mean that we wouldn't have to constantly worry about build costs and could be confident about not blowing our budget."

The 1930s house was a two storey construction, but its huge mansard roof created enough height for the new house to be arranged over three storeys while still retaining the same roof line. A small and shabby garage was also to be demolished so that the new house could be positioned further back on the site, substantially increasing the amount of living space to 250m2 and fulfilling planning requirements.

"The garage was designed for an Austin A30 rather than a modern-day Ford Galaxy," says John. "We could drive our car into the garage but

Jon and Jan wanted an open plan living area with a double height space above the dining area. ➤

there was no way we could open the doors to get out, so demolishing it seemed the most sensible use of space."

The family had specific requirements for their new home, which is highly insulated and almost completely glazed to the rear elevation. "We wanted an open plan living/dining room on the ground floor, with a double-height space above the dining table and easy access out into the garden," Jan explains. "Upstairs, the first floor is 'adult' space, with our bedroom leading onto a covered balcony, and a separate library for reading and relaxing. The children's rooms are up on the second floor, where we also have a guest bedroom, and it's an arrangement that works extremely well."

The plot is situated in an Area of Townscape Value, and the planners were keen that the contemporary new house should complement its more traditional surroundings. They allowed the steel and concrete building to be constructed with a flat rather than a pitched roof, but refused Jan's request for copper cladding – favouring blue render and brick slips which would emulate the slate roofs and brick walls of neighbouring buildings.

Once the plans had been approved the contractor, Optimum Building Products in Hull, could fabricate a prototype pod complete with wincows, wiring, plumbing, cladding and render which would also be light enough to lift by crane. Even the interior walls received an undercoat of paint. Eventually, the six large units which would make up the house could be produced – each measuring approximately 11 by

Inexpensive Ikea kitchen units have been fitted with fossil marble worktops for a luxurious finish. ➤

Glass balustrading and white walls help to complement the additional light drawn down by the lightwell.

four metres — and John and Jan were able to visit the factory, step inside sections of their new home and try to visualise how it would look.

During this time they moved out of their house, put their furniture into storage and rented a flat close to the site. The house could then be demolished and the eight-metre-wide site cleared — a process which John terms 'urban euthanasia'. "It was way past its best," he says. "A compendium of design and build mistakes spanning the past 75 years."

The new ground floor slab, footings and drainage needed to be particularly accurate so that, once the pods arrived, everything would match up exactly. "Before we could bring in the pods we had to tell our neighbours what was happening and ask if they would mind moving their cars," says John. "It's a tight site, and there was only about one metre between the new house and our next-door neighbours, so it was worrying to watch the rooms being dropped into place by a 100-ton crane. The low-loaders had a police escort from Hull, and everything was planned like a military operation to make sure that the vehicles could actually get down the road, but it was still the most nerve-wracking experience seeing the ground floor of our home swinging above other people's houses!"

The family watched with concern as their new home began to take shape, and were able to walk around the ground floor later that day,

"[THEY] WERE ABLE TO VISIT THE FACTORY AND STEP INSIDE SECTIONS OF THEIR NEW HOME."

although much of it was still hidden beneath a protective layer of plastic. On day two the low-loaders returned to Hull to load up the next two pods, and were back with their police escort the following day bearing the first floor. By day five the final storey had been lifted into position and the construction work came to an end.

"Although the majority of the house came pre-finished there was still a three-month period of connecting services, laying floors, decorating and installing the kitchen and bathrooms," Jan explains. "Three years after we bought the old house we were able to move into our new home, which was a far cry from its draughty 1930s predecessor.

"We wanted to make sure that the building would be nothing like the poorly built prefabs of the 1940s, and specified high-quality glazing and masses of insulation. With all that glass it can get quite warm in the summer, but the rear wall of the dining area can be completely folded back which allows cool air to circulate so that, although people look horrified when we tell them we live in a prefab, they soon change their minds when they see for themselves what a comfortable, modern home it actually is." ■

FLOORPLAN

The house has been designed over three storeys, with the children's bedrooms, bathroom and guest room on the top floor and the adults' bedroom, balcony, bathroom and library/lounge on the first floor. Downstairs, the open plan living room and double-height dining area overlook the rear garden through a wall of glass, with a separate study to the front of the house.

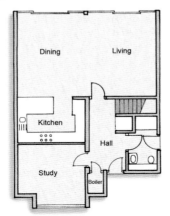

GROUND FLOOR

FIRST FLOOR

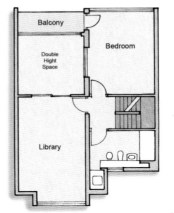

SECOND FLOOR

PREFABRICATED HOMES

Prefabricated homes were first built in 1944 to help relieve the post-war housing shortage, when thousands of these 'temporary' bungalows were built using asbestos, concrete, steel and aluminium. Prefabricated in factories, the homes were only supposed to last for around five years but many are still in use today.

Recently the interest in prefabs has been revived, with Ikea announcing that it will be selling flat-packed homes imported from Sweden aimed at first-time buyers who have been priced out of the housing market. The concept has already proved popular in Scandinavia and will help

John Prescott in his ambition to build 80,000 affordable new homes by the year 2010. Other companies are also taking up the prefab challenge and changing self-builders' negative preconceptions by offering inexpensive, well-insulated homes which are constructed almost entirely off site.

FACT FILE

Names: Jan Tallis and John Lock
Professions: Chief executive of School-Home Support charity and development manager for university
Area: East London
House type: Four bedroom prefabricated house

House size: 250m²
Build route: Prefabricated and erected by Optimum Building Products
Construction: Steel and concrete pods clad in brick and render
Warranty: Architect's Certificate
finance: BuildStore mortgage
Build time: Aug '03 – Aug '04
Land cost: est. £275,000
Build cost: £300,000
Total cost: £575,000
House value: £600,000
Cost/m²: £1,200

4%
COST SAVING

USEFUL CONTACTS

Architect – Bryden Wood Associates: 020 7253 4772; **Structural engineers** – DTA: 0121 233 1323; **Prefabricators** – Optimum Building Products Ltd: 01482 788355; **Brick slips** – Eurobrick: 0117 971 7117; **Render** – Sto: 01505 333555; **Timber flooring** – Boen UK: 0870 770 4322; **Glazing** – CSI: 01482 788355; **Folding sliding doors** – I-D-Systems: 01603 408804; **Ironmongery** – Dorplan: 01707 647647; **Radiators** – Stelrad: 01709 578950; **Underfloor heating** – Velta: 01484 860811; **Sanitaryware** – Villeroy & Boch: 020 8871 4028; **Roof** – Sarnafil: 01603 748985; **Kitchen units** – Ikea: 020 8208 5600; **Sinks** – C.P. Hart: 020 7586 9856; **Glass** – Pilkington Glass: 0121 328 1188; **Mortgage** – BuildStore: 0870 870 9991

CALIFORNIA DREAMING

CREATING A CONTEMPORARY WEST
COAST STYLE HOME IN DORSET

■ CALIFORNIA DREAMING

Alan Wood has built a light and spacious contemporary-style home designed around a central atrium living space and featuring an indoor pool.

WORDS: DEBBIE JEFFERY   PHOTOGRAPHY: NIGEL RIGDEN

"I BUILT THIS house in reaction to Poundbury," smiles Alan Wood. His spacious, contemporary new home in Dorset could not be further removed from the traditional urban design of the local development championed by the Prince of Wales. The architecture at Poundbury draws on the rich heritage of Dorset and, in particular, the attractive streets of Dorchester, using local and often recycled materials.

Although he does not deny the quality of materials and attention to detail of the village, Alan Wood's ideas are slightly more forward thinking. "Don't misunderstand me – I do appreciate why people like old houses," he explains. "I wanted to build something which was of our time, however, and to incorporate up-to-the-minute innovations and technologies. A totally contemporary house, without compromise. I'm not a revisionist – I want to move forward – but it proved impossible to buy a large modern house in this area."

Alan Wood wanted a modern house, suitable for entertaining large numbers of people, with generous expanses of glass to provide a light and spacious feel.

Inspired by his travels to the Far East, Alan – the Director of Buying for New Look, and a leading figure in the retail fashion sector – has stayed in more hotels than he cares to remember. "Places like Thailand and Japan ➤

"BROCKWOOD HAS OUTSTRIPPED
EVEN MY DREAMS, AND HAS
CHANGED THE WAY I LIVE…"

have had a lasting effect on me," he says. "There's quite a minimalist approach to their philosophy for life. Many of my ideas for the house came from modern hotels, which have impressive atriums and lots of natural light. Coming from a country that can be grey and miserable, and being a person who craves daylight, I just wanted to live in that kind of environment."

Set in four acres and surrounded by woodland, his site is sheltered from its neighbours but benefits from being within walking distance of the village pub. Previously owned by one of Alan's friends, the plot was overgrown and occupied by a small cottage which had been extended

in the 1960s and 70s. "To do anything with the existing house would have proved very expensive and restrictive," Alan explains. "I knew that I wanted to build something more fitting for such a unique site."

The central two-storey atrium is enclosed by a first floor gallery providing access between the four corner towers and lit by an impressive roof lantern.

After trawling through hundreds of books, magazines and web sites in search of buildings to inspire him, he approached architects Cheshire Robbins Design. An innovative house designed by the practice on a difficult site had caught his eye and, by pure coincidence, he discovered that they were also based in Dorset.

The result is Brookwood: a 658m^2 house with an internal swimming pool and detached lodge suitable for staff or visitors. Large areas of glass provide a light and spacious feel, whilst private spaces are secured within solid corners around an open plan core used primarily for living and entertaining.

The design was supported by the local planning department, but considered too modern for its conservation area setting by local councillors, and refused. A subsequent appeal was upheld, however, with the inspector stating: "It is certainly an unequivocally modern design, aiming to be an unashamed product of its own time — as are several of the principal houses in the area. I consider that the scheme is an exciting example of modern architecture, with the potential to enhance the conservation area by contributing to the continuing evolution of its architectural heritage."

A contract sum was negotiated with Poole-based contractor Edward Jackson, whose experience of civil engineering was considered to ➤

"I REALLY HAVE TO PINCH MYSELF AND
THINK HOW LUCKY I AM TO OWN SUCH A
FANTASTIC NEW HOME."

be beneficial to the type of construction required. "I explained to the architect that I wanted someone to build the house who would really put their heart into it," says Alan. The contractor, who had previously worked with Cheshire Robbins, was employed using a JCT Intermediate Form of contract, and work started on site in September 2000.

Enabling work included demolition of the existing dwelling, new fencing to the perimeter and de-watering to allow the construction of the swimming pool. The project was due for completion by mid-summer 2001 but overran until November due to excessively wet weather conditions: it rained almost non-stop for six months. Even so, everyone involved in the project remained on extremely good terms, and the standard of workmanship proved consistently high.

Foundations were short bored piles with in-situ ground beams, due to the high water table. The basic structural composition is load bearing stone and blockwork to the corner

The 'infinity' swimming pool – set in a single storey glazed enclosure lit by a bank of rooflights – appears to flow out into the landscape beyond through a full height window. ➤

The white kitchen and utility room units, as well as the kitchen in the lodge, were all fitted out for £25,000 including appliances and contrasting dark marble worktops. From K&B: 01722 334800

"THE VIRTUAL TOUR OF THE HOUSE WHICH CHESHIRE ROBBINS SHOWED ME BEFORE IT WAS BUILT MADE ME FEEL AS IF I HAD BEEN HERE BEFORE."

towers, with steel supports to the central atrium area. Beam and block flooring was specified for the corners of the first floor, with a timber 'silent floor' to the gallery.

Anti-cracking, white insulated render is the predominant external facing material, with feature stone walls providing a contrast. All doors, windows and rooflights are colour coated aluminium frames, with double glazed 'K' glass, and the main roof is finished with a 3-coat torch-on integrated waterproofing and insulation system, concealed beneath a parapet upstand.

Working in the fashion industry ensures that Alan Wood has his finger firmly on the pulse. Low voltage lighting was specified throughout Brookwood, with a central unit controlling different lighting moods, along with integrated audio and video facilities, plus fire and security protection.

"Like most people, I have worked my way up the property ladder –starting off in a modern flat, followed by a new house in a village setting and then moving to a property situated on a cliff in Weymouth," says Alan. "Brookwood has outstripped even my dreams, however, and has changed the way I live. I am now far more home based, and more active due to the swimming pool and workout area.

"Before, I tended to spend much of my time entertaining in restaurants – but now I can accommodate large numbers of friends at home, and I also have a working office here." Each bedroom has its own en suite bathroom, with friends debating who will stay in the 'round room', with its raised bathroom overlooking the bed (above right).

Despite its size Brookwood is not an overpowering building, and Alan is comfortable spending time there on his own. None of the living spaces exist in isolation, and there are no connecting passageways or corridors.

"The virtual tour of the house which Cheshire Robbins showed me before it was built made me feel as if I had been here before," he remarks. "One thing I had never experienced, however, is waking up, going for a swim and having a feeling of sheer joy at living in the house. I really have to pinch myself and think how lucky I am to own such a fantastic new home." ■

FACT FILE

Costs as of March 2003
Name: Alan Wood
Profession: Buying Director
Area: Dorset
House type: Four bedroom detached plus one bedroom lodge
House size: 658m²
Build route: Building contractor
Construction: Rendered blockwork and stone
Warranty: NHBC Buildmark
SAP rating: 94
Finance: HSBC
Build time: 15 months
Land cost: £300,000
Build cost: £660,000
Total cost: £960,000
House value: £1.5m
Cost/m²: £1,003

36%
COST SAVING

"I AM NOW FAR MORE HOME BASED, AND MORE ACTIVE DUE TO THE SWIMMING POOL AND WORKOUT AREA."

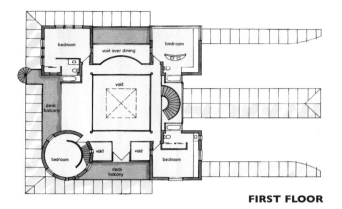

FIRST FLOOR

GROUND FLOOR

USEFUL CONTACTS

Architect - Cheshire Robbins Design Limited: 01202 473344; **Main contractor** - Edward Jackson Ltd: 07774 940240; **Structural Engineer** - Oscar Faber: 0117 9017000; Environs Partnership: 01305 250455; **Helical stairs** - Crescent of Cambridge Ltd: 01480 301522; **Windows** - Pennington Lacey & Sons: 02380 631555; **Flooring** - Peter Newman Flooring Ltd: 01202 747175; **Swimming pool** - Cresta Leisure Ltd: 01305 834969; **Fixings** - Allfix Distributors: 01202 519066; **Plumbing** - Colin J Brumble Ltd: 01305 766549; **Demolition** - Bermacross Ltd: 01258 473309; **Builders & Timber Merchants** - Jewsons Ltd: 01305 786611; Eagle (Wessex) Plant Ltd: 01305 775656; Roger Bullivant Piling Ltd: 01373 865012; **External render** - Marmorit (UK): 0117 9821042; **Special roof timbers** - Crendon Timber Ltd: 01305 847110 Cumberland Reinforcement Ltd: 01202 743311; **Portland stone** - Easton Masonry (UK) Ltd: 01305 861020; **Roofing** - Gorvin Roofing: 01202 676443; **Bricklaying** - R G Horlock: 01305 834134; **Groundworks** - T J Kelly: 01202 874129; **Painter** - T J Spears: 01305 787586; **Concrete** - Hanson Concrete & Aggregates: 01373 463211; **Electrics** - D Johnson: 01202 873257; **Carpentry** - R R Hobby: 01202 731420; **Plastering** - D J Taylor: 01202 733332; **Spiral stairs and railings** - Mowlam Metalcraft: 01305 250655; **Scaffolding** - Weymouth Scaffolding: 01305 783021

FLOORPLAN

Large, formal living areas are centrally positioned to the ground floor. Four first floor corner bedrooms are set around a gallery overlooking the central atrium, which draws natural light into the heart of the house. The swimming pool is positioned from the central staircase to create perfect symmetry.

ANOTHER LEVEL

Alan and Liz Whitehouse have built a spacious three-level home with dramatic contemporary-style interiors on a steeply sloping site.

WORDS: DEBBIE JEFFERY   PHOTOGRAPHY: JEREMY PHILLIPS

THE PENNINE TOWN of Holmfirth is surrounded by wild gritstone moors and boasts handloom weavers, cottages and dramatic scenery. It is most famous, however, as the home of the long running BBC TV series Last of the Summer Wine, and the success of the show has put the area firmly on the tourist trail. Understandably, the local authority is wary of any development in such an unspoilt Conservation Area —-particularly

buildings which do not echo traditional vernacular architecture. So when Alan and Liz Whitehouse decided to build their new home in the town, they had their work cut out convincing the parish council to accept their design.

"We did not set out to be self-builders," explains Liz Whitehouse. "We had lived in our previous 1970s house for 17 years and had become stuck in a rut. With our only daughter about to start university, Alan and I felt that the time had come for a challenge, but we were really looking for somewhere to renovate." The couple stumbled upon some land for sale, with planning permission for a dwelling, and were captivated by the views from the overgrown walled garden site and its quiet, convenient location only two minutes' walk from the centre of town. They were also impressed with an existing five bedroom design which architect Mark Lee had produced, and worked with him to scale down the size while retaining key features. They were also keen to introduce some of their own personal touches such as the unusual shower room and blue spiral staircase.

"What really interested us was the void which runs through the house," says Alan. "Instead of a garage we have a house on three floors, with two bedrooms at entrance level and a study at the bottom of the void, which ➤

The house is built on a 1 in 5 slope, with the ground floor cut into the land and semi-underground.

The layout is based around a large three-storey central void.

"ONE CONCERNED NEIGHBOUR WATCHED IN HORROR AS AN APPLE TREE ON OUR LAND MOVED ABOUT THREE FEET!"

is lit from above by rooflights, casting light through the core of the building. A traditional house would have been very dark and murky." The first floor is completely open plan, with the void passing right through it, and contains the kitchen, living and dining areas. A single storey conservatory doubles as Liz's office, whilst a tower houses the spiral staircase which leads up to the galleried landing and master bedroom situated in the eaves.

The Sheraton maple kitchen has black granite worktops, which complement the stainless steel accessories.

The parish council objected to the design, however, considering it too modern for a Conservation Area, in spite of the fact that it reflected many elements of the neighbouring Victorian villas, including a tower and pointed bay. The request was for something 'more cottagey'. Liz and Alan were happy to build their home in Yorkshire natural sandstone with ashlar surrounds to the doors and windows and a slate roof, ensuring that it would sit comfortably in its surroundings, but were adamant that their new home should not ape existing buildings.

Some changes were made to the windows, which echo those of the local stone mullioned weavers' cottages, and the application was referred to the conservation officer – who recommended that it should be ➤

"WE LOVE THE LIGHT AND AIRY FEELING THAT AN OPEN-PLAN HOUSE WITH SO MANY WINDOWS GIVES US."

approved. Planning permission was duly granted. "As we both have busy jobs and no previous knowledge of building, we felt that the sensible option was to employ a project manager – and the architect's practice offered their services," Alan explains. He and Liz were able to remain in their previous home thanks to an endowment policy which was due to mature, and visited the site on a regular basis to watch progress. A Norwich & Peterborough stage payment mortgage was secured to cover the build, which would be paid off from the sale of the old house.

"From the outset it was not our aim to make a profit on the house – we were aware that this was unlikely given the difficult nature of such a sloping site and the complexity of the house design," says Liz. "Even so, we could not have anticipated some of the problems the builders encountered. The land was cleared of undergrowth and existing outbuildings in October 2000. Then it rained and rained and rained. The site became waterlogged and work could not begin until January 2001."

Holmfirth is very steep and the house follows a local tradition of sinking the lower floors into the Pennine hillsides. Built on a 1 in 5 slope,

the design incorporates a three-layered rear retaining wall. "We had not accounted for the land above the site beginning to move once work commenced," Liz continues. "One concerned neighbour watched in horror as an apple tree on our land moved about three feet!" Work stopped whilst another seven foot high reinforced concrete wall was built across the site to hold back the neighbours' gardens, at an additional cost of £8,500.

The constricted plot – bounded by a road, a public park and neighbours above and below – meant that workmen encountered problems bringing materials on to the site and handling them once they were there. Such delays impacted on Alan and Liz who, having sold their house, were forced to moved into temporary accommodation for the remainder of the ten month project. "We only took our summer clothes with us, but it was October before we eventually moved in," laughs Liz.

The original build budget of £130,000 was exceeded by £50,000, but this final figure included all fees, site clearance, landscaping and

Joiners made the wardrobes on the galleried landing, spray painting the doors blue to match the spiral staircase.

fitted furniture, as well as underfloor heating, a mains pressure hot water system and higher than usual electrical specification. Finishes are indulgent, with Alan and Liz choosing Amtico, laminate and tiled flooring as they both suffer from allergies to house dust. One overspend was the blue spiral staircase, with oak treads which was specified to reduce noise. This staircase is set in the square tower – proving a logistical nightmare and costing over £5,000 more than initially proposed. The result, however, is striking.

"We love the light and airy feeling that an open plan house with so many windows gives us," says Alan, "and through the windows we have wonderful views in all weathers. The front overlooks the roofscape of Holmfirth, a jumble of old Yorkshire stone and slate, with the opposite hillside rising up above the town.

"The view up the valley is of dry stone walls and moorland. In sun, rain or snow it is always changing and is a constant pleasure. We would never have found such a beautiful and original home on a conventional, volume built development." ■

FACT FILE

Names: Alan and Liz Whitehouse
Professions: Broadcast journalist and charity manager for the Art Group
Area: Huddersfield

House type: Three storey, three bed
House size: 140m²
Build route: Architect-managed
Construction: Cavity walls, stone, reclaimed Welsh slate roof
Warranty: Architect's Certificate
Finance: Norwich & Peterborough
Build time: Jan '01 – Oct '02
Land cost: £42,000
Build cost: £180,000
Total cost: £222,000
Touse value: £275,000
cost/m²: £1,285
19%
COST SAVING

FLOORPLAN

The three storey house has three bedrooms and a study, with the single storey conservatory also doubling as a home office for Liz and living accommodation open plan to the kitchen.

GROUND FLOOR

SECOND FLOOR

FIRST FLOOR

USEFUL CONTACTS

Architect – One17AD: 01484 536553; **Quantity Surveyor** – David Bottomley: 01484 429667; **Roof** – Bradford Roofing Company: 01274 602025; **Plumbing and electrical** – Select Maintenance: 01484 319700; **Joinery** – Roy C. Smith: 01484 844405; **Sandstone** – Johnsons Wellfield Quarries Ltd.: 01484 652311; **Velta underfloor heating installation** – Underfloor Heating Company: 01484 860811; **Sanitaryware, floor and wall tiles** – South Yorkshire Ceramics: 01226 351112; **Painting and decorating** – Matthew Harding: 01226 770211; **Security and alarm** – de Taunton UK Ltd.: 01226 770211; **Paving** – Marshalls: 0870 1207474

LOW RISE LIVING

BUILDING A CONTEMPORARY-STYLE HOME ON ONE LEVEL

Mark and Gill Withers have built a contemporary-style single-storey house with exposed blockwork that somehow fits in perfectly with its rural location.

WORDS: DEBBIE JEFFERY PICTURES: PAUL DIXON

"BUILDING THIS HOUSE was definitely a family affair," says Mark Withers. "Not only was our son, Simon, the designer but our daughters also got involved – which made it really enjoyable."

Mark and his wife, Gill, had been living in a large Arts and Crafts house in London for a number of years. "We already owned some land in Kent, which we decided would make an ideal site for a new house," Mark continues. "Getting planning permission was not easy, however, as we were very keen to build a contemporary home."

Initially the Withers had plans drawn up by an architect which were approved by the local authority. Unfortunately, the couple decided that the two storey design did not entirely suit their requirements.

"We were difficult clients as we had not really identified our own needs at this stage," admits Gill. "Our son originally trained as a fashion designer, then became involved in buildings ➤

121

and took a second degree in architecture. While he was studying for this we asked him to work on designs for our house."

Led by their son, Mark and Gill became more adventurous and were heavily influenced by the architecture of Frank Lloyd Wright – who was one of the first to introduce the concept of open plan rooms which flowed and opened out to one another. Local vernacular also played an important role, with Simon drawing inspiration from simple farm buildings. The couple undertook their research in earnest, reading books and visiting houses in Chicago designed by Lloyd Wright.

"We have great confidence in Simon as a designer, he married contemporary architecture with the style of simple, agricultural pole barns found in this area," says Mark. "Pole barns are a relatively new invention, built from old telegraph poles with sloping corrugated roofs. The large windows of our house echo the apertures where tractors drive into the

barns, and the building has oak weatherboarding on three sides which is another local tradition. One of our neighbours commented that the design looked more like a farm building than a house – which we took as a compliment!"

The planners had specified that the house should be traditional in design, with a pitched tiled roof, but Simon persuaded them that the pole barn was another form of vernacular architecture, using a model to illustrate his point. As the house was to be built on the edge of a village, set amongst mature trees, the plans were accepted as appropriate to the site.

The single storey building has long slit windows set into the timber cladding, with the fourth façade containing larger glazed openings. From certain angles the roof appears to be flat, but is actually composed of a gentle slope from north to south (echoed in the ceiling below) which meets with a shorter slope of glazing in a drainage gully. Rooms lead off

"IT WAS VERY HARD WORK USING LARGE FORTICRETE BLOCKS, AND EACH BRICKLAYER WAS SHIFTING AROUND FIVE TONS BY HAND EVERY DAY."

from a single corridor, which draws natural light into the house through the glazed skylight – perfect for illuminating artwork.

Gill, an artist, has a spacious studio to one end of the house, with a guest room and shower situated next door. The study doubles as a third bedroom, and the master bedroom and bathroom are situated at the other end of the corridor. Between these rooms is a large open plan living/dining and kitchen space, with a long island unit and a 'services' area containing a larder and laundry.

"The house was designed for two, but we wanted our children to visit and bring their families. Our daughters, Sarah and Jane, became involved with design discussions and had their own ideas," says Gill. "The floorplan reflects the way we live. The whole family loves to

The internal exposed blockwork provides a low-maintenance neutral background for Gill's art and was inspired by an early Norman Foster house in Cornwall.

cook and there are often several people working in the kitchen. We wanted this room to be at the heart of the house, with other living areas radiating off from this central point."

The Withers sold their London house and moved into a mobile home on site for three years while their new house was being built. This meant that they were available for early morning deliveries and were able to labour on site.

A local builder was employed to complete the footings, with the rest of the build undertaken by local subcontractors, managed by Simon and Mark. "The bricklayer and the carpenter are brothers who were recommended to us by a friend, and they were able to put us in touch with various other local trades," explains Mark. "The quality of the workmanship was extremely high – although we did ask one electrician to leave as his work wasn't up to scratch." ➤

The house is built on shrinkable clay soil, close to several mature trees, and deep footings of between two and three metres were required to prevent movement. Gill and Mark had hoped that their engineer would come up with a raft solution, but the only option he offered was to spend several thousand pounds on additional concrete.

"We had hoped to build for £184,000, but ended up improving on the specification as well as making a few mistakes. Ultimately, we exceeded our budget, but all of our windows were hand crafted in American oak and the flooring is Rhodesian teak – reclaimed from County Hall – which cost twice as much as we first planned but warms up the interiors beautifully," says Gill. "We paid £2,000 for a quantity surveyor, who produced a detailed list of labour hours and material quantities with itemised costs – without which we would have been quite at sea."

From a distance the roof looks flat but actually consists of a gentle slope – echoing the vernacular pole barn construction

Although the Withers specified some expensive finishes, the basic structure of the house is simple cavity blockwork, left exposed internally to produce a low maintenance neutral background for the couple's art.

"It was very heavy work using large Forticrete blocks, and each bricklayer was shifting around five tons by hand every day," Mark recalls. "Originally, we considered building in stone, but good stonemasons are hard to find and Simon and the engineer both felt that blockwork construction with an insulated cavity was the best option. We had seen a house in Cornwall, designed by the young Norman Foster and Richard Rogers, which featured exposed blockwork – and this gave us the idea. The blocks actually appear to change colour in different light."

Gill and Mark tackled the garden design with the same enthusiasm as they had the house, visiting the garden of landscape architect Mien Ruis in Holland for inspiration. They then employed a local landscape architect to undertake the restrained and simple design. Gentle slopes

"WE HAD SEEN A HOUSE IN CORNWALL WHICH FEATURED EXPOSED BLOCKWORK – AND THIS GAVE US THE IDEA. THE BLOCKS ACTUALLY APPEAR TO CHANGE COLOUR IN DIFFERENT LIGHT."

were introduced to drain the clay soil, and the garden levels raised slightly above the surrounding arable fields to create the effect of a ha-ha, offering uninterrupted views and carrying the eye to infinity. Instead of being a one acre site the garden appears to stretch for miles.

"We both grew up in this area," says Mark, "and it has been wonderful to return in order to enjoy our retirement. The house incorporates everything that is important to us. It is low maintenance, bright and spacious with open plan living areas. We have the luxury of zoned underfloor heating and a kitchen where everyone can congregate and cook. Most importantly, it has given us the opportunity to work closely with our son and daughters to create a modern family home which everyone loves." ∎

The blockwork walls of the house have been clad on three sides with untreated green oak weatherboarding, which has dulled to a silver grey colour.

FACT FILE

23%
COST SAVING

Cost Breakdown:

Professional services	£22,400
Preliminaries	£3,399
Services	£2,548
Drains	£5,336
Pole barn	£3,000
Footings	£7,639
Slab	£8,581
Walls	£31,433
Roof	£24,939
Porch, spouts, pergola	£2,000
Windows and doors	£21,720
Electrics	£7,524
Flooring	£7,977
Boiler and plumbing	£7,650
Heating	£4,811
Heat exchanger	£3,372
Sanitary appliances	£750
Ceilings	£1,797
Bath and shower	£3,032
Fittings	£13,104
Landscaping	£18,388
Pavilion	£10,000
Misc	£500
TOTAL	**£211,900**

Names: Mark and Gill Withers
Professions: Retired printer and artist
Area: Kent
House type: Three bedroom, single storey
House size: 162m²
Build route: Self-managed subcontractors
Construction: Forticrete blocks
Finance: Private
Build time: Sep '95 – Oct '98
Land cost: £80,000
Build cost: £212,000
total cost: £292,000
house value: £380,000
cost/m²: £1,309

FLOORPLAN

The single storey house is arranged so that all rooms lead off from a single glazed corridor. The kitchen has been positioned at the centre, with open plan dining and living areas to either side. Gill has her own studio and the study doubles as a third bedroom.

USEFUL CONTACTS

Designer –Simon Withers: 0207 228 3205; **Kitchen, doors and joinery** County Joinery: 01424 871500; **Landscape architect** Tom La Dell: 01622 850245; **Blocks** Forticrete: 01924 456416; **Roofing membrane** ICB (International Construction Bureau Ltd.): 01202 579208; **Underfloor heating** Thermoboard: 01392 444122; **Flooring supplier** The Natural Wood Floor Co.: 0208 871 9771

LOFT-STYLE LIVING

Ian and Andrea Ward have replaced an old dormer bungalow with a remarkable contemporary-style home full of open, minimalist space.

WORDS HAZEL DOLAN PHOTOGRAPHY JEREMY PHILLIPS

IT ISN'T EASY to pin down the exact moment when Ian and Andrea Ward's plans for a major revamp of their mock-Georgian house were abandoned, and a new decision emerged: to build a radical, contemporary family home on a new site from scratch.

They had already begun to stock up on modern furniture and schedule the building work for Plan A, when they set off for a skiing holiday in Canada with their two young daughters. By the time their return flight touched down, a more ambitious idea had clearly crossed Ian's mind. Andrea remembers the jet lag, and the suggestion: "We could do something different entirely…?"

Three years on, Ian, Andrea and the girls, now 11 and eight, are thoroughly enjoying their bespoke 21st century house. Set high on a one-acre plot, the whole focus of their new home is turned towards the south-facing garden and its views of the Northumberland countryside beyond. Sleek, curving walls of steel framed glass fill the interior with light. A dramatic staircase in steel, glass and pale wood runs through a central, cylindrical shaft. The semi-open plan ground floor layout combines kitchen, dining and informal living spaces, while upstairs there are large bedrooms, smart bathrooms and a stunning balcony. It's about as far from neo-Georgian as you can get.

The Wards' decision to set aside the smaller-scale project made perfect sense. Even their planned alterations could never have stretched their traditional, former house to fit their real wishes. They wanted en ➤

Wrap-around windows bring extra light into the south-facing family sitting room and make the most of solar gain.

The semi-open plan layout was inspired by London loft living. High ceilings, pale maple flooring and the use of industrial materials give the space a contemporary feel.

129

Pale lavender units and subtle lighting effects in the kitchen help to soften the harder edges of minimalism.

"BUILDERS THOUGHT THAT [THE PLOT] DIDN'T HAVE THE POTENTIAL AND WE WERE CONCERNED WHETHER IT WOULD BE TOO SMALL."

suite bathrooms for each of the children, a large and light family kitchen they could all enjoy, and a contemporary style that they felt was not in keeping with the original building.

Accepting that they were seriously upping the expense and upheaval was an early hurdle, but they were soon sure that they were on the right track. Once they had found a promising site in their village, an easy commute to their law firms in Newcastle, it was a done deal.

As locals, they were already well aware that they were living within a property hot spot and that competition for likely plots in the area was going to be fierce – but they soon came across one that appeared to have been overlooked.

"The garden was very overgrown at the front and I think that people thought it was very narrow," says Andrea. "Builders perhaps thought it didn't have the potential and we were concerned whether it was too narrow ourselves – but it turned out to be fine.

"We didn't really know what potential there was. We didn't know if we would get planning permission for a two storey house when there were dormer bungalows both on the site and on either side. It was a bit of a gamble."

Having found their plot, they needed an architect. They had already admired Bill Hopper's work on another project, and so they sought him

Safety-glass balustrading panels keep the feeling of light and openness on the galleried landing, which is accentuated by flush in-built floor uplighting.

out. "The first thing he said was: 'Well, I don't do trad,' and we said: 'We don't want trad!' says Andrea. "He asked us to get a style guide together with different bits and pieces we liked from magazines. He came and had a look at the house we were living in, we showed him the style guide and he came up with three ideas."

Visiting friends at their airy, open plan London loft, they agree, was inspirational. As Ian points out: "We were really copying a loft and making it into a family-friendly house." Light maple floors, open spaces and the use of industrial materials all came into the mix.

"This house was designed from the inside out," explains Ian. "It was what it looked like on the inside that really counted, so we were not really sure until the late stages of the architect's concept what the outside was going to look like."

Bill's design belongs specifically to its site, with the south-facing, glazed rear elevation making the most of both solar gain and the garden view.

To the front, a subtly curved wall and the angular roof line give only the slightest hint of the fabulous geometry at the back.

As well as gaining planning permission, they had to satisfy local by-laws. "We had to get estate consent," says Ian. "There is an estate code of rules – how high you can build, how far your can build from the road frontage, how far from neighbours' boundaries you can be – things like that."

Guided by one of Ian's colleagues, Jan Bessell, the planning process proved refreshingly straightforward and speedy. "It was a battle we thought we were going to have that we didn't," says Andrea. "Jan was great and she went on to be Ian's sounding board throughout the whole build."

They kept to the footprint of the house they knocked down, but given the generous floor size of the bungalow and their own two storey design, that posed no problem. They decamped to a rented two bedroom flat in Newcastle, with plans to demolish in late 2002 and begin building in the New Year. ➤

"YOU GET TO THE STAGE WHERE YOU THINK, 'WHY SPOIL IT FOR A HA'APORTH OF TAR?' WE DECIDED WE WOULD GO THE EXTRA MILE."

Andrea recalls how she heard, via a neighbour's child at the school gate, that demolition was already under way. "It was knocked down maybe a bit earlier than we would have liked," Ian admits. "We'd lined up a good demolition contractor, but we hadn't actually pressed the button to go ahead. It was before we had decided who was going to build it and suddenly we were committed because it was knocked down." They dashed to see for themselves. "That was it," smiles Ian. "There was no going back."

For the build itself, they fielded a full squad. "Anyone who could be involved was involved," he laughs. "With us both being lawyers, we did it by the construction textbook – we had a quantity surveyor, structural engineer and a project manager. You need someone who knows the construction industry, understands everything and can check what is being done. It is an extra expense, but it is worth it,

because if you are working you haven't got time to project manage. You don't know what's right or wrong.

"Even with a main contractor, a project manager, an architect and a full team, never underestimate the amount of involvement the client has. There are so many decisions that you have to be involved in. And don't ever expect that it is going to be built within the build period," Andrea adds. "You can be as organised as you like, but you are still at the behest of other people."

They kept a good grip on the budget, but allowed themselves to stretch their spending to ensure a high-spec finish, as well as underfloor heating and integral sound system. "You get to the stage where you think 'why spoil it for a ha'aporth of tar?'" Ian points out. "We decided we would go the extra mile." By December 2003, despite no hard landscaping, and with a two-month wait ahead for the kitchen granite,

GROUND FLOOR

FIRST FLOOR

FACT FILE

Names: Ian and Andrea Ward
Professions: Solicitors
Area: Northumberland
house type: Contemporary detached five bedroom house
House size: 334m²
Build route: Architect, project manager and main contractor
Construction: Steel frame, curtain walling, blockwork, brick and render, with post and beam floor and concrete roof tiles
Finance: Private
Build time: Feb '03 – Dec '03
Land cost: £450,000
Build cost: £450,000
Total cost: £900,000
House value: £1.3 million
Cost/m²: £1,347

The ground floor layout is very open plan, with a double height gallery overlooking the family space. The master bedroom opens out onto a terrace.

DEMOLISHING OLD HOMES

The planning rules for replacing old homes with new ones vary from county to county — particularly in respect of the size of the replacement and the possibility of replacing a bungalow with a two storey house — but the practicalities are the same nationwide. Demolition costs are minimal (budget £3-10,000). Some materials can be reclaimed and either used or sold. There can also be a big saving on the cost of service connections such as water, sewers and electricity. Some plots also benefit from a mature garden.

USEFUL CONTACTS

Architect Bill Hopper: 0191 261 5336; **Builder** Stephen Easten Ltd: 0191 232 8638; **Fire** CVO Firevault: 020 7580 5333 **Furniture** B & B Italia and Ligne Roset at Barker & Stonehouse: 0191 261 6969; **Kitchen design** Paul Lamb Interiors: 0191 214 6238; **Legal advice** Dickinson Dees: 0191 279 9000; **Limestone tiles** Lapicida: 01423 560262; **Maple flooring** Stenhouse Flooring: 01670 713507; **Project management** Dave Southern & Associates: 01434 673772; **Sanitaryware** Wearside Plumbing Supplies: 0191 510 3993; **Windows** Fortress Architectural Systems: 0191 581 1000

---

they were more than ready to leave their rented flat and move in,.

Ian and Andrea have kept the decoration simple and fresh, with the strong, sculptural shapes of their new modern furniture set against off-white walls. "The key to a minimalist-looking house is storage," says Ian – and their home is no exception. A bank of built-in cupboards are perfectly fitted into the family room and the couple persuaded Bill to rework his design for the master suite to create extra wardrobe space.

The Wards would be the first to admit that combining demanding jobs, family commitments and a full-scale new build can be hugely stressful. "When you get through the agony, it's fantastic," says Ian. Andrea agrees: "Even though we moved in in less than ideal conditions, it was really, really exciting. We love it. It really works for the way we live and for our family." ∎

The tern coated steel roof appears to float over the house.

PERFECTLY FORMED

John and Eleanor Stewart have built a beautiful contemporary-style home with a cleverly compact layout that makes excellent use of space.

WORDS: CAROLINE EDNIE PHOTOGRAPHY: ANDREW LEE

HEADING SOUTH THROUGH the villages towards Aberdeen, a new addition to this relatively flat landscape has stopped more than a few passing motorists in their tracks. With good reason too. For the new home of John and Eleanor Stewart has thrown down the gauntlet in terms of presenting an alternative model to the samey and not very contextually savvy kit houses that currently pepper the Scottish landscape.

In fact the Stewarts' house, designed by Edinburgh based Richard Murphy Architects, is a cracking model of cool yet cosy contemporary design, that not only respects the integrity of the rural setting, but importantly has its feet firmly on the ground in terms of budget. Indeed, for the none too princely sum of £110,000, the Stewarts are now happily ensconced in a beautifully bespoke architectural gem, which just goes to show that it is possible to achieve a leading edge architect designed house without entering financial cloud cuckoo land.

Eleanor Stewart is, not surprisingly, very proud of her new home and unfazed by all the attention it's been attracting. "I'm hoping that it does generate interest because if you've seen the majority of housing being built locally, you'll appreciate what has been achieved here," she explains.

And what has been achieved is not "cobbling together a kit house to make it look like a typical one and a half storey Highland building," explains architect ➤

On a nice summer's day the whole house can be opened to the garden. In winter occupants can shelter within behind cherry-wood shutters that close off all of the windows.

Richard Murphy. "I totally reject that way forward, it's a horrible aping of the past," he adds. Instead the architects have adopted a very site-specific approach. "Our idea for the house was to be long and sleek in the countryside. The landscape is nothing spectacular as far as Scotland goes, so I was interested in making something low, horizontal and floating."

The architects came up with a linear, single storey design on an east-west orientation. The building is constructed by means of a galvanised steel frame and clear-stained timber window frames to the south, with dry-dash blockwork to the north elevation. Load bearing blockwork also features internally. A tern coated steel roof completes the "low, horizontal and floating" picture.

"The major difference between this house and other indigenous buildings is that other Highland houses tend to be dominated by the roof, so although ours is very conscious, it doesn't take the usual form," continues Richard. "Although it is still making a big statement about the whole idea of living under a roof, embracing the idea of shelter. It's a big roof that floats over the building."

The roof overhangs the southern glazed façade primarily to reduce the glare of the direct summer sunlight, yet it also succeeds in harnessing the lower winter sun in the living area. "The beautiful thing about an architect

"IN TERMS OF BUDGET, THIS IS AN EXTRAORDINARILY IMPRESSIVE HOUSE FOR A BUILD COST OF JUST OVER £100,000…"

designed house is that you can influence its orientation. In our case the sun hits our bedroom first thing in the morning, then goes down in the living area downstairs just above the fireplace. It's a beautiful effect. And in terms of solar gain we only need the heating on in the late autumn and winter. It's cosy enough without it," explains Eleanor.

And just in case extra cosiness was required, an all embracing system of insulated cherry wood shutters along the roof lights and glazed south façade means that the whole house can be completely cocooned. As Richard Murphy explains "the house has three manifestations of its skin. On a nice summer's day you can open the whole house to the garden, then on a normal day the house is collecting solar gain, and finally at night or in the winter you've got all the shutters closed. The whole thing about moveable insulation is that it's empowering the people in the house to make an energy efficient home. You have the insulation when you are in a situation of net heat loss, and you can take the insulation away when you are in a position of net heat gain. That's a very simple idea but very rarely built."

By way of a contrast to the ever changing personality of the south ➤

The kitchen
was supplied by
Aberdeen-based
Denmore Kitchens
(01224 826776).

The top level of the house features a decked balcony that enjoys views over Nottingham.

HEIGHT OF STYLE

Bill Hammond and Alex Brade have built a cutting-edge home over seven levels on a sensitive, urban, brownfield site.

WORDS: HEATHER DIXON   PHOTOGRAPHY: DAVE BURTON

WHEN DEVELOPER BILL Hammond transformed two Victorian schools in the centre of Nottingham into modern apartment blocks, he was left with a playground measuring just 374m2 in between. At first he considered building two townhouses on the awkwardly shaped site — but then he had a better idea. He decided to build a house for himself. Not a house which would blend in with the 19th century architecture on either side, but a radical, seven storey steel and glass structure which would become a significant landmark in Nottingham's architectural history.

"I liked the idea of creating something very modern in a conservation area and making it work with — rather than against — the neighbouring properties," he says. As an award winning property developer, Bill wasn't afraid of pushing boundaries to

New meets old. The house, the rear of which is clad in sand faced brick and almost three quarters of its facing in glass, sits next to Victorian properties in an urban conservation area. ➤

"BILL WASN'T PREPARED FOR THE COST OF CREATING A CONTEMPORARY DREAM…"

the limit – even in one of the city's most stringent conservation areas – but he had no intention of ruffling feathers.

In an unusual move, he decided to involve Nottingham's forward thinking planners, conservationists and, most importantly, his neighbours at the design stage of the build, to ensure there would be no unwelcome surprises when the site was developed. He also asked Nottingham based architects Julian Marsh and Jerzy Grochowski, who are nationally renowned for their innovative designs, to create a house which would be unlike anything else in the area, yet still complement the surrounding buildings.

"The planning department were extremely supportive and forward thinking," says Bill. "Although the design is in many ways quite radical, it still works well within the context of the site and its surroundings. People automatically assume that very modern houses won't work in a conservation area because they won't fit in, but if people had taken that attitude in Georgian times we wouldn't have the great Victorian buildings we see today. However, getting the design right was a tortuous process."

It took a year and four re-draws to reach a design everyone was happy with – but the biggest headache was yet to come.

In spite of his extensive experience with traditional properties, Bill wasn't prepared for the cost of creating a contemporary cream. His initial fit-out budget overran by almost £100,000, to a total of £250,000, ➤

Feature staircase. The £40,000 glass and steel staircase from Phillip Watts, which took 16 weeks to install, forms a stylish backbone to the house.

when he refused to compromise on the quality of the finishing touches. "Once I started there was no going back," says Bill, who bought the land from his own company, Watermeadows

The powder-coated aluminium windows are from Trent Valley Windows (01159 425050).

Ltd. "If it was worth doing, it had to be done well, even if it meant running way over the initial estimates. You can't create a home on this scale and then cut back on the quality and fittings."

Bill's wish list included the finest quality build materials he could afford and a hydraulic garage capable of housing six cars, to avoid parking problems in the narrow street outside. But the build almost ground to a halt before it had begun in May 2002, when it was discovered that conventional foundations would be totally inadequate in the sandstone ridge they were developing. The retaining wall had to be redesigned and the whole of the north elevation sheet piled to a depth of five metres, complete with buttresses.

Two months behind schedule, and £40,000 lighter, Bill finally saw the concrete housing for his six car hydraulic garage installed and the towering shell of the house being built. The build itself was relatively straightforward. The roadside elevation of four levels is block and brickwork, which is part rendered, with timber weatherboarding. The back, which ➤

Honed granite flooring
and a Bisque radiator
frame the ground floor
kitchen. Bill bought the
kitchen carcasses and
doors from different
manufacturers to get the
effect he wanted.

"WHAT THE BUILDING COMPANY DID, THEY DID WELL, BUT THE JOB OVERRAN BY SIX MONTHS"

includes three stories below ground floor level, is primarily brick, glass and exposed steel work. The property features a mixture of beam and block flooring and timber floor joists.

But Bill faced further setbacks and expense when the first window company he employed left him in the lurch without explanation and the building company – after a series of unnecessary delays caused, says Bill, by bad management – went into liquidation, leaving Bill to pick up the pieces. "What they did, they did well, but the job overran by six months which cost money," he says. This included 16 weeks for the installation of the stairs, laying of maple and Portuguese limestone floors and the installation of the £25,000 kitchen.

The house is a remarkable feat of design and engineering, filling the entire width of the frontage between the neighbouring buildings and falling away to dizzying heights at the back, where it overlooks acres of city centre parkland once owned by the Duke of Newcastle.

Built of sand faced brick with a terne coated steel roof and almost a quarter of its total wall area in glass, the 56ft high property measures more than 280m² over seven levels.

"It is the most exciting property I've ever been involved with – there's nothing else like it in Nottingham," says Bill, "and I loved the challenge of making this work in a conservation area. There's a lot of vanity in it. A lot of people said I was crazy to try to build something like this in an area like this, but I wanted to prove that it was possible." ■

Contemporary style can be expensive. The standard of the internal fitting-out was so high that, despite being an experienced developer, Bill underestimated his internal budget by £100,000.

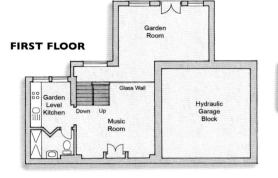

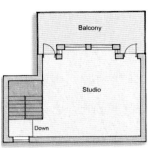

FIRST FLOOR

Garden Room

Garden Level Kitchen

Glass Wall

Down Up

Music Room

Hydraulic Garage Block

THIRD FLOOR

Balcony

Studio

Down

FACT FILE

Names: Bill Hammond and Alex Brade
Professions: Property developer and riding instructor
Area: Nottingham
House type: Seven storey self-build
House size: 288m²
Build route: Self-managed
Construction: Brick and block
Finance: Private
Build time: May '02 – Dec '03
Land cost: £150,000 (estimate)
Build cost: £524,000
Total cost: £674,000
House value: £850,000
cost/m²: £1,819

21%
COST SAVING

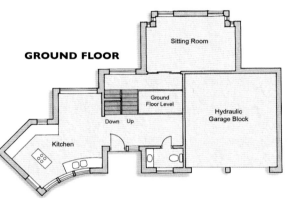

GROUND FLOOR

Sitting Room

Ground Floor Level

Down Up

Kitchen

Hydraulic Garage Block

SECOND FLOOR

Bedroom

Boiler

Bedroom

Bedroom

FLOORPLAN

The site sits on a sandstone ridge and the slope meant that the rear of the house has three floors below the original ground level. Each floor is split-level and so, in total, there are seven different levels. An unusual feature is the two storey garage made possible by using a hydraulic lifting system – it can store up to six vehicles.

USEFUL CONTACTS

Architects – Marsh & Grochowski: 01159 411761; **Engineers** – Price & Myers: 01159 507977; **Staircase design and installation** – Phillip Watts Design: 01159 474809; **Hydraulic six car garage** – Wohr Parking: 01993 851791; **Honed granite and limestone flooring** – Lapicida: 01423 501249; **Sanitaryware** – Cesame at WPS: 01472 824092; **Brassware** – Waterfront Ltd: 01865 371571; **Kitchen carcasses** – Mereway Ltd: 0121 706 7844; **Kitchen doors** – Trimdene: 0161 474 7189; PWS 01325 505555; **Internal American cherry doors and casings** – Brystewood

01623 870972; **Radiators** – Bisque: 01225 478500; **Underfloor heating** – Devi Mat: 01359 242400; **Powder coated aluminium windows** – Trent Valley Windows: 01159 425050; **Powder coated aluminium doors** – Castle Architectural: 01159 701000; **Stainless steel water feature** – Architectural Fabrications: 0115 8549548; **Lighting** – Genesis 1:3: 0208 845 8444; **Sockets and switches** – Forbes & Lomax: 0207 738 0202; **Contract floor laying** – Vitruvius of York: 07762 829472; **Landscape architects** – Graham Scott: 01949 850824

VISION OF THE FUTURE

BUILDING A MODERNIST-STYLE HOME

WORDS: CLIVE FEWINS   PHOTOGRAPHY: JEREMY PHILLIPS

Andrew and Paula Watson have created a groundbreaking house using the latest insulated formwork construction system.

WHEN THEY HAVE finally put the finishing touches to their new self-build home in a village near Nottingham, Andrew and Paula Watson are contemplating placing a noticeboard outside on which people can attach their comments. "I am not expecting them all to be polite," says Andrew, a chartered surveyor and developer, whose ambition for as long as he can remember has been to build his own house in a contemporary international style.

He has certainly succeeded. But if previous remarks are anything to go by, the comments on the board are likely to include the phrases "an eyesore," "like a fish factory," (Andrew's sister's comment) and "like an igloo."

The latter remark came from Andrew and Paula's five children and resulted from the main form of construction — the Beco permanent insulated formwork system, in which interlocking lightweight polystyrene blocks act as a mould for the concrete that is poured between them to form the walls and then stays permanently in position afterwards.

Some of the adverse comments originated during the seven-and-a-half month construction phase, when residents of the quiet, genteel lane in which the house is situated found themselves confronted almost daily by giant lorries carrying steel beams and large tankers full of liquid concrete. ➤

■ VISION OF THE FUTURE

The kitchen (left and this image) is from CP Hart (0161 214720).

They also had to contend with several visits from a 50 tonne crane that was used to erect the steel frame and lift the beam and block system supporting the first floor and roof.

The heavy concrete roof and massive steel frame is one area in which Andrew admits that his approach to building the house might have verged on overkill at times. "We could have saved a lot of money by using straightforward blockwork in the walls," he says. However he loves the highly insulated solid walls, and also their thickness. In the two storey section of the building – the kitchen is single storey – the walls are 470 mm thick, with the Beco blocks wrapped round the steel sections that form the frame. The concrete-filled blocks take up all but 32mm of this width, the rest being plasterboard on the inside and a render on the exterior.

As you might imagine, the U-values in the roof, floors and walls are very high, particularly as the south-facing frontage is largely glazed, including a striking glass clerestory running right along the front of the house. This brings light flooding into the full-height atrium, which is supported by nine full height round steel columns.

Outside, the fear of overheating is alleviated by a striking array of sun louvres above the ground floor windows at the south-facing front. Inside the plain white, Minimalist atrium, storage cupboards are concealed neatly behind plain white doors stretching right along the front of the house. The single-storey kitchen, breakfast room and playroom leads off it in a T-shape to the south. The house is awash with light from the front but the rear of the lounge, which is the full height of the building, is glazed to bring in additional light which bounces off the plain white walls in all directions. Like the large kitchen, the lounge is doorless.

Andrew and Paula are delighted with the way the house has turned out. ➤

"BECO IS MARVELLOUS FUN TO WORK WITH BUT WE HAD QUITE A FEW BURSTS WHEN THE CONCRETE BROKE THROUGH THE POLYSTYRENE."

"Andrew coped very well with some of the ruder remarks but I am a bit more sensitive than him about such things," says Paula. "But then this is a very quiet lane and the build did cause a lot of disruption. Fortunately our immediate neighbours were very supportive and our planning officer, Norman Jowett, was right behind us from the start. He took a lot of flack himself, although he told us that towards the end of the project he did receive a few complimentary phonecalls. Strangely enough the planning consent went through on delegated powers."

Andrew acted as project manager for the build. Having sold their previous house in a nearby village early in 2000 (their first self-build and home of five years) they lived in temporary accommodation nearby during the build. Andrew moved his office to a temporary building on a corner of the six acre site, which had previously contained a 1960s bungalow. From there he was able to supervise the seven-and-a-half month build at the same time as running his business.

The key builders were some of Andrew's own workforce whom he had known for ten years or so. Nevertheless he admits that some aspects of the technique demanded a steep learning curve. "Beco is marvellous fun to work with but we had quite a few bursts when the concrete broke through the polystyrene," he says.

For this he blames not the Beco system but

A six metre long gallery bridge, overlooking the living room (right), links the master bedroom and children's rooms (above). ➤

"OUR ONLY REGRET IS THAT OUR HOUSE IS NOT SITUATED IN CALIFORNIA OR SYDNEY, WHERE IT WOULD LOOK VERY MUCH AT HOME!"

This style of heating is ideally suited to the clean, crisp lines of the house. There is nothing out of place: the furniture, right up to the prototype designer chair, made by Andrew's oldest son, Seng, is carefully chosen.

The open fire on the ground floor is a two-way feature shared between the sitting room and the snug. Its steel flue, visible in the main sitting room, makes a strong statement. Another 'industrial' feature, in addition to the steel frame and the full-height atrium is the deep, frameless glass porch, while the roof is covered by a single ply membrane on a tapering bed of insulation – again an adaptation of an industrial system.

Another notable feature is the sliding screen between the two older children's ground floor bedrooms. This is repeated upstairs – again between the two other children's rooms. The object is to make the spaces more versatile when entertaining overnight guests.

From the upstairs children's bedrooms you pass along a six metre long bridge to the master bedroom. Reflecting much of the downstairs, this room has plain white walls and no curtains. There is a cleverly-designed permanent dividing screen situated behind the bed that leads to the dressing room, walk-in wardrobe and shower room and wc.

The main upstairs bathroom is at the other end of the house. It connects with the guest bedroom as well as the landing. The stunning slab containing the washbasins is cut out of solid marble, so heavy it had to be craned in. It was specially made at a cost of £2,500.

One big expense that Andrew and Paula had not anticipated was the cost of below-ground works, which involved 45 deep piles being built to support the beam and block ground floor slab. This was necessary because of the fears of shrinkage due to the clay subsoil and the large number of yew and redwood trees on site, all of which were subject to tree preservation orders. "Because of this and the £500,000 build cost, in terms of investment we have to take a long term view of the project," says Andrew. "The cost of the plot, which included the previous house but no planning permission, was very high. We did not aim to make an instant profit and although we have not ruled out another self-build, this will be it for a while. Our only regret is that our house is not situated in California or Sydney, where it would look very much at home!" ■

the way he and his team went about the job. "Some of the bursts were where the Beco blocks had to fit round the posts of the steel frame, which was a bit tricky," he says. "Many of the problems were caused because we were trying to do it too fast. The Beco formwork needed more support on both sides as the blocks were being filled. Also I think we did not control the rate at which we poured the concrete into the blocks as well as we might have done."

There is so much solar heat gain in the house that air conditioning is vital. The Watsons have had to use their gas fired underfloor heating very little.

A glazed atrium runs across the front of the house where the structure is supported by nine full-height round steel columns.

The striking white external render is from Marmorit (01179 821042).

FACT FILE

Costs as of Aug 2002
Names: Andrew and Paula Watson
Professions: Developer & housewife
Area: Nottinghamshire
House type: Six bedroomed flat-roofed contemporary-style house
House size: 423m²
Build route: Main contractor
Construction: Beco Wallform system around steel frame
Warranty: Zurich
SAP rating: 97
Finance: Private plus £200,000 mortgage from Lloyds TSB
Build time: Nov '00 – June '01
Land cost: £245,000
Build cost: £500,000
Total cost: £745,000
House value: £800,000
Cost/m²: £1,182

7%
COST SAVING

Cost Breakdown:

Substructure	£40,000
Drainage	£5,000
Steel frame	£20,000
Upper floors	£15,000
Exterior walls	£80,000
Roof	£35,000
Stairs	£10,000
Exterior windows and doors	£125,000
Interior windows & partitions	£25,000
Interior doors	£15,000
Finishes	£40,000
Fittings	£30,000
Mechanical and electrical	£40,000
Fees	£12,500
Misc	£7,500
TOTAL	**£500,000**

GROUND FLOOR

FIRST FLOOR

FLOORPLAN

The kitchen wing of the house is single storey, while the main living areas over two storeys contain six bedrooms.

USEFUL CONTACTS

Architect – Allison-Pike Partnership: 01663 763000; **Structural engineer** – Howard Stanley-Pratt: 0115 953 9993; **Builders** – Park Portfolio: 01949 829101; **Structural formwork** – Beco Products: 01652 651641; **Air conditioning** – Lynx Climate Control: 01522 788721; **Horizontal solar shades** – Swift welding: 01298 79381; **Underfloor he ating** – Rehau: 0161 777 7400; **Roofing membrane** – Trocal: 01753 522212; **Roofing contractor** – Metclad: 01623 720032; **Steel windows** – DNS windows: 0115 963 6361; **Clerestory windows on first floor** – Reglit: 0141 613 1414; **Glazing** – Vision Systems: 01843 825817; **External render** – Marmorit: 01179 821042; **Oak floors** – Floorco: 01933 418899; **Stone floors** – Stone Age: 01179 238180; **Marble floor** – Fyfe Glenrock: 01224 744101; **Kitchen and sanitary fittings** – C P Hart: 0161 214 7206; **Sliding room dividers** – Dividers Modernfold: 01269 844877

NATURAL WONDER
BUILDING A CEDAR-CLAD HOUSE USING STUCTURAL INSULATED PANELS

Scott Kemmis and Rachel Dovey successfully battled the planners to build their inspirational new home on an idyllic riverside site.

WORDS: DEBBIE JEFFERY   PHOTOGRAPHY: NIGEL RIGDEN

"LIVING SO CLOSE to the river brings with it certain responsibilities," explains Scott Kemmis. "If the water level rises I can be up every hour throughout the night checking that no debris has been caught in any of the eight sluice gates. It's like caring for a baby and can be extremely hard work, but the rewards of living beside such a beautiful stretch of water and fishing in the river are worth the odd sleepless night."

In 1993 Scott had decided to pursue a childhood interest and founded his own company, The Gardeners Ltd, specialising in park and garden maintenance, landscaping and garden design. One client employed Scott to maintain his formal park-like gardens in the market town of Romsey,

which included a stretch of the River Test — regarded as one of the most famous chalk streams in the world. When managing the weir and sluice gates became too difficult for their elderly owner, an agreement was reached whereby Scott would take over ownership of the lower two acres of garden, river, the remains of an old mill structure and a 'salmon ladder' — a man-made channel which assists the fish in making their way upstream.

The land came with no planning permission, but Scott and his partner, Rachel Dovey, decided to gamble on building a new house which would make tending the grounds and river a far easier task. The couple had been living in a Victorian terraced house in Romsey for eight years which they planned to sell in order to fund the project, and approached a local architect with the intention of drawing up plans for a contemporary new home.

"He took one look at the site and announced that it was beyond his ➤

Oriental-style sliding screens help divide the living space. There is also inspiration from Australian interior design.

"A NEIGHBOUR HAD WAITED UNTIL PLANNING PERMISSION WAS APPROVED BEFORE REVEALING THAT A RESTRICTIVE COVENANT EXISTED…"

capabilities," says Rachel. "Nobody thought that we would ever be given permission to build there until we met Peter Dowsett and just hit it off straight away."

The semi-retired architect seemed far more upbeat and excited about the challenge of building on such a beautiful site, which forms a hidden oasis right in the middle of town. He worked with Scott and Rachel developing a number of designs ranging from a cabin-like structure to the final proposal of a contemporary cedar clad house with a stainless steel roof. This was submitted to the local council for planning approval and was instantly and resolutely refused as an unsympathetic, overly large development on the riverbank.

"That's when the fun started," says Scott. "Years ago the council had allocated this land to be acquired as a future extension to their neighbouring War Memorial park, so we knew we had a real fight on our hands." He, Rachel and Peter Dowsett prepared for battle over a period of six months, employing a planning consultant and a landscape architect to assess the land. They encouraged the Environment Agency and English Nature to back their proposal, and even the police force supported the application on the grounds of preventing trespassers from tampering with the sluice gates.

"We sold our car and some shares to gamble £14,000 at the planning stage which we could easily have lost," Scott continues, "but we knew

we had to give it our best shot and gathered a huge file of evidence for the hearing."

Ultimately, their design for a predominantly single storey house featuring large sections of glazing was approved by the appeal inspector on Christmas Eve 2002 but, just as they were preparing to celebrate, another obstacle presented itself to the couple. "A neighbour had waited until planning permission was approved before revealing that a restrictive covenant existed which prevented any building except a fishing hut from being erected on the land," Rachel explains. "We were advised to pay for this covenant to be removed. At £60,000 it was a huge blow to our budget and we had to take out a bigger mortgage to cover it."

The couple continued to live in their previous house, taking out a bridging loan to pay for the build. They had hoped to start on site in July 2003 but work was delayed for a further two months when the planners queried some of the window shapes and requested a new planning application. After so many set-backs Scott and Rachel were becoming understandably despondent about the project but were hopeful of making up time by building with highly insulated SIPs — Structural Insulated Panels manufactured by sandwiching expanded polystyrene between two sheets of oriented strand board. "The panels were erected in just four days and are extremely versatile," says Rachel. "They allowed ➤

An integrated sun room acts as an informal dining space in the open plan kitchen arrangement.

External cedar cladding is fixed vertically, horizontally and diagonally to the various elements of the predominantly single-storey house.

us to have open plan living spaces with full height ceilings and no visible supports which, along with the hidden underfloor heating, help to give the house its clean, uncluttered lines."

Unfortunately the main contractor proved less than satisfactory, the project's momentum began to slow and the couple had to sell their home and move in with friends for eight months while the house was completed. Scott, a qualified carpenter, took time off from work to oversee the build and help out on site wherever possible.

External walls have been clad with softwood cedar cladding, fixed vertically, horizontally and even diagonally onto the various elements which make up the predominantly single storey house. This quirkiness is further highlighted by the series of unconventional windows in various sizes which adorn the property. Colourfast, weather-resistant Trespa panels — based on thermosetting resins homogeneously reinforced with wood fibres — have been used where tannin from the cedar would leach resin onto the stainless steel roofs below, and prevent the roof cladding from becoming stained or damaged.

Facing south-west and shaded by mature trees, which form a sheltered micro climate, the house benefits from large sections of glazing and a flexible, open plan layout achieved with the help of wide oriental-style glazed screens between the oak floored dining area and the sitting room.

Purpose-made Japanese-style acrylic screens may be opened to unite the ground floor living spaces.

Steps lead up from the seating area to a contemporary staircase, which winds up to the master bedroom and en suite shower room on the first floor, forming a steel vertebra with pale ash treads and handrails. At the base of this slender staircase further screens slide back to reveal an internal garden on the north side of the house, an indulgent glazed space which is filled with orchids, lush palms and planting.

Scott had spent his childhood living in Australia and was heavily influenced by what he describes as "the breezy, inside-outside style of Australian houses." He and Rachel stumbled upon a book entitled New Australia Style which, coupled with inspiration from their travels, led to them incorporating unusual ideas into their new home such as bathroom shutters which enable the bather to lie in the bath on the ground floor and look through an opening into the neighbouring internal garden.

The couple still have little time to relax and enjoy their new home, however, as their attention has turned instead to planning their wedding in Australia, to which their architect Peter Dowsett and his wife have been invited. When they return to Hampshire, the newly married couple have big plans for both the house and garden, which include a micro-hydro system to harness the power of the mill waterfall using a turbine to create electricity — an ambitious project which will further connect their new home to the beautiful stretch of river beside which it stands. ■

FLOORPLAN

The house is mainly single storey, with two bedrooms on the ground floor, a utility room and study. The kitchen opens directly into a conservatory dining area with screens between this and the lounge, where a delicate winding staircase leads up to the master bedroom and en suite.

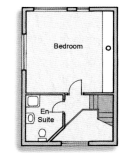

FIRST FLOOR

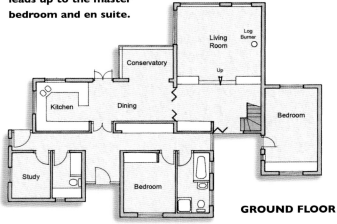

GROUND FLOOR

RESTRICTIVE COVENANT

A restrictive covenant is a legally enforceable restriction that can control the future development, alteration or use of a piece of land and the buildings on it, to protect the interests of a previous owner, their successors in title and/or the interests of neighbouring properties, especially on a single development or estate. Covenants can be relaxed subject to the agreement (often involving payment) of the beneficiaries, but, as Scott and Rachel found, doing so can be expensive. Very old or antiquated covenants may not be enforceable. Visit homebuilding.co.uk for more information.

FACT FILE

Names: Scott Kemmis and Rachel Dovey
Professions: Directors of garden landscaping business
Area: Hampshire
House type: Three bedroom detached
House size: 200m²
Build route: Main contractor, specialist subcontractor and selves
Construction: SIPs panels, stainless steel roof, cedar and Trespa cladding
Warranty: NHBC
Finance: Private and mortgage from NatWest One account
Build time: Sep '03 – June '04
Land cost: £60,000 to remove covenant and £14,000 planning costs

Build cost: £297,000
Total cost: £371,000
House value: £1,000,000
Cost/m²: £1,485

63%
COST SAVING

Cost Breakdown:

Supply and erection of SIPs walls and roofs	£52,000
Supply and fit of stainless steel roof coverings	£23,000
Aluminium glass structures	£28,000
Hardwood doors and windows	£16,700
Electrics	£3,700
Plumbing and underfloor heating	£13,000
Kitchen	£8,500
Kitchen appliances	£4,400
Stairs	£3,900
Oak flooring	£5,000
Tiling	£5,000
Sanitaryware	£4,800
Mini treatment plant	£2,500
Solar shades	£2,000
Cladding and Trespa panels	£26,000
Carport	£12,000
Decking and landscaping	£6,000
Main contractor	£80,500
TOTAL	**£297,000**

USEFUL CONTACTS

Architect – Peter Dowsett: 01202 419100; **Hardwood decking, landscaping and tropical planting** – The Gardeners Ltd: 01794 514765; **Planning consultant** – Southern Planning Practice: 01962 715770; **Landscape architect** – Integrated Design: 01425 277253; **Structural Insulated Panels** – BPAC Ltd: 01383 823995; **Hwam wood burner** – New Forest Wood burning Centre: 01590 683585; **Hardwood doors and windows** – Boylander Joinery Ltd: 01202 499499; **Glazed structures** – Conservatory Installations: 02380 667747; **Electrics, internal and exterior lighting** – Colin Stilwell: 01794 523760; **Sanitaryware** – Villeroy & Boch: 0208 871 4028; **Kitchen** – Shaston Ltd: 01962 863232; **Cladding panels** – Trespa: www.trespa.com; **Canton sliding screens** – Draks: 01869 232989; **Staircase** – Albini & Fontanot Italy: 390541 906111; **Hardwood flooring** – Boen UK Ltd: 0870 7704320; **Organic paints and stains** – Ecos Organic Paints: 01524 852371; **Sliding wardrobe screens** – Doors Direct: 01423 502040; **Sanitaryware supply** – The Bathroom Warehouse Winchester Ltd: 01962 862554; **Hall and kitchen floor tiles** – Nicobond: 01489 779700; **Solar shades** – Dales: 0115 9301521 info@doorsdirect.co.uk; **Blinds** – Hillarys: 0800 5876420

LIGHT INDUSTRIAL

Julian and Dinah Powell-Tuck have built a light-filled family home on a former commercial site in busy West London on a combined live-work basis.

WORDS: CLIVE FEWINS   PHOTOGRAPHY: PHILIP BIER

JULIAN AND DINAH Powell-Tuck's new self-build lies on a backland site which, just off the busy A4002, is an oasis of peace in one of the most highly populated areas of England. "We were amazingly lucky to find a site which allowed a 23 metre frontage on two storeys in this part of London," says Julian, who runs his own architectural and design practice from a separate but linked section of the new building.

Inside, the house is rather austere in its appearance and finishes, and highly functional in ▶

The property is set back and hardly visible from the road. Access is though an allyway between two existing houses

HOMEBUILDING & RENOVATING MAGAZINE

AWARDS 2003

WINNER BEST CONTEMPORARY HOUSE

167

■ LIGHT INDUSTRIAL

"IN MANY WAYS THE HOUSE HAS MADE THE BEST POSSIBLE USE OF A BACKLAND SITE OF THIS SORT…"

its design. This is partly a reflection of the lifestyle of the Powell-Tucks and their four children – Julian describes it as "rugged" – and partly because they could not afford more expensive finishes.

"We were absolutely determined to build for the price we got for our of our previous house – a four bedroom Victorian terrace in south-west London which we sold for £625,000 – and we were spot on," explains Julian.

It was partly a reaction to that house that led Julian and Dinah, a journalist, to come up with their design. "It seemed that in our previous house the whole family would congregate in the kitchen," says Julian. "So we have taken the kitchen and 'blown it out.'" Consequently, the kitchen, dining area and relaxation space is all one vast room of 86m² – approaching a third of the total size of the house.

Perhaps the most remarkable thing about the Powell-Tucks' house is the transformation it has brought about on the site. Previously the land was occupied by a car body workshop and paint spray works, that had, in turn, replaced a taxi garage on the site of what had originally been a large Victorian stable block for the London Omnibus Company.

Julian discovered the plot, but it was purchased by his neighbour and colleague in the project, for whom Julian had carried out several other design schemes in the past. The Powell-Tucks' section of the plot totals 25 by 30 metres and their neighbours' – whose house was built in parallel using the same contractor – is approximately the same size.

"We had few difficulties coming up with a design that fitted in with the building's long frontage with two separate entrances, whilst encompassing the 'live' and the 'work' sections of the building," Julian explains. "The main problem was the planning authority – Hammersmith and Fulham Council. Previously I had not had a 'live-work' project in mind, but it made sense to combine the two functions because of the size and shape of the site and because the policy in this part of London is to encourage schemes of this sort. However, the council wanted a 50:50 live-work split and we wanted the division to be 62 per cent house and 38 per cent office. It took two years and

The largely glazed first floor houses the main living areas and kitchen, which leads out onto a decked sun terrace. ➤

"THE HOUSE IS HARDLY VISIBLE FROM THE ROAD AND WE HAVE OUR OWN LITTLE PRIVATE SPACE."

an appeal to get consent. In a sense this did not matter because we had not yet bought the site — just made an arrangement with the previous tenants, who wanted to be freed of their legal agreement in order to move their business to a different location. However, it was very frustrating at times and took a lot of time and effort as well as costing around £2,000. Fortunately, it was quickly upheld at appeal."

Nevertheless, there were stiff conditions attached to the design, namely that they should not overlook any of the neighbours in what is mainly a residential area. This did not prove particularly difficult as the site the house occupies is not very close to any other houses, so these restrictions did not stop the family from creating a first floor that is largely glazed — with large sliding units 2.2m tall, all of which open. The light therefore floods into this upstairs living area on two sides as well as through the roof.

Part of the austere look comes from the plain concrete floor that stretches throughout the main living area. "We agonised over it a bit, but it is very functional and warms up well with the underfloor heating — and we were on a strict budget," says Julian. "We think it suits this upstairs living area, which is closer to the light and more private than living downstairs." Living upstairs has also enabled them to make the most of the very high ceilings they have been able to achieve beneath the flat, membrane-clad, highly insulated roof.

The site is very secure because they have retained the old 3.8m high wall of London stock bricks that surrounds it. Repairing this greatly added to the construction costs, as did their decision to build the main frame in reinforced concrete. "We chose a concrete frame because the contractors who were building this and the adjacent house were pouring a great deal of concrete, as our neighbour has a large basement with swimming pool. It made sense to continue with this means of construction," Julian explains.

The brick perimeter wall has greatly added to the character as well as the security of the site. "Even if we had wanted to, we would not have been allowed to demolish it because it forms the end of lots of other people's gardens," says Julian, who has also rather cleverly brought it

The library is entered via a huge sliding blackboard that serves as a door, a means of reducing noise, and a family reminder board. ➤

into the house by using it as a feature wall in the master bedroom and upstairs relaxation area.

While the upstairs has underfloor heating, the bedrooms downstairs are all heated by a rather novel arrangement. All the children's rooms step up to the exterior decking over a grid that contains the heating pipes. "Natural ventilation comes in throughout the year. All that happens is that it passes over hot pipes if the heating happens to be on as it passes through," explains Julian.

"It is a simple method of heating, but it works. And that underlines the real trick of building on a tight budget – the way you put things together. We used a local builder, but a highly skilled joiner. With his help and that of a few others we were able to introduce interesting elements."

Julian and Dinah are particularly fond of the high ceilings in all the rooms. "We like generous spaces and I believe that in Britain today people have

become too obsessed with the use of every little bit of space," says Julian. "It is nice to be generous with space and we have been lucky enough to be able to do this. It is a shame that we just could not run to a sixth/guest bedroom, and that we had to cut back on some of the finishes. It would have been good to have been able to afford something a bit less basic than the aircrete blockwork on many of the internal walls. But the building has a rugged, tough look and is tailor-made to suit our lifestyle.

The brick perimeter wall was very cleverly used as a feature wall in the bedroom

"The house is set back and hardly visible from the busy road and we have our own little private space with its three courtyards and sun terrace. We can also park the car in a garage – rare in this part of London. The building nestles into its surroundings and is honest and functional. In many ways it has made the best possible use of a backland site of this sort." ■

FACT FILE

Names: Julian and Dinah Powell-Tuck
Professions: Director of architectural and design practice and journalist
Area: West London
House type: Five bedroom

detached, attached to live-work unit
House size: 290m² (office unit: 178m²)
Build route: Self managed
Construction: Reinforced concrete frame, exterior walls: brick, block, horizontal cedar cladding and glass
Warranty: Architect's Certificate
Finance: Mortgage from Clydesdale Bank
Build time: April '00 - November '01
Land cost: £156,000
Build cost: £625,000
Total cost: £781,000
House value: £1,500,000
Cost/m²: £1,335

48%
COST SAVING

JUDGES' SUMMARY

HOMEBUILDING & RENOVATING MAGAZINE
AWARDS 2003
WINNER BEST CONTEMPORARY HOUSE

This is an exciting and bold new contemporary house that is coherent in all aspects of its design. The building's form, the colours and textures of the external materials, and its relationship with its private courtyard setting are all aesthetically very well balanced.

The relationship between the live and work aspects is efficient and unobtrusive to either function. The orientation and format of the living space makes optimum use of the overlooked urban backland site. The interiors – particularly the light filled first floor living spaces – are at once dramatic and elegant. The pragmatic use of honest, rough, inexpensive finishes in the interior creates a utilitarian aesthetic that perfectly suits the building's crisp linear architecture.

Most importantly, however, the building clearly functions very successfully as a family home for its owners and their four children. An exemplary new urban home that represents excellent value for money.

Once within the backland courtyard setting, the property is extremely private and secluded.

FLOORPLAN

The first floor is used for the main living spaces and kitchen, leading out onto a sun terrace. The five bedrooms are all downstairs along with utility spaces and games room.

GROUND FLOOR   **FIRST FLOOR**

USEFUL CONTACTS

Design – Powell-Tuck Associates: 020 8749 7700; **Quantity surveyors** – Stockdale: 020 8664 6373; **Structural engineers** – Whitby and Bird: 020 7631 5291; **Electrical and mechanical consultants** – E&M Tecnica: 01784 431333; **Site clearance, footings, walls, perimeter wall repairs and roof** – Epsom Contracts: 020 8959 7383; **Joinery and kitchen** – Becher Joinery: 020 8568 9488; **Glazing** – Compass Glass: 020 8946 8080; **Roof** – Allround Roofing: 020 8221 0100; **Roof membrane** – Integrated Polymer Systems: 01969 625000; **Metalwork** – Culmer Fixing: 020 7498 2026; **Sanitaryware** – C P Hart: 020 7902 1000

A CONTEMPORARY

THE DESIGNER OF THE NEW WEMBLEY STADIUM BUILDS HIS OWN HOME

CLASSIC

Renowned architect Ken Shuttleworth has created a dramatic crescent-shaped home that responds brilliantly to the conditions of its site, making the most of the views and available sunlight.

WORDS: CLIVE FEWINS   PHOTOGRAPHY: PHILIP BIER

YOU COULD DRIVE a small car through the fortress like front door of Dr Ken Shuttleworth's house on the edge of a Wiltshire downland village. The huge aluminium door – it has no windows and at first visitors are not even sure it is the main entrance to the building – is not the only surprise in the house.

Dr Shuttleworth is a partner in the London architectural practice headed by Lord Foster, and designer of Hong Kong Airport and the new Wembley Stadium. He is a man well versed in the use of glass, steel, concrete and aluminum, all of which he has a knack of making do all sorts of things other people might never think of. All four are used in profusion in his own 400m2 house, which has won a clutch of awards including a Concrete Society Millennium Award and RIBA Award 2000, since the architect, his

The south east facing curtain wall is 34m of toughened glass on two layers, from MAG Hansen on 0113 255111.

wife Seana and their two children moved in three years ago.

As if walking through the front door — once you have found it — of Crescent House is not enough of a surprise, the space you then enter is not so much a conventional hall as what Ken and his wife calls 'the gallery.' It leaves you aghast as you enter because of the height — it rises 5.4m — and the width reduces as you proceed.

The walls of the gallery, built like the rest of the house in cast concrete ►

"ALTHOUGH THE CURVE IS STRUCTURALLY SIGNIFICANT, THE GLASS WALL DOES NOT SUPPORT THE FLAT CONCRETE ROOF ON THAT SIDE…"

"I DON'T THINK BUILDING YOUR OWN HOME IS THE SORT OF THING YOU SHOULD DO TOO YOUNG… I THINK ABOUT 45 IS THE MINIMUM.'"

and plastered on the inside, are lined with paintings – some of them by the Shuttleworths' two young children – and the whole is surmounted by an 'upper gallery' – a small, narrow mezzanine running along the rear wall and accessed by two sets of samba stairs. These are stairs with split treads, allowing them to rise much steeper than a normal staircase and designed as a space saving device.

Halfway along the hall is a giant, 'brutalist' concrete fireplace set into the rear wall. It faces the vast horizontal space of the garden room, where the family cooks, eats, and relaxes and where Jo, 10, and Jaime, 6, play. It is at this stage that you realise the hall, which is lit by means of a high, 30m long, curved clerestory window in jointed glass, cast to form channels which interlock to form a cavity, is the key element that links the two crescent shaped wings.

The couple chose to build their home in Wiltshire because they had owned a house there since the late 80s and were very fond of the area. After a three year search they found a five bedroom, box like house dating from around 1925 on a five acre plot on the outskirts of a village they knew.

"It was built of single skin blockwork and had virtually no insulation. We knew we should knock it down and rebuild eventually but it was big enough for us to live in for 20 years if necessary," says Ken. They paid £180,000.

The family moved in 1994 and lived there for three years. Then they found – 'by luck', Ken claims – that together with a mortgage of £175,000 from Barclays, they could raise the £345,000 needed to build the sort of house they had decided upon.

"We were very apprehensive about approaching our neighbours – they had sold us the house and land and built a smaller property in which they were living on the adjoining plot," says Ken. "Fortunately when I showed them a model I had made, they quite understood what we wanted to do. We also found the planners

Ken designed the house so that there would be one main living space – including the cooking and lounge areas – that was bathed in light and took in the views of the garden. ➤

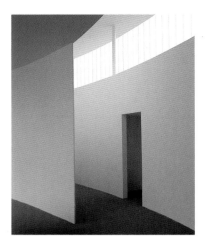

"THE HUGE ALUMINIUM DOOR HAS NO WINDOWS AND AT FIRST VISITORS ARE NOT EVEN SURE IT IS THE MAIN ENTRANCE…"

very supportive. They seemed to like the idea of the curved exterior and the way the building fitted into the site, which borders a large area of outstanding natural beauty. They thought the sort of house we planned would improve the area and did not seem to mind the fact that at 400m2, it was nearly double the size of the previous house. This was because the previous building had a number of outbuildings and workshops that spread over a considerable area."

Ken enlisted colleagues at Ove Arup and Partners to assist with the structural engineering because he knew that the complex design (geometry is his passion) of the flat-roofed structure required some careful engineering.

"The main thing was that we intended to use a large amount of glass

in the house" he says. "The entire 34m, south east facing curtain wall is glass. It comprises two layers " the outer 15mm layer of toughened glass and the inner 10.5mm laminated glass. There is a 16mm cavity with a Low-E coating on the inside of the outer skin. The whole structure was specially made for us. The way it is anchored into the ground is very complex. At £45,000 it was by far the single most expensive component.

Aluminium and vast amounts of concrete are what greet you as you approach the fortress-like entrance.

"We wanted one main living space – a garden room – that would allow all the day to day activities of cooking, eating relaxing and playing," says Seana. "There are no divisions in the room, which is bathed in natural light and gives generous views of the garden all the year round."

The keys to the whole structure are the two massive concrete 'shear walls' above the front and rear doors and the massive concrete chimney, which rises above the building. The chimney is both practical and the basis of a feature that was very important in the design specification – it houses a massive fireplace. "There is nothing like a log fire. It forms the whole focus of the living area in winter," says Ken.

"This is an extremely windy site. Despite the fact that we are not high here there is nothing between us and the Bristol Channel. We have planted 1,000 deciduous trees which will eventually reduce the effect of the winds but in the meantime we need great strength in the building to resist this.

"The whole concept was entirely site specific. It was not as though I said to myself, 'I am going to build a house like this whatever the site. The most attractive outlook is on the south east, where we face open country leading across to the Wiltshire Downs. It was to make the most of this that we decided on a semi-circular house, which essentially turned its long back on what we wanted to block out and concentrated its gaze through the glazed wall onto the best views and over the garden."

"The orientation actually helps to prevent overheating in the summer and if it does get too hot we simply swing open the two large glass doors at either end of the south east crescent," Ken explains. The other advantage is that as the sun moves round and hits the solid and translucent walls, the very heavy structure acts as a heat store. ➤

"WE BELIEVE WE HAVE SUCCEEDED IN THE BRIEF WE SET OURSELVES – TO CREATE A HOUSE THAT IS ENVIRONMENTALLY FRIENDLY… BUT FUNCTIONAL"

The five bedrooms – all situated within the north west crescent – are windowless apart from narrow skylights against the rear wall. The main source of light is a continuous glazed strip that brings light in from above. "You can lie in bed and focus on the sky and stars," Ken says. "These private spaces, being small and low, give a strong sense of intimacy, security and protection."

The bedrooms are all irregular shapes, with variants of a crescent in them. The washbasins are all cast in concrete. Except for the vast bulk of the cast concrete chimney and the shear walls, the interior surfaces are all white, intended to reflect the whitewashed walls of traditional Wiltshire buildings. The colour comes from the furnishings and objects within. The Shuttleworths change towels, cushions, bed linen and other items four times a year to reflect the changing seasons – blue for winter, yellow for spring, green for summer and red for autumn.

In addition to the massive fireplace in the 'gallery' there is a warm water trench heating system fired by bulk bottled gas.

"The house was originally going to be a retirement project but we managed to bring it forward," says Ken. "However, I don't think building your own house is the sort of thing you should do too young. I think about 45 is the minimum age. I am 47 now.

"We believe we have succeeded in the brief we set ourselves – to create a house that is environmentally friendly and low maintenance which is not lavish, profligate or precious but calm and functional. Considering the house is currently valued at around £1.3m, I do not consider the building price of £345,000 bad value." ■

FLOORPLAN

The shape of the building was not a whim but a response to site conditions. The curved walls deflect strong prevailing winds and the glass curtain wall makes the most both of the views and available sunlight.

"THE HOUSE WAS ORIGINALLY GOING TO BE A RETIREMENT PROJECT BUT WE MANAGED TO BRING IT FORWARD."

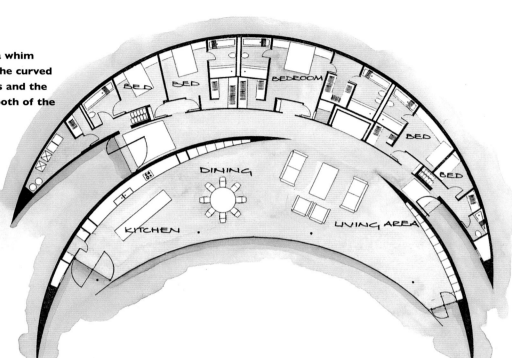

FACT FILE

Finance: Private
Build time: Jun '96 — Mar '97
Land cost: £180,000
Build cost: £345,000
Total cost: £525,000
House value: £1.3m
Cost/m²: £862

60%
COST SAVING

Costs as of Feb 2001
Name: Ken and Seana Shuttleworth
Professions: Architect and artist
Area: Rural Wiltshire
House type: Single storey, flat roofed
House size: 400m²
Build route: Main contractor
Construction: Solid concrete walls and masonry externally insulated
Warranty: NHBC
SAP rating: 85

Cost Breakdown:

Preliminaries	£64,300
Demolition of old house	£1,900
Substructure	£33,400
Frame and roof	£63,600
External walls	£88,200
Windows and external doors	£8,800
Internal walls and partitions	£5,500
Wall floor and ceiling finishes	£12,300
All services	£53,500
Sundries	£13,500
TOTAL	**£345,000**

USEFUL CONTACTS

Architect - Ken Shuttleworth: 020 7794 4574; **Structural Engineers** - Ove Arup and Partners: 020 7636 1531; **Main Contractors** - Dove Brothers: 01375 392391; **Roof Membrane** - Fenland: 01223 840772; **Glass curtain wall** - MAG Hansen: 0113 255 111; **Clerestory Glazing** - Reglit: 0141 613 1414; **Fireplace** - A W Knight: 01225 891469; **Services Engineers** - Roger Preston and Partners: 01628 623423; **Quantity Surveyors** - Davis Langdon and Everest: 020 7497 9000; **Heating** - Drake and Scull: 01703 641641; **Metalwork** - Nic Greening: 0860 836487; **Aluminium Doors** - Trapex: 020 7739 5845; **External Insulation** - Sto: 01505 324262; **Main Joinery** - Unit 22: 020 7278 3872; **Lighting** - Erco: 020 7408 0320

BUILDING A RADIACL HOME IN A
SENSITIVE WATERSIDE LOCATION

OFF THE WALL

The O'Sullivan House has it all, but building this contemporary retreat as a visual extension of the sea wall in Devon stretched both architect and engineer to the limits.

WORDS: DEBBIE JEFFERY
PHOTOGRAPHY: NIGEL RIGDEN

WITH ITS COPPER barrel-vaulted roof, fortress-like stone faced walls apparently growing up out of the water, and projecting timber clad bay complete with an armoured glass floor, Roderic and Sue O'Sullivan's house is architecture with a capital A. Taking the term waterside home to new extremes, its feet literally dabble in the estuary at Salcombe, Devon, and with its ravishingly masculine good looks, taut, clean lines and sharply defined spaces, the breathtaking views and problematic site conditions became the raison dêtre for the design.

Almost more grittily interesting than the house, however, is the man who designed it. Stan Bolt, a native Devonian rightly proud of his "working class roots," admits to initially feeling intimidated when training as an architect. His determination fuelled from the age of thirteen by the careless remark of a clueless careers advisor to "be more realistic" in his ambitions, Stan was going to prove his undoubted talents come what may — which he eventually did by winning a RIBA Award for a lavatory and utility room extension, the smallest project ever to win such a prize.

The O'Sullivan family were aware when they purchased this piece of land that building on it would not prove easy. "We enjoy sailing and had owned a flat in Salcombe for over twenty years," explains Sue, in

The dining room is dominated by the glorious external views over the estuary.

telling how the family came to build in the area. "We first saw the site from the water whilst out on our boat, and were immediately interested in finding out more."

Formerly a corner of the neighbouring villa's extensive gardens, the site came complete with planning permission and was advertised for sale by auction — with Roderic warned that it would achieve an enormous sum and prove even more expensive to build on. "We gave up and didn't even attend the auction," he recalls. Only later did the family discover that the plot had not reached its reserve price and negotiated privately to purchase the land for a comparatively small (and undisclosed) five figure sum.

Ensuring that both the site and the house were secure and fortified in such an exposed location was of prime importance. Situated at the foot of a steep, almost inaccessible wooded slope overlooking Salcombe Estuary, a planning restriction was imposed requiring all materials and plant to be transported to the site by barge.

"Our architect, Stan Bolt, approached the project extremely methodically, working closely with structural engineer, John Grimes," ➤

The exterior of O'Sullivans house is designed to become part of the sea wall – one of the clever concessions that enabled such a radical home to get through planning.

states Roderic. It was necessary to stabilise and support the coastal slope to prevent slippage and collapse, and the O'Sullivans, who have four children, decided to play safe and attempt to develop the plot in two distinct

The fireplace from Croydon Fireplaces (020 8684 1495) acts as a partition between the two main living areas.

stages — determining that they could physically and financially build a house only once the necessary preliminary work had been undertaken. This involved clearing the site, rebuilding and repairing the existing sea wall in four hour time slots as the tides allowed, excavating and piling. The coastal slope was cut back to correspond to the 10m contour of the land and stabilised with the construction of a high level concrete retaining wall and an extensive system of rock anchors prior to laying the ground floor slab. Phase one alone was to total £388,000 and took eight months to complete. "I was very keen on a belt and braces approach," remarks Sue.

The existing site of the proposed dwelling, at 3.6m above Ordnance Datum (AOD), had experienced flooding as a result of waves breaking over the sea wall. This, coupled with predictions that tide levels may rise by up to 420mm over the next 70 years due to global warming, resulted in rebuilding the sea wall with a wave deflector – calculated by the consulting engineer to combat a potential wave height of up to 1.5m – and raising the ground floor as high as practically possible on the site.

The house is a reverse level affair, with a large open plan living room leading out onto decked terraces and cantilevered balconies and taking full advantage of the views. This first floor was constructed in an altogether different manner to the robust reinforced concrete walls which contain the bedrooms and bathrooms below. The loadbearing masonry of the ➤

"THE ELECTRICIANS REFUSED TO WALK ON THE GLASS FLOOR AND TRIED STRETCHING OVER IT… BUT IT REALLY IS PERFECTLY SAFE!"

ground floor supports the first floor exposed steel frame, terminating in the gentle curve of the copper roof.

The stunning see-through floor in the study area is made of reinforced glass.

"We gave Stan a detailed brief of our needs," says Roderic, whose primary residence is a chintzy and traditional London flat which now feels cluttered when compared to the contemporary new house. "This included the need for plenty of bathrooms to accommodate our children, and we now have a really big walk-in shower room, with a large utility area for washing and drying clothes. The design aesthetics were left almost entirely to Stan, however, and when we first saw the drawings we were quite shocked – it was not what we had imagined at all – although we immediately warmed to it. He has given us more from the site than we ever thought could be achieved."

It has to be said that the minimalist style dwelling would not suit an untidy family. Each room is streamlined to within an inch of its life: a row of bedrooms leads off from the lower hallway through grey doors, with all beds made up in pristine white linen to complement the black carpet and grey built-in wardrobes. Light reflecting from the water outside ripples on the ceilings. Bathrooms are identically tiled in white, with slate

"[STAN BOLT] HAS GIVEN US MORE FROM THE SITE THAN WE EVER THOUGHT COULD BE ACHIEVED…"

floors and perfectly folded grey towels. It is almost a shock to stumble upon the single room featuring primary colours, in the form of duvet covers on bunk beds.

Upstairs, the glass floor holds a child-like fascination for most visitors and is highlighted by the fact that this screened workstation bay does not feature forward facing windows. Such a clever conceit provides a degree of privacy and contrasts with the vast expanses of glass on this level, drawing your eye downwards to the lapping waves beneath your feet and, surreally, a bobbing red buoy. Your mind tells you it must be safe to stand on, and yet somehow it takes a superhuman effort to tread here.

"The electricians refused to walk on the glass and tried stretching over it," laughs Stan, forcefully leaping up and down to prove his point, "but it really is perfectly safe!" ■

FLOORPLAN

The house is a reverse level affair, with a large open plan living room leading out onto decked terraces and cantilevered balconies. The ground floor has been constructed using robust reinforced concrete and houses the bedrooms and bathrooms.

GROUND FLOOR

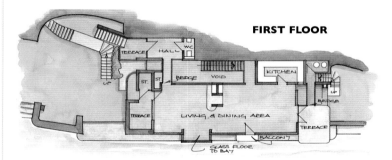

FIRST FLOOR

USEFUL CONTACTS

Chartered Architect — Stan Bolt: 01803 852588 **Structural Engineer** — John Grimes Partnership: 01752 690533 **Services Engineer** — Dodd, Cumming & Love: 01752 253559 **Main Contractor** — Dean & Dyball Construction Ltd: 01392 460500 **Steelwork** — JCR Engineering: 01803 520232 **Walling stone** — Lakeview Quarry: 01458 224033 **Steel windows** — Monk Metal Windows Ltd: 01213 514411 **Glazing** — Pilkington UK Ltd: 01744 692000 **Flat roofing** — Sarnafil Ltd: 01603 748985 **Copper roof** — W H Joyce & Sons: 01752 668381 **External doors** — Martin Roberts: 01795 476161 **Internal doors** — D. W. Archer: 01179 710294 **Entrance door** — Sharman Joinery: 01271 375481 **Timber floors** — Junckers Ltd: 01376 517512 **Western Red Cedar** — D W Archer: 01179 710294 **Balau Decking** — Morgan & Co: 01634 290909 **Joinery; bathroom, utility room, window cills & staircases** — Fitzroy Joinery: 01752 562452 **Fireplace** — Croydon Fireplaces: 020 8684 1495 **Slate flooring** — Delabole Slate: 01840 212242; **Light fittings** — Concord Lighting Ltd: 01273 515811, Marlin Lighting Ltd: 020 8894 5522 **Sanitaryware** — West One Bathrooms Ltd: 020 7720 9333 **Kitchen units** — Applied Shopfitting Ltd: 01364 643855

FACT FILE

Costs as of Sept 2001
Names: Sue and Roderic O'Sullivan
Professions: Teacher and solicitor
Area: Devon
House type: Four bedroom detached
House size: 282m²
Build route: Main contractor
Construction: Loadbearing masonry supporting exposed steel frame
Warranty: Architect's certificate
SAP rating: 100
Finance: Private
Build time: 16 months
Land Cost: Undisclosed
Build cost: £808,542
Current value: £1.3m
Cost/m²: £2,867

Cost Breakdown:

Phase One

Preliminaries	£206,000
Demolition/site clearance	£3,000
Sea Wall	£51,250
Piling/ground floor slab	£52,250
Rock excavation and high level retaining wall	£43,500
External works/drainage	£32,000
Total	£388,000

Phase Two

Preliminaries	£133,989
External Walls	£22,739
Internal Walls	£10,940
Upper floors	£8,633
Staircase	£3,989
Roof	£47,737
Frame	£23,531
External doors/windows	£22,059
Internal doors	£5,212
Balconies and terrace	£13,856
Wall finishes	£15,160
Floor finishes	£16,275
Ceiling finishes	£4,334
Fittings and furniture	£23,807
Mechanical/plumbing and electrical installation	£48,506
Fireplace	£4,772
External works	£11,448
Drainage	£3,485
Total	£420,542
TOTAL	**£808,542**

BUILDING A SUPER E
CONTEMPORARY ECO HOME

SPIRIT OF THE PIONEERS

Sarah and Doug Stewart have built the first bespoke Super E airtight house in the UK from an imported Canadian kit.

WORDS: DEBBIE JEFFERY PHOTOGRAPHY: NIGEL RIDGEN

"AS A CHILD I always wanted to be a builder, and started out working as a bricklayer – which meant that it took me some time before I realised the benefits of building with timber frame," says Doug Stewart. "I'm currently doing a degree in Building Processes, which has made me far more aware of sustainable options, and attended a seminar promoting Super E housing which really inspired me."

Doug's interest in sustainable construction has led him to be among the first in the UK to embrace the state-of-the-art technology embodied in the Super E programme: the recognised brand name for high quality Canadian housing, designed to help Canadian exporters deliver healthy, energy efficient housing to other countries. This airtight construction with a heat recovery ventilation system, high levels of cellulose insulation and underfloor heating, is extremely comfortable to live in and drastically reduces heating bills.

Doug is managing director of DGS Construction Ltd, a building company based in Milton Keynes which specialises in building and renovating individual houses and small scale developments. Recently, the company has entered into a partnership with DAC International, a Canadian company producing bespoke Super E homes. The result of this collaboration is the first bespoke self-build Super E home to be built in the UK.

Doug and his wife, Sarah, had spent five years searching Cornwall for ➤

Next generation eco house. Super E airtight construction incorporates a heat recovery ventilation system, high levels of cellulose insulation and underfloor heating.

"TACKLING SOMETHING NEW IS ALWAYS GOING TO BE FRAUGHT WITH PROBLEMS…"

Bamboo flooring only takes four years to grow at source, compared to oak which takes a minimum 100 years, and has been laid in the majority of rooms – with ceramic floor tiles chosen for the wet areas.

a suitable site on which to build their new house, eventually discovering a piece of land near Torpoint, on which stood a tumbledown timber clad bungalow. The 0.3 acre plot was overgrown with brambles and littered with old cars and refrigerators, but the stunning elevated site is situated in open countryside within walking distance of the sea, and was exactly what the Stewarts had been waiting for.

Convincing the planners to allow them to replace the dilapidated bungalow with a two storey house proved far harder than Sarah and Doug had imagined, however. "Catchfrench, our architect, took our concept from a rough sketch and made a convincing case to the planners, and we had great support from the Super E supplier in Canada," says Doug. "We had to prove residential status, and I went into the village and asked around until I found the last two occupants, who gave written evidence which satisfied the planners. It was a struggle, and I didn't tell Sarah just how difficult things had been until after planning permission was granted, as I knew she would worry."

The new house has been designed with flexible accommodation in the form of two spacious flats, enabling Sarah and Doug to live primarily on the first floor. "It was only when I stood on the roof of the old bungalow and looked over the hedges that I realised what wonderful views the upstairs rooms would have," Doug explains. "This fact has influenced the whole design, and we have our master bedroom suite and main living spaces

upstairs, with three additional bedrooms, a kitchen, bathroom and lounge downstairs for guests. If you are considering building a Super E house it makes sense to experience what it is like to live in one, and we hope to be able to offer accommodation to other self-builders who would like to find out more about this kind of building."

Doug visited Canada and spent three days working closely with kit supplier DAC International, its design team and the frame erector. He was extremely impressed by the detail and quality of the timber frames and the technical support.

"Bringing three huge containers into the country from Canada proved to be a real learning experience," Doug recalls. "Not only did we have to navigate the red tape to pass customs, but we were shocked to discover that VAT and import duty would have to be paid up front before customs would let the containers into the country. We were able to reclaim the VAT at the end of the project, but it was still an unwelcome addition to the budget."

Building a new home 250 miles from where you live and work was never going to be easy, but Doug's son, Matthew, ran the family business in Milton Keynes while Doug stayed in Cornwall. Sarah was very supportive, but refused to move into the shack on site where Doug camped throughout the summer of 2003. Later, some neighbours rented the couple a holiday property close by, which enabled Sarah to become ➤

The house has spacious rooms and cathedral ceilings on the first floor, and is flooded with light from large glazed gables.

195

"PEOPLE WRONGLY ASSUME THAT WITH AN AIRTIGHT HOUSE YOU NEED TO KEEP ALL THE WINDOWS SHUT, WHICH JUST ISN'T TRUE."

"We were fortunate to find subcontractors who were interested and sympathetic to our requirements — even if they did not always agree with our ideas," says Sarah, 41. "Our Cornish neighbours were sceptical at first, but always offered a helping hand, and even the use of their forklift truck."

One of Doug and Sarah's biggest setbacks occurred when the house failed to pass the air pressure test which is required for Super E certification, and is based upon the Canadian R-2000 standard, adapted for local climates. "Most houses in the UK can expect at least ten air changes an hour — but 1.5 is required for certification, and we finally achieved 0.9 following remedial work to the garage," Doug explains. "Air had been getting in through this area, and there was a moment of panic during the second test when we thought the house would fail again — until we realised that someone had left the plant room door open!"

A sophisticated heat recovery and ventilation system minimises heat loss by maintaining between 0.5 and 1.5 air changes per hour at 50 pascals of pressure, and a ground source heat pump supplies heat to the underfloor heating and hot water from underground heat collecting panels, with independent hot water cylinders on each floor which have the facility to add solar heating in the future. The heat pump converts 1kW of electricity into 4kW of heat.

"People wrongly assume that with an airtight house you need to keep all of the windows shut, which just isn't true," says Sarah. "In the summer we open the windows, which are fitted with fly screens to keep insects out of the house. The Super E system really comes into its own during the winter, however, and we have yet to turn on the underfloor heating because the house has been so warm. We've also installed Scandinavian soapstone log burners on each floor, which are 95 per cent efficient and require an external combustion air source to maintain the building's air tightness."

"I am very keen to keep pushing the boundaries of sustainable building," says Doug. "Tackling something new is always going to be fraught with problems, but we were very impressed with the Canadian package, which included everything we needed to build the shell of the house — from the low-e, argon-filled double glazing to the cedar cladding. Hopefully we will inspire more people to take this route, because the house has exceeded our expectations and is really wonderful to live in." ■

involved with fitting out all of the house interiors.

In addition to designing the house and project managing the build, Doug was responsible for constructing the foundations, drains and central core, which incorporates the chimneys although he travelled to Cambodia once the timber frame had been erected, leaving Sarah to organise the roofing.

Soapstone wood-burning stoves have been fitted in the two living room areas.

Renewable and sustainable resources were used wherever possible. The engineered timber structure with panelised walls has been clad with cedar on a local stone plinth. Heavy Fermacell boards, produced from recycled paper and gypsum, were used for the floor, walls and ceilings instead of plasterboard and chipboard, providing a tougher finish, enhancing fire retardancy and limiting the transfer of sound within the house. Excel Warmcel cellulose insulation, made from recycled newsprint, has been blown within the 140mm frame, and every effort was made to ensure the building would be as airtight as possible.

FLOORPLAN

The house has been designed with flexible accommodation which may be used individually as two flats. Sarah and Doug tend to live on the first floor, which has an open plan lounge, dining and office space, contemporary kitchen and one bedroom with an en suite bathroom and balcony. Downstairs there are three further bedrooms, a bathroom, kitchen/breakfast room, lounge which connects with the entrance vestibule and verandah, and a garage with adjoining plant room.

FIRST FLOOR

GROUND FLOOR

FACT FILE

Names: Sarah and Doug Stewart
Professions: Retired florist and MD of family building business
Area: Cornwall
House type: Four bedroom detached
House size: 280m²
Build route: Self-managed subcontractors
Construction: Engineered timber frame, stone plinth, cedar cladding, slate roof
Warranty: Zurich
Finance: Norwich & Peterborough self-build mortgage
Build time: April '03 — April '04
Land cost: £90,000
Build cost: £300,000

Total cost: £390,000
House value: £650,000
Cost/m²: £1,071

Cost Breakdown:

DAC timber frame package, incl. cedar cladding, doors and windows	£101,000
Import logistics and tax	£3,671
Services	£2,500
Roofing	£17,000
Carpentry	£40,000
Stone plinth	£5,000
Scaffolding	£2,500
External works	£10,000
Plumbing, heating etc.	£24,264
Electrical/ventilation	£10,000
Decorating	£6,000
Warmcel insulation	£5,000
Floor finish	£6,500
Kitchen	£14,054
Other items & materials	£31,806

USEFUL CONTACTS

Super E design and construction consultant – DGS Construction Ltd: 01908 503147; **Architect** – Catchfrench: 01503 240781; **Canadian timber frame kit** – DAC International Inc: 1-613-839-0888, dac@magma.ca; **Frame erector** – Timber Build (SW) Ltd: 01404 811833; **Scaffolder** – Apex Scaffolding: 01392 460099; **Carpentry** – SM Woodhouse: 01579 345574; **Roofing** – Roofing Contractors of Cornwall: 01208 74736; **Electrics** – Taylor Kirkham Electrics: 07860 679849; **Warmcel insulation** – PC Builders: 01548 821413; **Plumbing** – SAS & Trewarthas Plumbing & Heating: 01579 340505; **Ventilation** – PRW Electrical Services Ltd: 01761 419909; **Leakage rate measurement** – Retrotec (Europe) Ltd: 01453 836700; **Super E information** – www.super-e.com

HOMEBUILDING
&RENOVATING
MAGAZINE

AWARDS
2003

HIGHLY
COMMENDED

THE
LIGHT
HOUSE

BUILDING A FOUR-STOREY
CONTEMPORARY HOME

■ THE LIGHT HOUSE

James and Kirsten Crinan have built a remarkable new contemporary-style four-storey home on the south coast.

WORDS: CLIVE FEWINS   PHOTOGRAPHY: NIGEL RIGDEN

JAMES AND KIRSTEN Crinan's new white-walled, curved four storey house is situated in an exclusive neighbourhood on the outskirts of Bournemouth, just a few hundred yards uphill from the sea. It has large glass towers which stand above the surrounding houses and a striking curved roof – a dominant feature from the outside. Inside there

seems to be barely a room without at least one curved wall or a curved balcony, which is one reason why it caused a few headaches for the builders, as well as local planners.

It caused a few for James as well. He took 18 months off work during the build and although he did not touch a trowel during the laying of the dual skin blockwork walls or the exterior rendering, he acted as main contractor, clerk of works, sourcing supremo, general factotum and part-time driver, as well as keeping the entire project on schedule. He also played a lead role in casting onsite the flight of ten concrete steps that lead to the front door.

Despite the size of the house James has been careful with space, declining an entrance hall in favour of an open plan entrance/living space.

Despite all the traumas, and dealing with a difficult hillside site with a very steep access, James and Kirsten have come out smiling. On winter nights they now sit in their rooftop hot-tub – invisible from ground level – and gaze out over their curved garden paths and surrounding treetops. "At night up there we could be on safari in southern Africa," German-born Kirsten quips.

The house – they are thinking of naming it 'The Light House' because of the huge variety of angles in which the light enters and the large areas of glass in the roof and walls – is unashamedly self-indulgent. It is 433m², excluding the 33m² garage beneath.

"There are only three bedrooms – each en suite – but all the rooms➤

are large and extremely carefully designed," says James. "If you spend as much as we did – more than £600,000 – on a build, you have a right to expect to get everything exactly as you want it: a high quality build that is going to need hardly any maintenance for the next 10 years."

James' background is in jewellery design, but from his early years he always wanted to design and build his own property. However, he and Kirsten made a false start when they left London for Dorset 12 years ago. "We tried to self-build in Christchurch," explains James. "We had bought a plot but found getting permission for what we wanted impossible and failed to get the project off the ground." Someone else took over the project and the Crinans bought a New England style house half a mile away from where they are now. The dress rehearsal for their present

The staircases are lit by a full height arrow window in four sections on the north-east side. The top landing is awash with light from a glazed section of roof.

"DOING INTERESTING THINGS WITH GLASS IS INCREDIBLY EXPENSIVE. AT TIMES I GAVE UP COUNTING."

home was renovating and extending it and adding a pool complex. After that James felt far more confident when their present plot came up in 1999 for £350,000.

"On the plot was a very tired-looking and dated 1970s chalet bungalow which was not very well built and had been left to deteriorate into a very poor state," says Kirsten. "Even at £350,000 it was a good price. Similar houses in the road are changing hands for around £700,000 nowadays."

James and Kirsten were determined to build something that would have a much more enduring pedigree. "The intention was to build ➤

The two main flights of steps are unsupported steel plates, clad in beech, that are cantilevered straight out of the wall.

■ THE LIGHT HOUSE

something to be a statement of contemporary architecture, a home which will not rapidly date. Ideally I'd like people to be saying in 60 years time that it is a house that still works," says James.

They had few preconceived ideas about the house design, but in order to gain planning permission thought it best to keep to the same footprint as the house they demolished. This meant it would have to be tall if they were to have the amount of space they wanted. It was at this stage that the Crinans fell foul of a group of local residents, one of whom started a petition and presented it to the planning authority, Poole Borough Council, opposing the project on the grounds of its height.

Eventually, after a height reduction, the plan went through without the need to go to appeal. "It was all a bit odd because quite a number of local people told us how they liked the project," says James. "For example, the elderly couple who live just below – they are both in their late 80s – were great supporters from the onset and love the house and its 'different' design. The irony is that the house ended up with a

Commendation from the planning authority in its 'Pride of Place' Award scheme."

Architect Phil Easton, of Dorset-based Western Design, says it was "little short of miraculous" that the project received approval. Although he is head of the practice, most of the design fell to one of the younger members of his staff — Matthew Haley. "Matt absolutely lives his architecture," says Philip. "He puts a huge amount of time and effort into his designs. This was an exceedingly complex project because of the full height, large curved internal wall that provides so many interesting shapes and because it is on so many levels. There were 150 separate drawings, and at the time it took up a large chunk of Matt's life as well as James'."

Although Phil says he had to rein in some of Matt's wilder flights of fancy, there are still many exciting features in the house. Amongst these is the roof. It comprises two curved sections, with a plywood clad steel ➤

The kitchen is located on the first floor and features a glazed wall opening into a balcony. The furniture is from Dream Design (01425 279525).

"I SPENT A HUGE AMOUNT OF TIME CHASING PEOPLE, KEEPING SUBCONTRACTORS ON THEIR TOES."

structure beneath. The two sections are separate and at right angles, with the north-west section – which is partially glazed – a metre higher. All the concealed guttering and close fitting downpipes match the colour of the roof membrane.

The curved roof sections give interesting shapes to bedrooms two and three. The original intention was to leave these open to full roof height but later on in the scheme it was decided to make more use of their height by adding mezzanines. However, it is still possible to see the shape of the roof from below as well as from the mezzanine platforms, which are approached by a curved timber staircase in bedroom three and a spiral stair in the neighbouring room.

It was a disappointment to James that he was unable to have the curved glass balustrading that he wanted fixed to the end of each stair riser. It would have cost about three times as much. "Doing interesting things with glass is incredibly expensive," explains James. "At times I gave up counting. The cost of glazing was one of the main reasons why the house cost about double what I had originally anticipated. One of the problems with building a house like this is that subcontractors think: 'Big house, big car, expensive area, big money and big profits'. But throughout the project Kirsten and I have sought value for money. On the whole we think we have got it, and we are delighted.

"However, it was a constant battle. I spent a huge amount of time chasing people, keeping subcontractors on their toes and the project on schedule. If we build again – as we plan to – I'll favour a single storey glass and steel frame. It should avoid all the hassle of brickies, renderers and plasterers. If I had not been running the project myself and been here virtually every day we would not have got anything like the quality we have achieved. The house would have had the same form but as far as I am concerned it would have been 'wrong' in many ways." ■

The initial plan was to leave all of the bedrooms open to double height, but James felt he could make more of the space in the two guest bedrooms by incorporating mezzanine levels.

FLOORPLAN

SECOND FLOOR

GROUND FLOOR

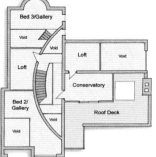

FIRST FLOOR

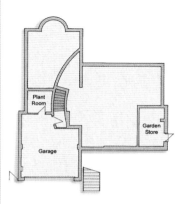

BASEMENT

USEFUL CONTACTS

Designer – Matthew Haley, Western Design Architects: 01258 455239; **Engineer** – Paul Hansen: 01590 682087; **Demolition and main shell** – Sandcroft Homes: 01202 887499; **Glazing contractor** – WHI: 01392 275287; **Glazing consultant** – Paul Trigg: 01179 615395; **Roof construction and erection** – BJ Galvanising: 01202 871448; **Roof membrane** – Alwitra: 01202 579208; **Roofing contractors** – Dawes Roofing: 01202 881150; **Guttering** – Guttercrest: 01691 663300; **Heating and Plumbing** – Chris Rampton: 07870 908281; **Electrics** – Kevin Wilkins: 01202 529197; **Stainless steel handrails on stairs and balconies and casings for fireplaces** - Hayeswood Technical Services: 01202 683883; **Spiral staircase** – B J Galvanising: 01202 871448; **Specialist glazing** – Dorset Glass: 01305 785745; **Kitchen** – Dream Design: 01425 279525

JUDGES' SUMMARY

This is an impressive new house that stands out as a landmark both by day, thanks to the striking curved roof atop its four storeys, and by night when under illumination, it takes on a new life. Although strongly contemporary in design, the exterior also has a Period Art Deco flavour that befits its south coast setting. The semi basement garage makes good use of the site's topography — as does the building's height which affords sea views from the top floor. Inside, the 470m2 of accommodation is of exquisitely high quality, with spacious open plan interiors, vast expanses of glazing bringing in light from all directions and a spectacular staircase with treads cantilevered from the walls. This is an unashamedly indulgent house yet one which has proved excellent value for money thanks to astute timing and meticulously efficient project management.

FACT FILE

Names: James and Kirsten Crinan
Professions: Company director and housewife
Area: Dorset
House type: Three bedroom detached
House size: 470m² (inc. integral basement garage)
Build route: Self-managed
Construction: Dual skin rendered blockwork
Warranty: NHBC
SAP rating: 97
Finance: Private
Build time: October '01 – March '03
Land cost: £350,000
Build cost: £613,000
Total cost: £963,000
House value: £1,800,000
Cost/m²: £1,304

68% COST SAVING

Cost Breakdown:

Architect's and other fees	£21,000
Glass construction and installation	£70,000
Demolition of existing house and construction of main shell	£195,000
Kitchen	£31,000
Floors	£35,000
Electrics, inc. lighting	£36,000
Stairs	£30,000
Balustrading for stairs and balconies	£31,000
Door furniture	£1,250
Sanitaryware	£11,000
Fireplaces	£2,000
Plumbing and heating materials	£9,000
Plumbing and heating labour	£9,000
External paintwork	£10,000
Rendering	£28,000
Roof	£37,000
Joinery	£17,000
Miscellaneous	£40,000
TOTAL	**£613,250**

The oak framed house is clad in brick at ground floor level with weatherboarding above. The south-east facing elevation is largely glazed.

NEW DIMENSIONS

BUILDING A CUTTING EDGE OAK FRAME HOME

WORDS: CLIVE FEWINS
PHOTOGRAPHY: ROB JUDGES

■ NEW DIMENSION

Clive and Helen Hicks have built a cutting-edge contemporary-style timber frame home with spacious open-plan ground floor.

:PEOPLE EITHER LOVE or loathe our new house," says Clive Hicks, and his wife and fellow self-builder Helen agrees. It is easy to see why. Not everyone would like the rather stark modern lines of the long brick and timber frontage, nor the house's somewhat isolated riverside position half a mile from the Thameside village near Reading where they live.

On the other hand there are the river views, the peace, privacy, sense of space, fishing, canoeing and boating and, as Helen says, the fact that it is an ideal place in which to bring up their two daughters aged 12 and 10.

The interior of the oak framed house is one many lovers of contemporary style houses would die for. It has a large open plan downstairs relaxation and kitchen area and a striking flat roofed glazed link containing the main staircase and front entrance that joins the two main sections of the house together. Add to this the large amount of glazing and the controversial linear frontage — which fits in well with the low-lying site and incorporates a mix of interesting and 'different' materials — and the result is an exciting new build with a number of distinctive features.

Among a long list, these include the 4.5m high dual storey double glazed sliding door in the glass fronted south-east elevation, several internal glass 'secret doors' and a bank of 32 rooflights (12 of which open) all along beneath the ridge at the front of the house and on both sides above the double height living room.

For Clive and Helen it all started in January 2000 when they bought the one acre site, occupied by a large 1950s bungalow that had been extended many times. It was a short distance up the road from the house of Clive's brother and business partner Richard, who had lived there for six years — long enough to know that there was a good sense of community and that the threat of flooding was minor.

However, although they had bought the house largely for the plot, Clive and Helen did not take the decision to demolish and rebuild until the following year, when Clive sold his share in the software company he had run with his brother. "Clive had always been interested in building his own house and my background is in design," says Helen. "When we ➤

Large glazed sliding doors to the rear and an open plan interior layout mean that the house is full of natural light.

"YOU HEAR PEOPLE SAYING SELF-BUILDERS ALWAYS GO OVER BUDGET, BUT OFTEN THIS COMES DOWN TO BAD PLANNING."

realised that the existing house was poorly built we decided to make the most of a wonderful opportunity and start again from scratch."

They found architect Paul Bell through friends. He had previously worked in London for architect Terry Farrell, but has since returned to practice in his native city of Newcastle-upon-Tyne.

"We found Paul very sympathetic to what we wanted. He immediately realised that we were not seeking an architect's 'temple to himself'," Clive says. "He also proved amenable to our 'back to front' concept, with the main glazed elevation at the rear, and suggested that to avoid the house looking too linear at the front that we should insert a small L-shape where the ground floor, snug and upstairs office area jut out beneath a flat roof on the side facing the road.

"During most of the 16 month build Paul came here for three days a week and worked with me from the site office. This meant that we spent a great deal – £52,000 – in fees, but it has resulted in a radically 'different' house with all sorts of influences. Some people think it Japanese in style, others say Scandinavian, but we like to use the phrase 'Contemporary

Barn Style' and have tried to use a variety of materials that connect with this area of the country, such as the oak framing and the large expanses of brick cladding with handmade two inch bricks." Clive has always been keen on timber, so where it is not glazed, the upstairs of the exterior is also clad with horizontal oak weatherboarding.

Large sections of the oak frame are exposed in the interior, while light enters the building through a bank of 36 rooflights.

A major design consideration was the flat riverside setting and its propensity to flooding. "We considered setting the house on stilts but the land and soil surveys we commissioned showed that it would be not be necessary," Clive says. "We did a lot of research and found that there were only two serious instances of flooding near here, in 1896 and 1947. We then engineered the ground so that the flood risk was alleviated. Having done all this there was serious flooding soon after we moved in last winter, and the house next door but one flooded. Fortunately our calculations proved correct and all the neighbours finished up parking their cars on our dry patch. We found ourselves using our Land Rover to ferry some elderly neighbours to the shops."

For the vital task of installing the glazing, including the glazed stair banisters, Clive and Helen chose Somerset based Specialist Cladding Services. "We chose them because of the 'can do' attitude of MD Jim Rush," says Clive. "They are really window manufacturers rather than installers, but they are also adept at designing specialist 'one-off' profiles such as our 'architectural' guttering, which is integral and discharges ➤

into the downpipes on two levels, thus protecting both horizontal weatherboarding on the upper storey and the brick on the ground floor."

To Clive and Helen the outside elevations were as important as the spacious and largely open plan interior layout. As well as the unusual front elevation – it still causes raised eyebrows locally – Clive and Helen particularly like the asymmetrical south-west elevation at the end of the main 'living' section.

"Good planning really was vital to get the design approved," Clive says. "During the preparation stage, which took a full year, we had a meeting with Paul every month. I think this was a major reason why we gained planning permission first time round. We would advise any self-builder to think ahead. Planning ahead also gave us time to find some excellent subcontractors. Very often going over budget comes down to bad planning.

"We did have one major hiccup which proved quite expensive. All the stud partition walls on the first floor had to be moved as we realised,

after they had been largely constructed, that they made the bedrooms too small and the corridor they run off too wide. It was one of those things that sometimes just can't be visualised from a two-dimensional drawing."

The Hicks' other main piece of advice to fellow self-builders is to be prepared to roll up your sleeves. "Somehow it helps to keep the workforce motivated if you are prepared to weigh in as much as Clive did," says Helen. Her role was more on the support side, producing vast numbers of bacon sandwiches from their temporary home at Richard's house just up the road and delivering them to site daily.

"We were totally involved with the build from Day One," Clive says. "I think it paid off both financially – we built for less than £750,000 when the QS had indicated a figure of £850,000 – and also because there is virtually nothing we would want to change now it is finished. It really is our dream home." ■

'Architectural' guttering protects horizontal weatherboarding on the upper storey and the brick on the ground floor.

HOMEBUILDING
&RENOVATING
MAGAZINE

AWARDS
2003

SHORTLISTED
CONTEMPORARY
HOUSE

FLOORPLAN

The downstairs consists of a large open plan kitchen, dining and relaxation area and features a large double-height space. The sitting area is overlooked by a galleried family room reached by a spiral staircase.

FIRST FLOOR

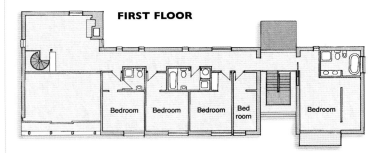

GROUND FLOOR

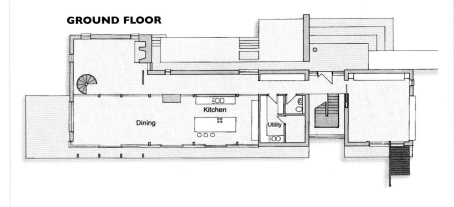

FACT FILE

Names: Clive and Helen Hicks
Professions: Company director and yoga practitioner
Area: Berkshire
House type: Five bedroom detached
House size: 440m²
Build route: Self-managed
Construction: Oak frame with brick and timber cladding
Warranty: Architect's Certificate
SAP rating: 85
Finance: Private
Build time: Sept '01 – Dec '02
Land cost: £650,000
Build cost: £728,000
Total cost: £1,378,000
House value: £1.5m
Cost/m²: £1,655

8%
COST SAVING

Cost Breakdown:

Prelims/connections	£27,000
Demolition/clearance	£9,000
Glazing and metalwork	£136,000
Timber frame/structural package	£100,500
Groundworks/drainage	£39,000
Professional fees	£52,000
Plumbing and heating	£35,800
General building materials	£34,600
Staircases	£29,500
Kitchen	£29,400
Bricks and blockwork	£29,400
Carpentry	£28,800
Rooflights	£20,000
Electrical work	£20,000
Wall finishes	£20,000
Oak cladding and flooring	£14,000
Stone flooring	£13,600
Bathroom sanitaryware	£16,000
Roofing	£13,700
Plastering	£12,000
Bespoke joinery	£9,500
Insulation	£7,700
Lighting	£7,100
Structural steelwork	£3,700
Borehole and water pump	£2,300
Sewage processing plant	£3,000
Alarm system	£2,400
Miscellaneous	£12,000
TOTAL	**£728,000**

EUROPEAN HARMONY

Allan and Lindsey Taylor used a German timber frame company who designed and erected their new home in just 12 weeks.

WORDS: SUE FISHER   PHOTOGRAPHY: STEVE RUSSELL

ALLAN TAYLOR WAS pleasantly surprised when he first stumbled on the Huf Haus show home at Weybridge by accident. It was a dream date – he already had the perfect site, he was looking for the right house to build for himself, his wife and two teenage children, and he loved the design and the concept behind Huf.

"I had just bought a bungalow that I knew I was going to knock down," he says. He had already submitted one design for planning permission, only to have it rejected, and decided to change his ideas completely and go for a Huf kit structure instead.

"The refusal was good in a way because it made them commit themselves to the reasons why they didn't want it," says Allan. The Huf Haus design answered the planners' objections although the unconventional plan raised a few eyebrows in Allan's ▶

Allan's house is the first Huf Haus in the country to use grey specially treated and laminated Swedish spruce rather than the usual black.

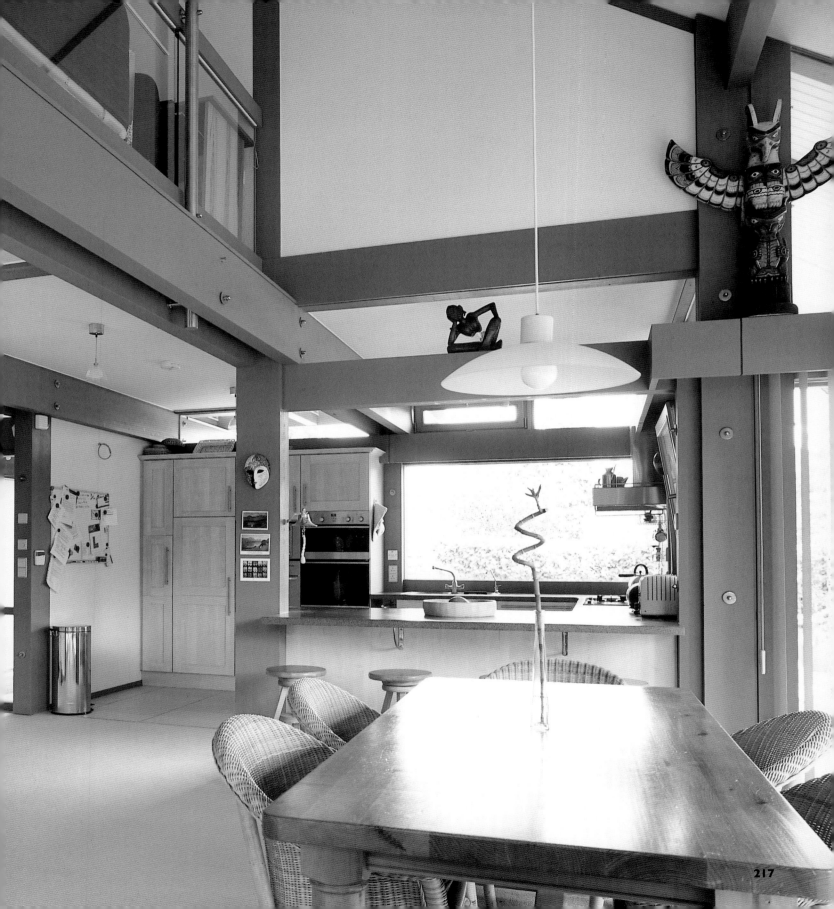

■ EUROPEAN HARMONY

"IT'S BEEN WHAT EVERY BUILDING
PROJECT SHOULD BE. BUT I'M AFRAID
IN THE UK IT'S THE EXCEPTION
RATHER THAN THE RULE."

sedate Hertfordshire town, with complaints from several neighbours.

The more Allan saw of the Huf set-up, the more he was impressed by the design and high standards of workmanship. He went to the German show village twice to look at the varied layouts and finishes before deciding which combination would be best suited to him and his family.

"When I went to Germany they treated me like royalty," he says. He was equally impressed with the company's five-strong team when they arrived on site in January 2003. "They brought everything with them when they came here except the crane, the toilet and the sand – they even brought the cement," he says. "They work extremely hard and their attitude is very different – they have a laugh, they behave and they come here the next day and get on with it again. It's been what every building project should be but I'm afraid in the UK it's the exception rather than the rule."

The basic house, which was erected in just four days in January, is the only one in the country finished in grey as opposed to the more usual black finish, which Allan initially liked but then decided against. "It's a very sharp contrast and it got on my nerves," he says. "And the white was just too clinical."

The grey timber is a specially treated and laminated Swedish spruce which matches the concrete roof tiles and blends with the white wall panels and doors. It will only need painting every five years and the interior every 10.

Allan's five-bay design sits at the end of a conventional cul-de-sac of mixed housing and had to fulfill the criteria for a chalet bungalow to satisfy the planners. Allen considered excavating a basement but Huf came up with enough space to make even a cellar superfluous. Not only have the Taylors got a large open plan ground floor, they also have a TV room, cloakroom, study and utility room downstairs as well as four bedrooms, one en suite, a family bathroom and a wide gallery, all set into the eaves. There are also balconies on the east and west side with access through French doors from all four bedrooms.

"We messed about with the standard design a bit to get a TV lounge for the kids. Being open plan is OK but you've got to change your lifestyle and they need somewhere of their own," says Allan, who runs a small property development company in south London and has built two houses for himself before: one in Hemel Hempstead and one in Hitchin. Despite his background as a building surveyor and his experience, he is still amazed at the high specifications and innovation in the Huf design. They include cables hidden inside the post and beam structure, overhangs

The supply and installation of the kitchen – from an English company – provided Allan and Lindsey with one of the few hiccups during the project.

on the roof to reduce window cleaning to an annual event, and the use of Pilkington low emission double glazed glass containing argon gas for insulation, giving a U-value for the window element of 1.1.

The Elco Klockner pressurised boiler sits like the controls of a spaceship warp drive in the utility room but Allan was determined that it shouldn't take over the room. "This is a utility room with a boiler, not a boiler room with a washing machine," he says firmly. The system has worked perfectly with instant hot water anywhere in the house. No detail has been forgotten – walls preserve privacy where necessary upstairs but glass panels have been used elsewhere to maximise light. ➤

"THE SPEED OF CONSTRUCTION WAS AMAZING. THE STRUCTURE WAS ERECTED IN FOUR DAYS."

Mezzanine or loft space can be fitted against the roof in the bedrooms.

The Taylors chose a mixture of white floor tiles and cream carpet for the house, which has underfloor heating throughout that can be adjusted from a central control panel as well as in each room. The tiles complement the smaller ones chosen for the kitchen, shower room and bathrooms, giving the bungalow a great sense of unity.

All the tiles and the Villeroy and Boch sanitaryware was chosen in Germany because Allan felt it would be easier. He was proved right – the only hassle he and Lindsey had was with the English kitchen fitters.

The speed of the construction was amazing. The basic structure was erected in four days, the electricians were finished in a week, followed by the plumbers who took just two weeks from start to commissioning both hot water and heating. The floor screed was laid in week four and the Taylors moved in just over three months after the arrival of the German vans.

Allan decided to get a double garage built himself rather than buying one from Huf. It has been designed, with their blessing, to blend with the bungalow but uses more traditional building methods. All has gone well but it has thrown up some interesting points. "The garage has taken longer to build than the house!" he laughs. The family moved in at Easter and spent the summer adding finishing touches, especially to the outside where

The design is largely open-plan although Allan amended the basic layout to incorporate an enclosed TV room for the children.

they have created a terraced area around the house with 2" red granite chippings.

They are thrilled with their new home – Lindsey loves the light and the site has proved even better to live on than they thought

The upstairs rooms are all set into the eaves, making maximum use of the available floorspace.

with its large sycamores, horse chestnuts and an oak. "The location is ideal, at the end of a cul-de-sac, totally quiet and surrounded by birds, squirrels and muntjac," says Allan.

Reaction to the house has generally been positive and several people are now considering building similar homes nearby — a reaction the builders predicted. "People either love it or hate it and those who hate it are definitely in the minority," says Allan. One minor problem with the large glass areas has been bird strikes, with one mortality in the first few weeks. Mostly they have recovered and flown off groggily after an hour.

Now Allan is hoping to interest others in the Huf Haus concept and encourage them to build their own version. "I am more than happy to show anyone around if they are serious," he says. He is also prepared to share some of the tips he has gained during the exercise and smooth their way. He certainly has no regrets about the project – in fact he is so enamoured of his new home that he and Lindsey have even considered doing it all again, but in the West Country.

One quirky detail he noticed is the stillness of the house. "There is a complete absence of any structural creaking and noises," he says. "In normal houses you always get something moving but there is absolutely nothing here at all. The first two nights we lived here I couldn't sleep because of the total silence." ∎

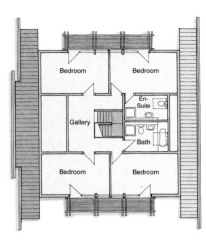

FIRST FLOOR

FLOORPLAN

The ground floor is largely open plan. Upstairs all four bedrooms lead on to a balcony through French doors.

GROUND FLOOR

FACT FILE

Names: Allan and Lindsey Taylor
Professions: Property Developer
Area: Hertfordshire
House type: Four bed chalet bungalow

House size: 300m²
Build route: Package supplier
Construction: Timber frame post and beam
Finance: Private
Build time: Nov '02 – April '03
Land cost: £375,000
Build cost: £425,000
Total cost: £800,000
House value: £975,000
Cost/m²: £1,416

18%
COST SAVING

USEFUL CONTACTS

Design and construction – Huf Haus: 01932 828502 www.huf-haus. de; **For information on all aspects of the home contact Allan Taylor:** 01462 454555 taylor@hitchin.co.uk

The home is clad in polymer render and western red cedar, which has weathered to different tones on different sides of the house owing to effects of the sun.

BETTER BY DESIGN

Jack and Sophie Burt's new contemporary style home is designed to meet the family's very specific living requirements.

WORDS: CAROLINE EDNIE   PHOTOGRAPHY: ANDREW LEE

WHEN IT COMES to diametrically opposite living experiences, the Burt family really can claim to have the last word. For doctors Jack and Sophie, and their sons Calum, 12 and Aedan, 10, have gone from the most bijou 16th century cottage, replete with teensy nooks and crannies, to the wide open spaces of a brand spanking new bespoke contemporary home.

Jack says that the family are delighted with their traditional to modern switch, particularly since they didn't have to abandon the charming coastal village that they have grown to love. In fact, the new Burt home forms a very elegant contemporary feature in one of the loveliest areas in the 'Kingdom' of Fife —arguably Scotland's hottest property spot.

The Burt family's decision to swap intimate historical for spacey contemporary was not, however, simply a matter of 'build it bigger, bolder and better' aspirations. Rather, it was to meet the important needs of Jack and Sophie's son Aedan. "The house was very much built around Aedan," explains Jack. "He is paralysed from the neck down, and in a wheelchair, so the house had to be suitable for him.

"When Aedan had his accident in 1996, we were living in one of the old 16th century cottages right in the centre of the village. It was lovely but totally unsuitable for anyone in a wheelchair: you couldn't even get in the ➤

The kitchen looks highly contemporary but has also been subtly designed around Aedan's needs, with the breakfast bar installed at a wheelchair height and lots of wide open spaces.

front door. It was a listed building so there was no way we could modify the house, and the advice we received from the doctors at the spinal injuries unit where Aedan was being looked after was that even though you can adapt houses, it is never as good as starting from scratch. So, the medical staff put us in touch with NJSR McLean Architects who had had experience with this type of bespoke design."

The result of this unusual three-way collaboration between the Burt family, architects and medical consultants is undoubtedly a triumph of space and accessibility which subtly caters for all of Aedan's needs. Yet, according to Jack, "we were very keen that the house didn't look like a hospital or a medical centre." And this desire has been fully honoured, because the Burts' new house is quite simply a cracking family home: architecturally striking, with a clever combination of impressively extrovert light-filled living areas, with cosy introverted bedrooms and hideaway spaces.

Approaching the Burt family home is actually quite an event, particularly when viewed against the backdrop of the mediaeval village. Indeed, Jack laughs when he describes how "tourist buses actually stop outside to look at the house." This is due in most part to its unusual form. "Due to the scale of the house, there was a concern that it might dwarf the surrounding houses, so there was a desire to break down the mass," admits architect Don McLean. "We designed the house as a series of disparate parts, and introduced different textures, surfaces and materials. So, there's a timber 'extension', a stone tower, garage, and finally, timber bedroom blocks."

The idea for the design, which is based around the theme of 'flotsam and ➤

"WE DESIGNED THE HOUSE AS A SERIES OF DISPARATE PARTS AND INTRODUCED DIFFERENT TEXTURES, SURFACES AND MATERIALS."

Aedan's living quarters are in the tower part of the house, which enjoys views over the garden space.

jetsam', was very much influenced by Aedan. "When we spoke to Aedan about the house at the time, he was into pirates, and this got itself into the brief," continues Don. "The kitchen, which sits at an angle and where the roof lifts up and there's glazing round it – that's meant to be the lid of a treasure chest lifting up. The tower is reminiscent of a sandcastle, and the bedroom blocks reflect upturned boats. These were our methods to introduce different elements into the design, and the house is near the beach so it does make sense."

"The collaboration between ourselves and the architects was very straightforward," explains Jack. "Craig Govan, the project architect, spent some time with us to find out what type of people we were, and discussed ideas with us. Some of the ideas were Aedan's, and Sophie and I liked the idea of the tower reflecting the form of a Pictish broch, given our love of Scottish history and archaeology."

The house took four and a half years to complete. This was due in part to a lengthy design process, which had to take into account the specialised brief. And according to the architects there were also difficulties getting it through planning, which was more to do with local objections than design issues with the planners. The construction itself took around a year. The house essentially comprises a masonry structure featuring cavity concrete blockwork, with elements of steel frame included for support, particularly in the tower area, which is finished in brickwork and render.

"The house was built as a long-term enterprise, so if Aedan wants this to be his home for life then it is. If, however, he decides at 18 that he wants to leave, then he can do that too," explains Jack. As a result of this long-term vision, the couple have understandably opted for the very best finishes. These include polymer render; Penrhyn Heather Blue Welsh slates on the main roof and lead roofing on the conservatory and kitchen/dining block; NEG glass blocks above the entrance to the house; Nor-Dan double glazed windows; and finally western red cedar cladding. The cedar cladding has weathered in rich red tones on the north-facing side, whereas a more silvery ash shade has developed on the south-facing bedroom block side of the house due to the sun.

Although the house was built on a site which had previously received planning permission for two houses, the architects believed that ideally the house would have been bigger. "The size of the house was restricted, and in some rooms, there isn't really enough space – for example the bedrooms could have been bigger. But a bigger house wasn't going to be approved as it didn't leave enough garden space," claims Don.

Jack admits that "we were limited by the size of the plot, but the size of our bedroom doesn't matter to us. Basically what we were looking for was lots of space around the house for Aedan to be able to manoeuvre in his wheelchair – this is why the corridors are so wide and there are various doors that open themselves electronically. And due to the fact

that he can't regulate his own temperature we also have to have constant air conditioning in his quarters – the garage is bigger than most people's houses, as it contains the air conditioning plant," explains Jack. "These were the fundamental things that we needed.

"This is not the house that was originally designed by the architects," continues Jack. "It was originally designed as a bungalow. However, it soon became apparent to us that it wasn't going to be big enough. There wouldn't have been enough space to store all of Aedan's equipment, or for the rest of the family to live comfortably. So we ended up changing it to two storeys, with the second storey giving us room to incorporate separate living quarters for Aedan's carers, as well as affording great views over the Forth which we wouldn't have been able to achieve with a bungalow. It actually worked out better for everyone in the end."

In terms of living accommodation Jack claims that "we stipulated that we wanted two sitting areas – one for general purpose use and a nice main one upstairs. We spend a lot of time in the sitting area downstairs – it's very cosy – and although we don't really need the wood burning stove that's there, it's good for toasting marshmallows and the like." Adjoining the cosy downstairs sitting room is a south-facing conservatory which leads to the spacious kitchen, finished by means of simple Magnet units and granite ➤

"We wanted a lot of light and lots of nice pale wood finishes. We were also keen to have as much colour as possible," explains Jack.

worktops. The breakfast bar is also just at the right height for Aedan's wheelchair.

"The only thing Aedan needs help with is the (eight person standard) lift. Otherwise he can go anywhere he wants," explains Jack. And one of the areas in which the two boys spend a lot of time is the first floor play area which is located directly above Aedan's quarters in the tower. From here a light-filled open plan connecting area features Sophie's work space.

The design is based around 'flotsam and jetsam' and that means lots of textures and different materials.

The main sitting area on the first floor, complete with balcony and south-facing views, is the spatial jewel in the Burt house's crown. "We enjoy the uninterrupted views over the Forth to Bo'ness in the upstairs living area – the sea changes all the time," says Jack.

The house clearly gives Jack and his family a great deal of pleasure and as well as meeting a very practical requirement it succeeds from a purely aesthetic perspective. "There is nothing major that we would change about the house," concludes Jack. ■

FACT FILE

Names: Jack and Sophie Burt
Professions: Doctors
Area: Culross, Fife
House type: Two storey detached, for special needs
House size: 530m²
Build route: Architect and builder
Construction: Cavity concrete blockwork
Finance: Private
Build time: March '01 – April '02
Land cost: Undisclosed
Build cost: Undisclosed
Total cost: Undisclosed
House value: Undisclosed

SPECIAL BUILDING REQUIREMENTS

Although Part M of the Building Regulations sets minimum standards for the design of new and extended homes to meet the accessibility requirements of wheelchair users, designing a home around the particular needs of a family member requires a skilled hand to produce a home that meets those needs and yet isn't dominated by them. For more information read the Phillipa Harpin Adaptations Manual (020 7720 8055) and visit the Disability Show held annually at the NEC in Birmingham.

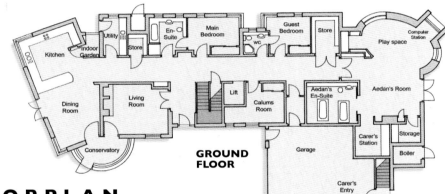

GROUND FLOOR

FLOORPLAN

A wide corridor runs through the heart of the house giving easy access to all the rooms. Self-enclosed carer's accommodation is provided with a different entrance.

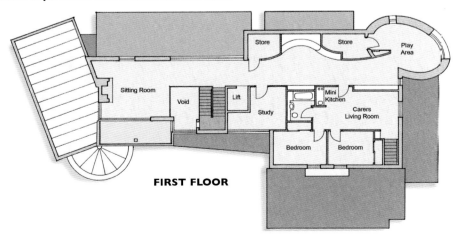

FIRST FLOOR

USEFUL CONTACTS

Architect – NJSR McLean: 0141 353 2040 www.njsrmclean.co.uk; **Landscape architect** – McGregor McMahon: 0131 229 0966; Lateral Technologies & Solutions Ltd: 01698 464470; Robin Swinton: 01882 634279; **Quantity surveyor** – Doig Hart Consultants: 0141 248 9635; **Main Contractor** – Trentham Construction (in receivership); **Exterior finishes** – Sto Render: www.sto.co.uk; NEG glass blocks: 01253 858333; **Roofing** – Alfred McAlpine Penrhyn Heather Blue Welsh slates: www.alfredmcalpine.co.uk; **Windows** – Nor-Dan UK: 01698 383364; **Heating** – Zehnder: 01342 305420; **Kitchen manufacturer:** Magnet: 0118 979 3990; Neff: www.neff.co.uk; **Bath and shower** – Armitage Shanks: 01543 490253; Arjo (Belfast): 028 9050 2000; **Tiles** – H & R Johnson: 01782 524000, Fired Earth: 01494 769150; **Flooring** – Junckers: 01376 534700; Tarkett: www.tarkett.com; **Doors** – Leaderflush Shapland (Internal): 0870 240 0666; Nor-Dan UK: 01698 383364; **Garage door** – Hormann: 01530 513000; **Insulation** – Kingspan: 0870 850 8555; **Specialist fittings** – Contracts Direct (passenger lift): 01928 571919; **Wood burning stove** – Morso: www.morsoe.com

AN EXTRAORDINARY NEW CONTEMPORARY FAMILY HOME

SURBURBAN CHIC

James and Hayley Keates have created an exciting modern family home with elegant living spaces on an infill garden plot in an ordinary suburban setting.

WORDS: JUDE WEBLEY PHOTOGRAPHY: MARK WELSH

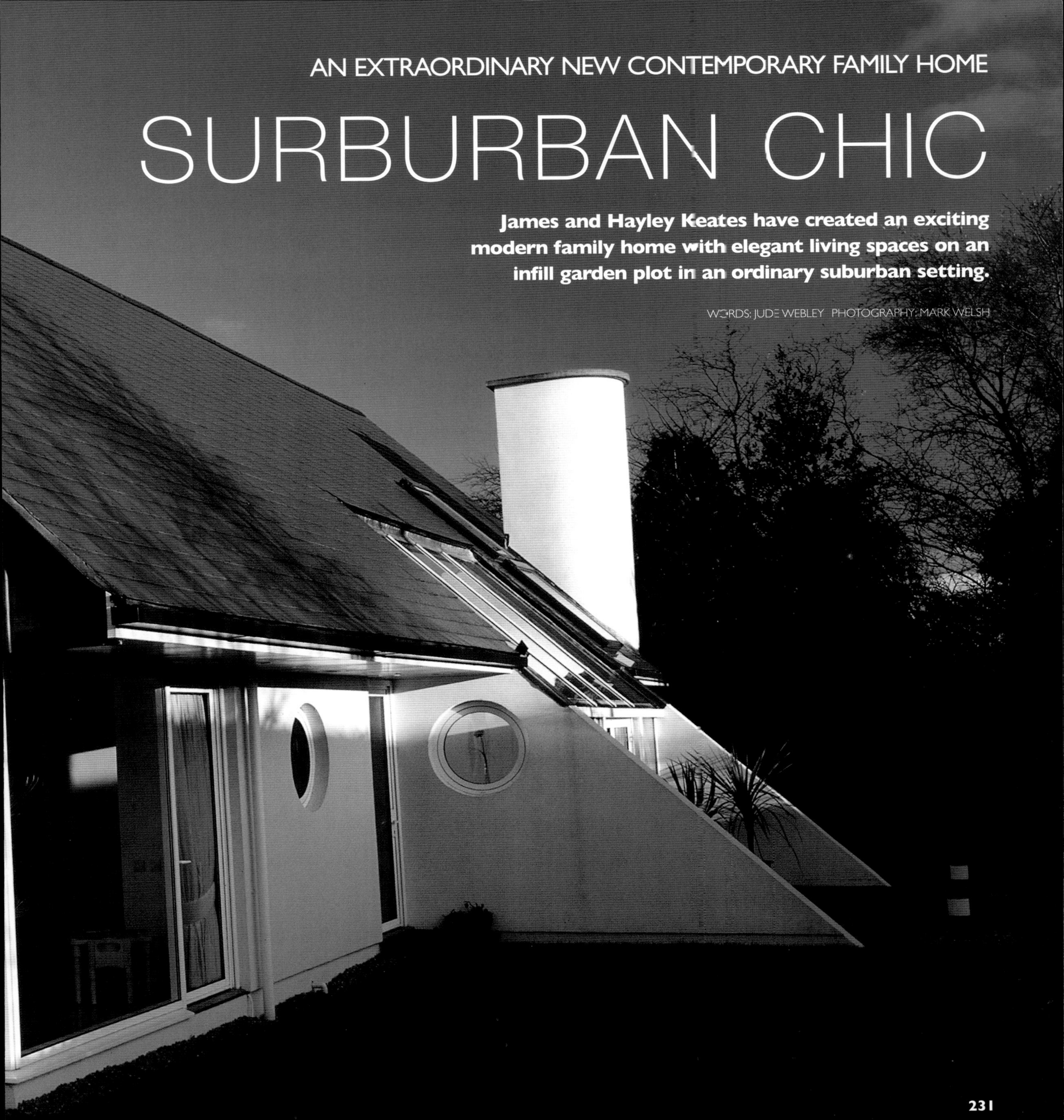

A fabricated steel staircase fitted with beech laminate treads and risers leads to the first floor from the dining area. Shadowline mouldings in place of skirting and architrave, and internal doors which go all the way to the ceiling add cost but contribute to the atmosphere.

DOES A FAMILY home have to follow the traditional mould? Not according to James and Hayley Keates, who in their late twenties have built a successful contemporary home that blends in happily with the leafy suburbs of an everyday Staffordshire town.

The front door leads to a hallway and on into a double height dining area with a huge glazed section overlooking the gardens.

Their home is more than a piece of stylish London Loft minimalism. It has bags of atmosphere and combines open plan living with a successful function as a real home for two young professionals and their two very young children. There cannot be too many young parents who would not be pretty pleased to have built themselves a home of this style and quality. All the more amazing considering it is their first home.

How did they manage it? James and Hayley are the first to acknowledge that they had a pretty good start. Hayley's father is an architect (Roy Manning of Eaton, Manning and Wilson). Keen on contemporary design, he worked with the couple designing this home and donated his services for free. If that was not enough of a bonus, they were able to continue their full time jobs as James's father, Laurence, a retired Planning Officer, volunteered to act as Site Agent and co-ordinate all the subcontrators and the ordering and delivery of materials.

"We were happy to take all the advantages we could get," smiles Hayley with no trace of embarrassment. "I've always lived in modern houses and wanted to carry on when I left home," she says. "We were both living at home with our parents but when we got engaged we started looking for an existing house with the intention of changing it. ➤

"WE WERE KEEN THAT THE GARDEN, WHICH WOULD BE VERY VISIBLE… WOULD BE TREATED ALMOST AS AN EXTRA ROOM…"

The trouble is you have to pay a lot for the original house and then a lot more to turn it into the house you want."

Roy heard of a suburban infill plot about to come on to the market and the couple decided to pull out of buying a house they were pursuing and offer the asking price of £50,000, which was accepted. The plot had outline planning consent for a dormer bungalow. Roy then set about his task. His conception of what a dormer bungalow might look like is certainly challenging.

"We gave Roy a free hand at the design," explains James. "We said that we wanted a spacious open plan layout, plenty of glass and high ceilings in the upstairs rooms. We wanted the walls to be white internally and externally – to link inside and out – and we were keen that the garden, which would be very visible from the house due to the large amount of glazing, would be treated almost as an extra room of the house. Roy got something down on paper which we had a look at. We decided against the spiral staircase for safety reasons as we were intending to have kids and we changed some of the windows but we liked Roy's ideas."

Amazingly, planning sailed through as there were no objections to the scheme but on site things were destined to go more true to form. Since they were building a large house to a budget and had the free services of ➤

At the far end of the dining area is the main reception area, a generous and elegant space with floor to ceiling windows on two walls.

Junkers Beech flooring is used throughout the ground floor. The Keates opted for a warm water underfloor heating system from Wirsbo which has proved very successful.

"WE REALLY SUFFERED FROM THE CONTRACTORS DISAPPEARING TO OTHER JOBS IN THE MIDDLE OF OUR OWN…"

a project manager, it made sense to use subcontractors. Both families had a good range of builder contacts and spent time going to visit reference projects before deciding on who to work with. "We worked mainly with people on a fixed price package of work," explains James, "and definitely found that this was an easier way of going about things than paying people on a day rate."

The main difficulty was not so much technical as to do with the perennial problem of keeping the men on site. "We really suffered from the contractors disappearing to other jobs in the middle of our own," recalls James. "Since we were originally in a rented house and latterly living rent free in the home of a departed grandparent, we weren't in a huge hurry to move in. But things did drag on and getting the project completed was difficult. My father came to the site every day and looked after ordering materials, co-ordinating the activities of the different contractors and pretty much everything else. We couldn't have done it without him!" Roy also kept an eye on things in his role as inspecting architect, issuing architect's certificates at the usual stages.

James and Hayley have clearly been blessed with extreme good

Low-maintenance, powder-coated aluminium doors and windows were used, fitted with energy-efficient Pilkington K Glass.

FACT FILE

Costs as of Aug 2001
Names: James and Hayley Keates
Profession: Solicitor and teacher
Area: Staffordshire
House type: Contemporary
House size: 310m² + 36m² garage
Build route: Local subcontractors managed by parents
Construction: Masonry with rendered blockwork
Warranty: Architect's Certificates

Finance: Staffordshire BS
Build time: May '96 — Mar '00
Land cost: £50,000
Build cost: £176,500
Total cost: £226,500
House value: £300,000
Cost/m²: £509

25%
COST SAVING

Cost Breakdown:

Groundworks	£27,000
Superstructure	£57,000
Roof	£38,000
Heating & plumbing	£8,500
Lighting & electrical	£10,000
Plastering	£7,000
Finishes	£9,000
Kitchen & bathrooms	£15,000
Landscaping	£5,000
TOTAL	**£176,500**

FLOORPLAN

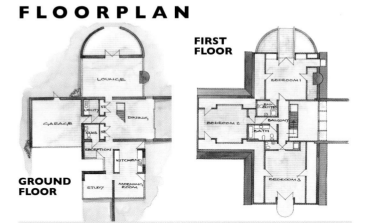

GROUND FLOOR

FIRST FLOOR

fortune and there is plenty about this tale that sounds rather sugar coated. The lack of struggle will not ring true with many self-builders. They have ended up with a fabulous house and all the family relationships appear to still be intact. One disagreement between architect and 'client' involved James' and Hayley's insistence that they wanted to have Velux rooflights in their bedroom to increase the natural light and give views of the garden. The architect did not want the purity of his roofline spoiled. "It was a difficult dinner," sums up James succinctly.

Design purity also had to meet cost reality in a number of areas. Large spans of clear unsupported patent glazing were switched for a cheaper alternative. Stainless steel sockets and switches were substituted by plastic. Designer bathroom fittings will have to come later. "You've got to get the best quality design at a price you can afford," concludes James. ■

USEFUL CONTACTS

Architect — Eaton, Manning, Wilson & Assoc: 01782 711822
Low-e Glazing — Pilkington K Glass: 01744 28882 **Wooden Flooring** — Junckers: 01376 517512 **Underfloor Heating** — Uponor: 01455 550355 **Reconstituted Rooftiles** — Marley-Eternit: 01675 468400 **Garage Door** — Crawfords: 01782 599899
Sanitaryware — Ideal Standard: 01482 346461 **Aluminium Powder Coated Windows and Doors** — Quality Glass: 01782 289700 **Stairs (glass balustrade)** — Quality Glass: 01782 289700
Stairs (timber treads) — Lancaster & Tomkinson: 01782 614156
Stairs (steelwork) — Reynolds & Litchfield: 01782 319029

SPLIT LEVEL LIVING

WORDS: CLIVE FEWINS PHOTOGRAPHY: NIGEL RIGDEN

■ SPLIT LEVEL LIVING

John and Jane Thompson have created a three-storey 'upside down' home on a sloping site.

JOHN AND JANE Thompson's new 316m2 'upside down' house, in a village near Bristol, is a fascinating mixture of influences. More than anything, John says, the dual level, exterior decked balconies at the rear, connected by an external timber staircase, were inspired by a Californian house where they once stayed. However, the house, which has a crisp, free flowing interior, also has Japanese and Arts and Crafts influences.

There is certainly a lot going on, and inside, the house is full of surprises – such as the lightwell at the front of the building that imports light into the five partially underground bedrooms on the lower ground floor. There are also nine separate internal windows used to 'borrow' light and pass it from one room to another.

Most of all there are the two huge, full-height round oak poles, shaped from individual trees, that frame the stairs, support the three floors and carry through to act as roof supports. These give the house a rugged feel that is continued by the use of coloured earth plaster in the hall,

"TO USE A SLOPING SITE LIKE THIS – IN WHICH YOU ENTER AT FIRST FLOOR LEVEL – TO ITS MAXIMUM, YOU HAVE TO TUCK AWAY THE BEDROOMS BENEATH THE LIVING AREA." ➤

The first floor living space is overlooked by a long gallery, which separates the study and informal TV room.

"TOO MUCH OAK WOULD HAVE LOOKED CLUTTERED, WE WANTED A MODERN, RATHER MINIMALIST INTERIOR WITH CLEAN LINES."

conservatory and one wall of the master bedroom. These surfaces, plus the use of stone inside the hallway, are carefully contrived to break up the large areas of plain white walls. Even if he feels he is not a Modernist in the fullest sense of the word, architect John likes open plan interiors and has created a feel that tends towards the minimalist.

He has similarly gone to deliberate lengths to create a rather stark frontage. The elevation that faces the road and presents itself to the visitor has small windows and a large amount of plain render. John calls it "not friendly," while he describes the rear, with its two galleried decks and mass of glass, as private. "It was quite deliberate. The plan was to have a softer, more open finish at the rear."

He has also gone to great trouble to vary the textures of the outside. The front outer skin has

The kitchen has uninterrupted views of the village below and to the east, and has been carefully designed to make the most of the sun. ➤

two sections of local stone, which contrast with a coloured render, and some vertical cedar boarding on the south side, while at the rear there is stone and vertical and horizontal weatherboarding, as well as large sections of glass.

The whole house has been carefully designed to suit the 0.3 acre plot. "It is 100 per cent a function of the plot. That's what architecture is all about – location," says John, a director of the Bristol-based Barlow Henley architectural practice. "You start with the sun and the plot."

The house uses the sloping site to the full. "Apart from the fact that this is the wrong side of Bristol for my work, it was just what we were looking for," says Jane. "It was the last of three plots on the site of an old orchard on the edge of the village. We had been searching for about 12 months and consider ourselves very lucky, particularly because of the splendid views over the surrounding countryside. We were very keen to have a site like this because we had enjoyed uninterrupted views over the Severn estuary from our previous 1930s semi-detached house on the north side of Bristol, where we lived for 15 years."

The site gave John and Jane scope to create all the features they wanted, especially to maximise the use of glass at the rear, which both pulls in light and makes the most of the views. "To use a sloping site like this – in which you enter at first floor level – to its maximum, you have to tuck away the bedrooms beneath the living area," John says. "I think there is something wrong with a house where you come in at first floor and go down to the reception rooms."

In addition to the main open plan hardwood staircase, the irregular-shaped, two storey, oak-framed conservatory on the south side has its own staircase. This leads down to the lower floor, where the family hot tub is positioned. The top floor is taken up with a "breakfast gallery." Entry is via the ground floor from the front of the house and, internally, from the living room. The conservatory wraps round the end of the house ➤

The open tread staircase varies in width and has a clever second step that continues round a corner to form a balustrade at the top of the flight that descends to the floor beneath.

"IT IS 100 PER CENT A FUNCTION OF THE PLOT. THAT'S WHAT ARCHITECTURE IS ALL ABOUT – LOCATION."

and is a key element because it acts as a sun trap. Two centrifugal fans connected to ducts draw in heat from the conservatory to three of the five bedrooms positioned on the lower floor and the main living room.

The top floor is a modern version of the traditional long gallery. At the south end of the upper floor is the study area for the Thompsons' two schoolboy sons, Robbie and Jack, and the other end houses the TV room. This leads directly to the deck above the garage, with its timber pergola above – complete with timber balustrading – which is a combination of two subtly different shapes, the object being to achieve an amorphous feel, rather than something with regular patterns. It is also subtly different

from the split laths of sweet chestnut that form the balustrading on the gallery at the rear of the main living floor, at the rear of the house.

The construction is mainly of dual skinned insulated blockwork with a concrete reinforced core in the lower sections where there are also retaining walls. "At first we wanted an oak frame house," says John. "Having built five for clients, I was keen to build one for ourselves. However here I felt too much oak would have looked rather cluttered for the style we were after. We wanted a modern, rather minimalist interior with clean lines, and this is what we have achieved. However our next self-build may be rather different…" ■

FLOORPLAN

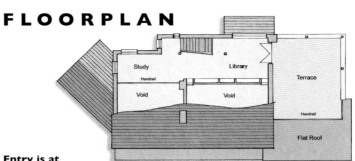

SECOND FLOOR

Study | Library | Terrace
Handrail
Void | Void
Handrail
Flat Roof

Entry is at ground floor level, with the bedrooms situated below. The study and library are placed on the second floor.

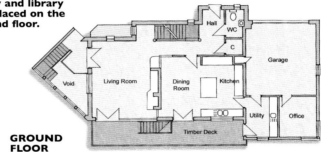

GROUND FLOOR

Hall | WC
C
Void | Living Room | Dining Room | Kitchen | Garage
Utility | Office
Timber Deck

LOWER GROUND FLOOR

Light Well | Bath | Linen
Garden Room | Bed 5
Bed 1 | Bed 2 | Bed 3
Bed 4

FACT FILE

Names: John and Jane Thompson
Professions: Architect and local government officer
Area: Near Bristol
House type: Five bed detached
House size: 316m²
Build route: Self-managed
Construction: Insulated blockwork with concrete reinforcement in the below ground sections
Finance: Private and Alliance & Leicester
Build time: 12 months
Land cost: £105,000

Build cost: £226,200
Total cost: £331,200
House value: £475,000
Cost/m²: £716

30%
COST SAVING

Cost Breakdown:

Groundworks + prelims	£31,500
Water supply + drainage	£4,800
Substructure +retaining walls	£21,500
Windows and doors	£12,900
Stairs	£4,600
Rooftiles	£5,700
Roof	£8,400
Steelwork + retaining walls	£13,500
Joinery	£15,600
Sanitaryware	£3,200
Floor + wall finishes	£19,000
Kitchen	£7,600
Conservatory	£14,500
Heating and plumbing	£21,500
Internal walls	£7,600
Electrics and lighting	£11,500
Ceramic tiling	£2,800
Miscellaneous	£20,000
TOTAL	**£226,200**

USEFUL CONTACTS

Architect – John Thompson at Barlow Henley: **0117 944 1777; General building** – Geoff Hammet: 01275 340190; **Electrician** – Frank Rawson: 01454 413771; **Plumber –** Andy Lewellyn: 01291 621634; **Natural Stone –** Pensford Natural Stone: 01761 452356; **Precast store** – Dabro: 01761 490664; **Oak** – Morton Timber: 01454 413307; **Circular oak posts –** Westwind Oak: 01934 877317; **Other timber** – Patchway Timber: 0117 969 1356; **Kitchen –** Ikea: 0845 355 2264; **Windows –** H&K Joinery: 0117 960 2849; **Roof slates** – Ogder Industries: 01924 261281; **Tierrofino coloured clay plaster** – Construction Resources: 0207 450 2211; **Cullarend render** – Weber SBD: 01525 722100

ALL HANDS ON DECK

BUILDING AN INNOVATIVE
TIMBER-FRAMED HOME

■ ALL HANDS ON DECK

Roger Hipwell and Pat Walker's new timber-framed home is a fine example of how to design around a unique, sensitive and relatively small site.

WORDS: CLIVE FEWINS   PHOTOGRAPHY: ROB JUDGES

ROGER HIPWELL AND Patricia Walker's new house, built on a highly sensitive site in the heart of a Suffolk coastal village, yet unnoticeable to the visitor or the passer-by, was created by renovating and extending an existing 15m2 pavilion in the rear garden of their former home. The result of clever design and siting, the project presents an object lesson for many self-builders in how to get the most out of a difficult site — not only within a Conservation Area, but also an Area of Outstanding Natural Beauty.

The project came from an idea of Pat's. She suggested that as they grew older, rather than moving to a more convenient house in another village, they should consider building in their garden. They wanted a house that suited their lifestyle rather better than the small two bedroom cottage they had owned for 10 years. "House prices had risen greatly here and we came to the conclusion that if we could make the scheme work, we would be better off staying put," explains Pat who together

with Roger runs an IT marketing consultancy.

At this stage they did what Roger calls "two very sensible things." They got a good planning consultant – Jeremy Hancock – and they found a good architect, Howard Nash. "Jeremy, who had previously worked for our local authority, Suffolk Coastal, told us at the outset that he considered we had a 50/50 chance of gaining planning permission," Roger says. "We were lucky with Howard because we knew from our village contacts that he was capable of exciting and imaginative work.

"Howard's scheme cleverly made use of the sloping nature of the site to step the main house down," says Roger. "The split-level design also overcame the major problem of a large public sewer that runs right across the site and beneath the proposed house. This was because it incorporated a full-width cellar in reinforced concrete, which both protects the sewer and acts as a valuable storage space for the items we would otherwise place in the roof space we do not possess."

The style of the building was to have nautical hints, with a timber framed main structure and a south-facing frontage in timber and glass with a full-width balcony supported by inclined timber masts with stainless steel cappings top and bottom.

"To our surprise, despite a local petition against the project, the parish ➤

The main open-plan ground floor living space, accessed downstairs from the entrance level, opens out onto the garden through glazed sliding doors.

"WE ARE DELIGHTED THAT THE HOUSE IS SO NEAR THE VILLAGE CENTRE AND YET SO PRIVATE AND TUCKED AWAY. WITH ITS LOW ROOF IT REALLY MAKES VERY LITTLE IMPACT."

The timber framed main structure has a full-width balcony, supported by inclined timber masts with stainless steel cappings top and bottom.

"WE DEMONSTRATED THAT WE WERE PREPARED TO COMPROMISE AND ACCEPT A SLIGHTLY SMALLER HOUSE THAN WE ORIGINALLY DESIRED."

council supported it – something that is almost unheard of round here," says Roger. "Even the Suffolk Preservation Society liked the design, but they were concerned, as were the planners, about losing so much of the garden – considered one of the 'lungs of the village' as it is so close to the historic market place. "However, by placing the house to the side of the plot we retained much of the garden."

Subject to some changes – reducing the width by just under a metre and sinking the building in the ground by an extra half metre – the plans were passed when they were presented to the planning committee for the third time.

"It had taken three months and we agreed to replace the section of sewer beneath with low-maintenance modern piping, but all that, including the £1,500 it cost us to employ a planning consultant, was a small price to pay," says Roger. "I think the other thing we had

demonstrated was that we were prepared to compromise and accept a slightly smaller house than we originally desired."

The search then began for a good builder. Roger and Pat asked four builders for detailed responses to the tender document. They chose Seamans of Stowmarket, 30 miles away. "They are a medium-sized family firm and were recommended by a friend," says Roger. "They put in a far more detailed and professional response to the tender document and were £25,000 less than the other three firms we approached. "They provided a full breakdown of their estimated costs and added 15 per cent for their charges and overheads and were prepared to invoice us net of VAT.

Although it was the renovation and extension of an existing pavilion within the garden of an existing house, Roger managed to persuade HM Revenue and Customs that the project constituted a new dwelling under the terms of Notice 719, VAT Refunds for 'do it yourself builders and converters' and was, therefore, eligible for zero-rating of VAT. Had the project not been accepted as a new dwelling, it may never have proceeded. "We were originally looking at a budget of around £200,000, but when the tenders started coming in we realised it was going to cost ▶

■ ALL HANDS ON DECK

us, all in, nearer £300,000. VAT on top of this would have added over £50,000 – enough to kill the project," says Roger.

The bathroon displays a modern sleek glass basin supplied by Igloo Glass: 01766 512652

Despite receiving an initially sceptical response, stating that the project was unlikely to be accepted as a new build because the pavilion was not being demolished, three weeks later a letter arrived saying that the project had been accepted as it created an additional dwelling which was 'wholly within the enlargement or extension' and 'designed as a dwelling'.

Despite having gained confidence on their two previous projects – renovating and extending the original cottage (for which they won a RIBA Award) and building the pavilion – Roger was keen not to supervise the build. Their architect, Howard, who spends most of his working week in London, felt he could not supervise the job, so they negotiated a price that incorporated having a foreman on site all the time. "Once the job got going we remained in our cottage home in the garden, but kept away during the daytime," says Roger. "We did not want to get in the way. In any case, we were busy running our small company.

"There were one or two minor hiccups and Howard had to come

out from London a couple of times, but on the whole the builders did a very good job," continues Roger. "They were so good, in fact, that Howard is now using them on a remodelling project on his own cottage in the village."

The new house faces south and is so enclosed by its surrounding trees and bushes that you barely notice the striking south-facing frontage that looks out to sea as you walk down the small path from the village centre. "It attracts so much sun that we shall need more solar shading – possibly some nautical-style canvas awnings that we can stretch between the tension rods that hold the timber masts in position," suggests Pat.

"We are delighted that the house is so near the village centre, and yet so private and tucked away. With its low roof it really makes very little impact on the surroundings yet it is a splendid example of modern design that makes the most of the site.

"We still have a reasonably sized garden and yet are able to do all the entertaining we enjoy so much by spilling out through the sliding glass doors downstairs. In addition, we have lovely views over the rooftops towards the sea from the two south-facing bedrooms upstairs. We had worked on the project for so long and so hard that we both felt totally at home with it from they day we moved in." ■

FACT FILE

Names: Roger Hipwell and Patricia Walker
Professions: Self-employed IT sales and marketing consultants
Area: Suffolk
House type: Four bedroom house with detached garage
House size: 182m²
Build route: Main contractor
Construction: Timber frame

with cladding of glass, and larch boarding, zinc roof
Finance: Private, plus £250,000 Bank of Scotland loan raised on previous home
Build time: Oct '04 – July '05
Land cost: Already owned
Build cost: £350,000
total cost: £350,000
house value: £700,000
cost/m²: £1,923

50%
COST SAVING

Cost Breakdown:

Main contract	£300,000
Fees	£30,000
Kitchen and utility room fitting	£17,000
Miscellaneous	£3,000
TOTAL	**£350,000**

USEFUL CONTACTS

Architect Nash Parker: 020 7229 1558; **Structural engineer** Ellis and Moore: 020 7281 4821; **Planning consultant** J Hancock: 01473 603944; **Main contractor** O Seaman and Son: 01449 676161; **Steel and glazing contractor** Amtin Ltd: 01379 388385; **Zinc roof** Rheinzink: 01276 686725; **Windows** Scandinavian Window Systems: 01777 871847; **Underfloor heating** Warmafloor: 01489 581787; **Oak floors** Floor Dimensions: 01449 615012; **Limestone floors** Mandarin: 01242 530500; **Kitchen and utility room** Ashford and Brooks: 01473 737764; **Oak doors** Anglia Joinery: 01449 720070 **Rooflight** The Rooflight Company: 01993 830613; **Sanitaryware and hand basins** CP Hart: 020 7902 1000; Igloo Glass: 01766 512652; Avalon Bathrooms: 01349 895006

FLOORPLAN

GROUND FLOOR

Living Area

Cellar

Existing Pavilion

Dining

Kitchen

The living accommodation is based around the view of the garden, with the bedrooms leading out onto a balcony through sliding doors.

Master Bedroom

Utility

Existing Pavilion

Study/ Second Bedroom

Hall

FIRST FLOOR

JUDGES' SUMMARY

Timber frame homes are very much part of the building mainstream these days and it is an example of how far this method of construction has come that, for Roger and Pat, the decision to choose to build in timber was of little consequence to their plans. The daring and cleverly engineered rear elevation, with a full-width balcony suspended from suspended timber posts, demonstrates the versatility of timber as a structural building system. The real success of this project, however, is the way it makes the very most of a difficult and highly sensitive plot through careful design and siting, creating a unique contemporary home in the heart of the village yet unnoticeable to tourists and passers-by.

ECONOMIC ELEGANCE

Chris Mortimer and Lucrecia Luque created an exciting, contemporary-style open plan home on a remarkably modest budget.

WORDS: CAROLINE EDNIE   PHOTOGRAPHY: ANDREW LEE

CHRIS MORTIMER OFTEN refers to luck as one of the key factors at the heart of his and wife Lucrecia's first homebuilding project. Indeed, Lady Luck seems to have been smiling on the couple as they surfed the net and happened upon a Scottish property website offering a perfect and affordable plot of land; and she also apparently had a hand in persuading the couple to abandon plans to build a standard kit house and go for a bespoke beauty instead, after they spotted, by chance, an article on a firm of local Skye-based architects.

➤

The house is constructed via a bespoke timber frame, and clad in Siberian Larch, which has been left untreated allowing it to weather to an attractive silver colour. A Spanish slate pitch roof tops the structure.

Yet for all this intervention of good fortune, when it came to netting the best site as well as a quality designer and builder, Chris and Lucrecia perhaps underestimate their own contribution in terms of canny project management skills, shrewd budget sense and openness to the spirit of collaboration. And it's essentially the alchemy of these important factors, as well as a dollop of luck, that has resulted in the successful realisation of the Brighton-based couple's two bedroom Highland gem 'An Tigh Learaig' (House of Larch) – completed for under £66,000.

"Lucrecia and I love hill walking and we spent a lot of time on and around Skye, so when we saw a plot advertised on the internet we went and had a look at it," explains Chris. "It's on the outskirts of Achmore, near Plockton. We saw the site and realised that it had this wonderful view, and fell in love with it. It's only about an eighth of an acre – it's really, really small, but the views are big, and there's nothing in the way, as the site drops away towards the river."

At this point there was nothing on the site. "Initially we were going to use a standard timber frame kit house," claims Chris. "We discussed it with the local timber frame kit house specialist, and we actually received planning approval. The problem was that he manufactured and erected the kit but he didn't do any of the groundworks or the fitting out, and being so far away in Brighton it would have been very difficult for us to manage the process of having a number of different contractors."

But during this period of planning the couple saw an article about a house by Skye-based Dualchas Building Design. "The article featured the house of Mary Arnold Forster, of Dualchas. We loved it and thought that this was something we really needed to explore, because here was ➤

A feature corner window frames scenic views of the surrounding countryside The original design was for a protruding/jetty style window design, but Chris and Lucrecia wanted to keep it flush and simple to fit in with the rest of the exterior

a local practice doing interesting housing, and with the building contract there could be a single point of contact all the way through. That, we thought, would take away all the things we were concerned about," admits Chris. "So we arranged to visit Mary and she was very excited about the prospect. That afternoon we drove over to her house and had a good look around."

Glazing was crucial to the success of the house, which enjoys spectacular views over Skye.

The couple liked what they saw and subsequently asked Dualchas to design their own home. "I suppose, to be really boring, the thing we had in mind for our own house was the budget – and keeping within the budget," says Chris. 'We gave a brief to Mary for a two storey house making the best use of the views, with a kitchen, dining, and living area downstairs, and two bedrooms and a bathroom upstairs. But apart from that we let her get on with it. There's no point in appointing an architect and then not giving them freedom to design. You really should give them the opportunity to make their mark, particularly early on in the process."

The design that Mary came back with is essentially the one that has been substantially built. In fact the couple's only intervention came in the form of requesting a larger window in the main bedroom in order to maximise the views over Loch Carron. And they also suggested a simplification ➤

"IT'S A NICE CONTRAST… ENCLOSED INTIMATE ROOMS UPSTAIRS, OPEN SOCIAL AREAS DOWNSTAIRS."

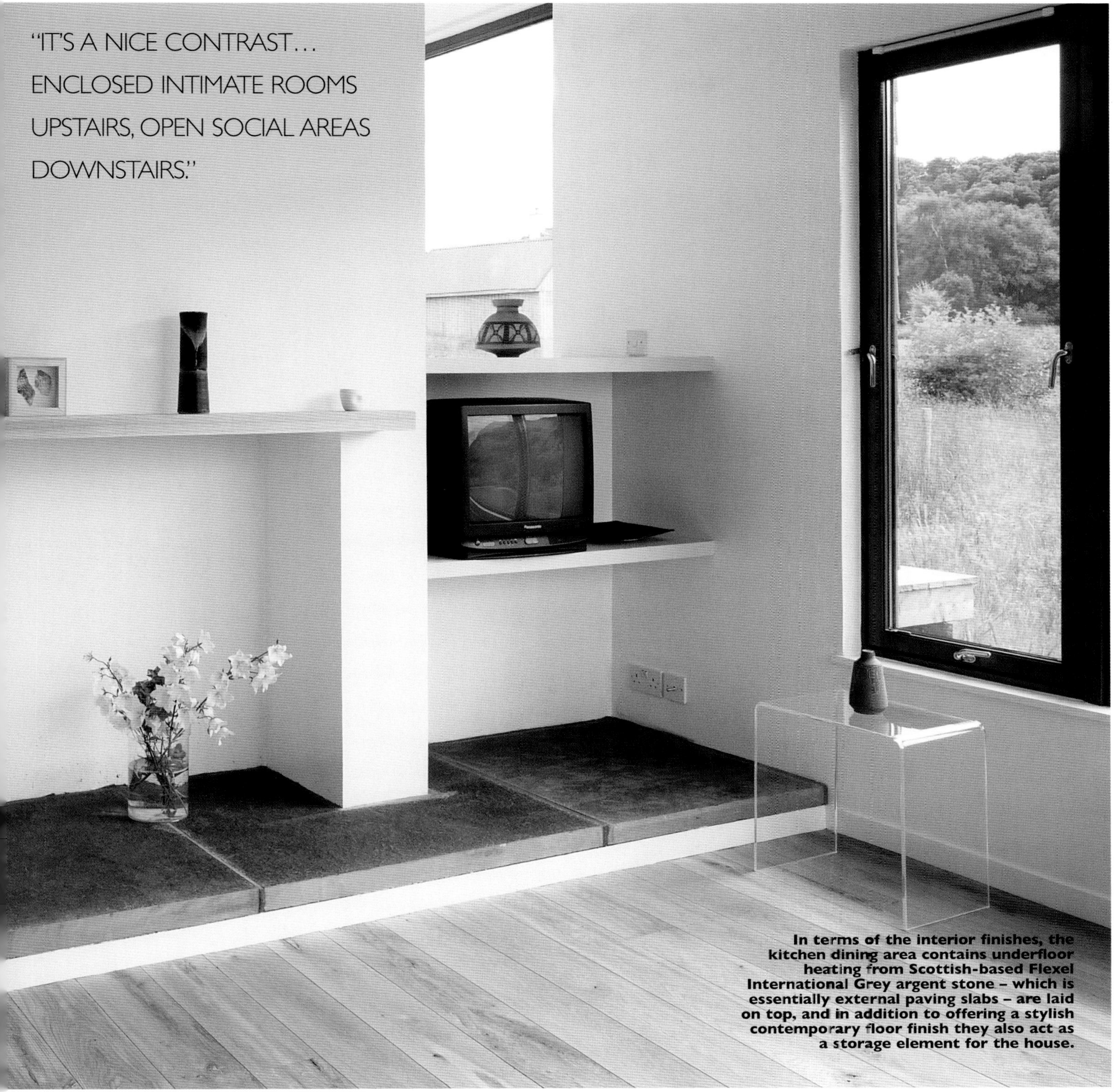

In terms of the interior finishes, the kitchen dining area contains underfloor heating from Scottish-based Flexel International Grey argent stone – which is essentially external paving slabs – are laid on top, and in addition to offering a stylish contemporary floor finish they also act as a storage element for the house.

"EVEN THE CONTRACTOR PULLING OUT AT THE LAST MINUTE DIDN'T AFFECT THE PROJECT."

of the form of the dramatic west corner window, which the architects had originally designed to project outwards. "We thought that although it's a really nice idea, it looked like it may have involved another feat of engineering, and that we wouldn't be able to do it within our budget," explains Chris. "But I think the house is better with the simpler window. I believe simplicity is important, I wanted a simple aesthetic with the house, and that's something that we wouldn't have got from a kit house."

In terms of the ongoing process Chris believes it was "an enjoyable experience. We corresponded a lot by email, and there weren't that many disagreements. Neil Stephen of Dualchas Building Design was the project architect and oversaw the contract – he was the contract administrator. And the architects had a good relationship with the local planners so that it all ran relatively painlessly." Even the main contractor pulling out at the last minute didn't seem to affect the on-budget and relatively on-time project.

"It was due to finish in July but actually finished in October," explains Chris. "We had arranged to come up and paint the house ourselves in October to make savings on the budget so in this respect it was a bit of an inconvenience. But it actually worked out well, we turned up in October

and we were painting the house while it was being finished. It was just one guy – a joiner – and it turned out fine because we all worked very well together."

The house is built on a downhill site, and in order to accommodate this step into the design, the kitchen (which is a simple Jewson's off-the-shelf design) and dining area effectively change level down into the beautifully oak floored living area. The step from stone to oak, and an 'open' dividing wall comprising a slate fireplace and series of two-way shelves, succeeds in retaining the connection between the living and dining area yet also effectively separates the areas as well. "It's a very clever device," admits Chris. Completing the picture on the ground level there's also "a little lobby at the door for us to dump our outdoor gear. On a functional level the house works really well," says Chris.

"Upstairs, we wanted to keep the two bedrooms very simple," explains Chris. "They're more enclosed spaces, and even though they've got the angle of the roof there's still plenty of room. It's a nice contrast to have the enclosed intimate rooms upstairs and the open social areas downstairs."

It's little wonder that Chris admits "we will eventually want to spend more and more time here." He also concludes that "we were so lucky to get the land and build the house when we did as we probably couldn't afford to do this now. Sites are very few and far between, and land and tender prices are also going up all the time." So, it seems that good luck might be the prevailing factor after all. ■

The architects persuaded the couple to abandon plans to build a standard kit house and go for a bespoke beauty instead

BUILDING A NEW CONTEMPORARY-STYLE HOME FOR JUST £66,000

FACT FILE

Names: Chris Mortimer and Luce Luque
Professions: Project manager and author/English language consultant
Area: Achmore, Ross-shire
House type: Two bedroom timber frame holiday home
House size: 100m²
Build route: Main contractor
Construction: Timber frame
Warranty: Architect's Certificate
Finance: Private
Build time: March '03 – Oct '03
Land cost: £10,750
Build cost: £66,000 plus fees
Total cost: £76,750
House value: est. £100,000
Cost/m²: £660

23%
COST SAVING

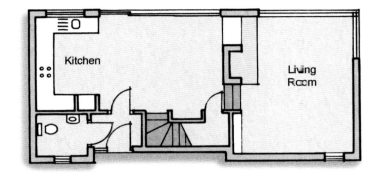

GROUND FLOOR

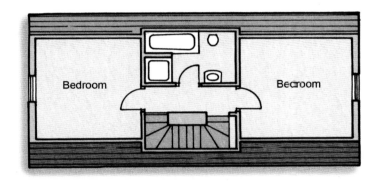

FIRST FLOOR

FLOORPLAN

The kitchen and dining areas effectively change level down into the living room to accommodate the way the house is built on a downhill slope. An 'open' dividing wall with a slate fireplace and series of two-way shelves effectively separates the areas. In contrast to this open plan layout, upstairs the layout has been kept simple, with intimate enclosed rooms.

USEFUL CONTACTS

Architects – Dualchas Building Design: 01471 833300 (Dualchas also operates a kit home company called Hebridean Homes which builds houses across the UK and Ireland www.hebrideanhomes.com); **Structural engineer** – John Addison of Peter Stephen and Partners: 0131 221 7020; **Main Contractor** – Donald McKerlich and Son Ltd: 01599 534259; **Exterior finishes** – Siberian Larch, Russwood Ltd: 01540 673648; **Roofing** – Spanish Slate, H.S.B.S: 01463 712666; **Windows** – Nordan UK Ltd: 01698 383364; **Heating** – Electric, Flexel International Ltd: 01592 757313; **Kitchen** – Jewson: 01471 822602; **Bath and shower** – Ideal Standard: 01482 346461; **Tiles, ceilings, linings and doors** – H.S.B.S: 01463 712666; **Flooring** – Prime grade oak by Russwood Ltd: 01540 673648; **Argent slabs** – Marshalls: 01484 438900; **Insulation** – Kingspan: www.kingspan.com **Specialist fittings** – Selkirk twin flue, Selkirkflue Ltd. Devon: 01271 326633

BUILDING A HOME ON A BUDGET

The key element in building a home on a budget is limiting the size of the dwelling; those looking to spend less than £100,000 should aim for a floor area of no more than 130m². Other ways to keep down costs include staying with a simple building form and choosing contract quality internal fixtures.

MADE TO MEASURE

A CONTEMPORARY HOME FOR A NARROW URBAN SITE

Terry and Gilly Pawson have built a spectacular contemporary-style four-storey home on a narrow urban site.

WORDS: DEBBIE JEFFERY PHOTOGRAPHY: RICHARD BRYANT

IF THE PAWSON house needed to be summed up in just three words, they would be: tall, light and handsome. Due to the restricted nature of its site, this innovative building is only one room wide and very tall — which is something of an oddity for a property newly constructed within a conservation area in Wimbledon. With the current trend for present-day housing to appear subservient to its period predecessors, planners are usually adamant that newly-built homes keep a low profile.

The site may have dictated the design parameters, but it also brought with it a whole series of construction dilemmas. "When we purchased our house we were aware that the property had been underpinned by a previous owner under an insurance cover," Terry Pawson explains. Despite this problem, he and his wife Gilly were attracted by the mature gardens, pleasant location and small price tag, and lived in the converted coach house with their two sons before realising that the cause of the subsidence had not been rectified.

"No-one knew that an extensive land drain ran below the property, which was broken and had continued to leak. Deepening the foundations in the clay soil had done nothing to alleviate this problem."

Ultimately, the family decided that the small brick cottage would have to be demolished and a replacement house constructed. With no insurance pay-out, they had a relatively tight budget and an extremely tight site. "It wasn't an ideal scenario," Terry continues, "but we had to make the best of the situation and start again."

The two storey cottage occupied a long thin strip of land on the east facing slope of the ridge that runs right across Wimbledon. At five metres wide, the site is actually narrower than an average three bedroom terraced house, but extends to some 80m in length. A mature oak tree, the unusual proportions of the plot and its prominent position among imposing 1900s villas have all influenced the final design.

"We approached the planners very early on to discuss the various issues," says Terry. "There were a lot of consultations but, from day one, they were very positive and supportive. We never asked for anything unreasonable which could not be justified, and the response from the officers was encouraging."

With the building only one room wide, a feeling of complexity has been created within the section of the house. The interior deliberately plays with the perception of space: compressing and then opening

Situated on the upper ground floor above the kitchen, the living room 'platform' has a barrel vaulted ceiling, glass balustrade and views across the garden. ➤

"THE CONSTRAINTS HAVE ULTIMATELY LED TO A MUCH MORE INTERESTING BUILDING"

out in an unexpected direction to create a series of changing volumes, with sunlight penetrating into every corner.

An oak clad tower sits on a reinforced concrete base, and has a bedroom and bathroom on each of its four floors, whilst a brick cube holds the stairs. Living spaces have been positioned beneath a planted, vaulted roof, and are able to open out fully onto the garden — blurring the division between inside and out. Each space has a different aspect: from the skylit hall to the rooftop terrace, set amongst the upper branches of the oak tree.

Terry — principal of Terry Pawson Architects — decided that this project would provide the opportunity to act as architect, client and main contractor — allowing him the freedom to explore new ideas and construction techniques.

"I was responsible for all aspects of the building design, procurement and funding," he says. "The building was constructed over an extended

The exposed concrete staircase with its slim handrail provides a dramatic feature in the toplit hallway, which is filled with natural light.

period of time, using a combination of direct labour and specialist contractors. This provided the opportunity to develop details on site from a practical, rather than a theoretical viewpoint, and to be actively involved and personally fabricate some elements of the house. Although I had never really tackled anything like this before, I helped to put up the timber structure and partitioning, decorated and generally laboured on site where I could."

This approach meant that the project management was carried out on a part-time basis at weekends and early mornings — a necessary consequence of the constraints on both time and finance. Terry admits that more time spent on the issue of purchasing materials would have improved the overall efficiency of the process, but feels that the experience allowed him to develop a better understanding of a self-build project.

"We put our furniture into storage and moved in with my mother during the build," says Gilly, a curate. "The whole process has taken four years, and was prolonged because Terry was also setting up a new practice during this time. For almost a year we did nothing about the house. I think ➤

The wall between the dining room can be folded back, so that the double height room opens directly onto the terrace.

This oak clad tower sits on a reinforced concrete base, and has a bedroom and bathroom on each of its four floors, whilst a brick cube holds the stairs.

"ALL THE CONCRETE ELEMENTS WERE CONSTRUCTED IN ONE PHASE, CREATING THE LOCALLY RENOWNED SIGHT: 'THE STAIRCASE SCULPTURE'!"

the neighbours were extremely glad when we finally finished!"

Structurally, the building comprises three distinct components: a concrete podium ground floor and basement; a timber framed superstructure to the front three storeys and a steel framed external envelope enclosing the main double height spaces to the rear.

"Terry wanted a simple form to unify the lower ground floor spaces and link with the upper storeys using a central staircase," says structural engineer, Bob Barton. "Concrete seemed the obvious choice and, given the concern about the site's settlement problems, we decided to use a reinforced concrete structure throughout — including the ground floor. This was designed to be a watertight box, which also acts as a damp proofing system. All the concrete elements were constructed in one phase, creating the locally renowned sight: 'the staircase sculpture'!"

A simple platform frame system was used for the three storey bedroom tower, with timber stud walls and a timber joisted floor. This has been clad externally in oak boarding, whilst the central circulation space was to be clad in brick. Here, an intricate steel frame was devised which was carefully integrated into the fabric of the external walls, and accommodates the glass slots and recesses in the ground floor storey. The steel solution was also used for the rear extension, which steps down the slope of the garden.

Internally, the finish materials are restricted to white painted walls, with floors of either oak or black slate. Elements of the structural in-situ concrete are also left exposed, principally in the main staircase and the concrete platform set above the kitchen — on which the upper ground floor sitting room is positioned. This has a barrel vaulted roof, glass balustrade and overlooks the mature gardens to the rear.

"Nobody would choose to build on such a difficult site," says Terry. "But the very constraints have ultimately led to a much more interesting building which responds directly to its location and yet feels spacious and generous inside.

"I'm extremely pleased with the quality of natural light within the house and the way the building connects to the garden. It has taken time, but we have learnt a great deal from building our own home and are now simply enjoying living here." ■

FLOORPLAN

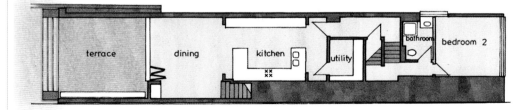

GROUND FLOOR

terrace | dining | kitchen | utility | bathroom | bedroom 2

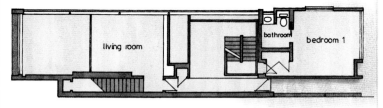

FIRST FLOOR

living room | bathroom | bedroom 1

SECOND FLOOR

roof | bath | bedroom 3

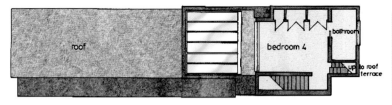

THIRD FLOOR

roof | bedroom 4 | bathroom | up to roof terrace

To take advantage of the narrow sloping site the ground floor spaces have been lowered using a reinforced concrete box structure. The four bedrooms and bathrooms are contained within the four storey oak clad tower at the front, topped off with a roof terrace. The living rooms and kitchen have been positioned in the two storey steel framed section to the rear.

FACT FILE

Costs as of Feb 2003
Names: Terry and Gilly Pawson
Professions: Architect & Curate
Area: South West London
House type: 4 bedroom detached
House size: 186m²
Build route: Subcontractors – self
Construction: Concrete, timber, steel + brick
Finance: NatWest loan
Build time: Three years
Land cost: £200,000
Build cost: £320,000
Total cost: £520,000
House value: £1.5m+
Cost/m²: £1,720

65% COST SAVING

Cost Breakdown:

Concrete, groundworks + drainage	£55,000
Steel frame	£10,000
Timber frame/cladding	£21,000
Roof coverings/flashings	£8,000
Windows and glazing	£26,000
Heating and plumbing	£13,000
Electrical and lighting	£4,000
Sanitaryware	£6,000
Building work	£143,000
Landscaping	£3,000
Kitchen	£7,000
Doors and ironmongery	£7,000
Timber + slate floor finishes	£17,000
TOTAL	**£320,000**

USEFUL CONTACTS

Architect – Terry Pawson Architects: 020 8543 2577 www.terrypawson.com; **Structural Engineer** – Barton Engineers: 020 7928 9099; **Timber supply** – Chelsea Timber Merchants Ltd: 0208 7700448; **Bricks** – Baggeridge Brick PLC: 01902 880666; **Oak cladding** – Layton Timber: C1491 613222; **Stainless steel cladding fixings** – Stainless Threaded Fasteners Ltd: 01902 490490; **Glass and glazing** – Compass Glass & Glazing Ltd: 020 8946 8080; **Sliding windows, rooflight** – Sunfold Systems: 01362 699744; **Louvre windows** – Ruskin Air Management Ltd: 0151 527 2525; **Underfloor heating** – Eurogauge Co Ltd: 01342 323641; **Planted vaulted roof** – Index Building Products Ltd: 020 7409 7151; **External paints** – Keim Mineral Paints Ltd: 01746 714543; **Ironmongery** – Hafele UK Ltd: 01788 542020; **Slate flooring** – Kirkstone Quarries Ltd: 01539 433296; **Glass mosaic tiles** – Edgar Udny and Co: 020 8767 8181; **Lighting** – Concord Lighting Ltd: 01273 515811; **Insurance** - DMS Services: 01909 591652

ELEGANT SIMPLICITY

Sarah and Stephen Gee have created a new home with beautiful contemporary style living spaces concealed within a simple, economic, steel-frame structure.

WORDS: DEBBIE JEFFERY   PHOTOGRAPHY: LEIGH SIMPSON

■ ELEGANT SIMPLICITY

SIX YEARS AGO we decided to buy a piece of land in Hurstpierpoint, Sussex, where I grew up," explains Sarah Gee. She and her husband, Stephen, were on holiday in the Dominican Republic when Sarah's mother phoned with the news that a large site with planning permission for a detached dwelling was for sale by sealed bids. "We knew the 14th century barn and old farmyard set in seven acres, and decided there and then without hesitation, that we would make a bid whilst we were abroad," Sarah continues.

After successfully purchasing the land, she and Stephen sold their Victorian house and moved into rented accommodation with their two children – later living in a large mobile home on the site for almost four months. "Life in the mobile home started out as an adventure and became a bit of a chore, as we had only packed enough things for a short stay," Stephen explains.

"I don't think that we would have considered building our own home

without the help of my brother, Nat, who is an architect. We wanted something modern and innovative, and I took two years off from working as a lecturer in beauty therapy in order to give the project my full attention," says Sarah, who decided to enrol in a design course at Brighton University to gain a greater understanding of the project.

The dramatic circular hallway and curved stone staircase were inspired by a visit to the opera.

"Nat is thirteen years older than I am, which meant that we were at very different stages in life when we were growing up," Sarah explains. "This project has given us a chance to spend time together, and we would meet two or three times each week and speak on the phone every day. It was fantastic because we had such similar ideas, and I felt extremely privileged to be able to have that time with him."

Self-build is quite obviously in the blood, as both Sarah and Stephen's parents have built their own homes. "We lived abroad, and my parents ➤

■ ELEGANT SIMPLICITY

built a very modern house in Fiji," says Sarah. "Although we had our traumas, Stephen and I found the whole process extremely exciting – being able to design a house exactly to our family's requirements."

Sarah and Stephen had regular design meetings with Nat, who drew up a detailed brief based on their requirements –including a mezzanine overlooking the sitting room, which gives Sarah a private study area with fine views, with a separate TV and hi-fi room helping to define public and more private spaces. "It was extraordinary just how alike our opinions were," says Nat. "I don't think we fell out over anything important."

Sarah and Stephen wanted underfloor heating, a system for collecting rainwater from the roof and storing it for use in the bathrooms, and a laundry chute from the bedrooms down to a basement uility room. "I was dubious about constructing a basement at first," says Sarah, "but Stephen felt that it would be perfect for containing all the service areas – and it has proved invaluable for hiding boilers and the laundry room."

The house has been built on the site of an old farmhouse which burned down 20 years before, with the new property positioned adjacent to the existing barn in order to benefit from maximum sunlight, and to take advantage of views towards the lake and fields beyond.

Externally, 'Big Edgerley' itself resembles a timber clad barn with giant ➤

Lighting was an important consideration, and a Lutron computerised lighting system has been preset for a variety of effects and moods, whilst an integrated hi-fi system allows music to be played in every room.

The chapel-like double-height sitting room has a curved ceiling, with panels of glazing giving views of the countryside and lake.

entrance doors, and is clearly visible from a well used public footpath. Even though the planning officer and the majority of the planning committee supported this design it still took almost a year to develop the brief and gain full planning permission for the house.

While they waited, Sarah and Stephen spent time dredging the lake and restoring the existing barn as a store and garage. "We then went on to use the same builder who had worked on the barn to build the house," says Stephen.

Archaeologists inspected the site for potential mediaeval remains before the foundations could be dug, with Stephen and Sarah deciding to use some of the spoil to create their own 'mediaeval mound' in the grounds. At this time, bad weather conditions meant that the plot closely resembled a muddy battlefield – with the JCBs struggling to cope.

Ease of construction, coupled with the need for large spans, led Nathaniel to specify a prefabricated steel frame – which was erected in just two weeks. Next came the blockwork walling and an external cladding of horizontal iroko weatherboarding, which has been left untreated to weather to a silver grey and blend with the surroundings.

"We asked Nat to design something which respected its setting and utilised natural materials and local tradesmen where possible. Traditional Sussex materials include square knapped flint and stone, with natural slate to the roof," says Sarah. "After much searching for a specialist in knapping – including as far afield as Suffolk – we eventually found a craftsman living locally who knapped all the flints to the front elevation, and laid them between the stone banding."

Built by a cabinet maker to Sarah and Stephen's linear design, the kitchen features a French limestone floor, teak work surfaces and sliding doors which conceal all the appliances and clutter. ➤

"WE LOVE ITS SPACIOUSNESS...
AND THE AMOUNT OF LIGHT
WHICH COMES IN THROUGH THE
LARGE WINDOWS."

"THE BUILDING [HAS]
A SIMPLE FORM
EXTERNALLY. THE
NOTION OF SURPRISE
WAS KEY TO THE
WHOLE CONCEPT."

**Clad in knapped
flint and iroko
shiplap, Big Edgerley
resembles a simple,
rectangular barn.**

"To clad the entire building in stone and flint would have been rather extravagant and hugely expensive, and so these materials have been limited to the front facade," Nat explains. "I designed the rectangular building as a simple form externally, giving no clues regarding the circular stairwell and double height spaces inside. The notion of surprise was key to the whole concept."

Windows were also an important factor, with different combinations of square glazing echoed internally with square lights and glass door panels. The master bedroom benefits from a large triangular window above the entrance doors which runs across the full width of the building.

"To me, the view from inside the house is far more important than the appearance of the outside," explains Nathaniel. "Windows have been positioned to maximise the outlook – and the sills on the first floor were set deliberately low to prevent them from dissecting these views, which meant that a metal safety rail was required."

Nathaniel decided that, as a country house, the property should have a grand entrance: oversized 'barn' doors lead into a circular atrium around which the rest of the house is based. A cantilevered limestone staircase is lit from above by a large skylight, whilst the hallway is floored in limestone and provides a perfect space for entertaining.

"I was inspired by a visit to the opera, which featured a dramatic curved staircase on the set," laughs Nat, "and decided that this space should set the tone for the rest of the house. In addition to the aesthetic appeal, the curved stairwell set into a rectangular space left four triangular corners, which were perfect for vertical service runs hiding flues, pipework and the laundry chute."

Sarah sourced many of the materials herself, working closely with Nat on every last detail. "We must have spent five hours just discussing door handles," she laughs. "I searched through adverts in magazines, travelled to London and phoned around to get the best deals.

"Following the Wembley Stone Show we contacted a French limestone quarry – cutting out the middle man and shipping over our own limestone at a fraction of the retail price.

"Looking back, the children did grow rather tired of constant discussions about lights and door hinges, although they also got to see a great deal of their uncle.

"Now that we are living in Big Edgerley we love its spaciousness, the underfloor heating and the amount of light which comes in through the large windows – especially in the living room. It is a unique design, tailored specifically to our requirements.." ■

FLOORPLAN

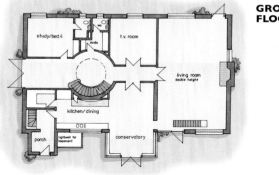

GROUND FLOOR

study/bed 4 | t.v. room | living room double height | kitchen/dining | porch | lightwell for basement | conservatory

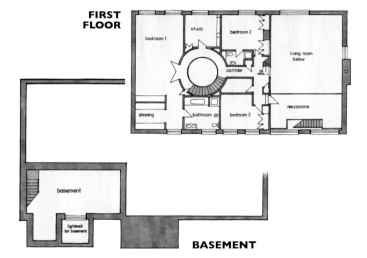

FIRST FLOOR

bedroom 1 | study | bedroom 2 | corridor | living room below | dressing | bathroom | bedroom 3 | mezzanine

BASEMENT

basement | lightwell for basement

USEFUL CONTACTS

Architect - Nathaniel Gee: 020 7524 7755; **Structural engineer** - Jampel, Davison & Bell: 020 7272 0562; **Main contractor** - Wedgecourt Ltd: 01273 440017; **Structural steelwork** - Prefab Steel Co.: 01273 597733; **Glass & glazing** - The Glass Centre: 01273 776688; **Steel gratings** - Thielco Gratings Ltd: 0208 681 2839; **Sanitaryware** - C P Hart Group: 0207 902 1000; **Knapped flints** - Duncan Berry: 01243 371071; **Joinery & iroko cladding** - Ace Joinery: 01273 439651; **Heating and plumbing engineers** - P J Fraine: 0208 317 9089; **Electricians** - Jarrards Ltd: 01707 262884; **Boilers & central heating pipework** - HCC Systems Ltd: 01400 250572; **Radiators** - Hudevad Britain: 01932 247835; **Electrical faceplates** - Mr Resistor: 020 8874 2234; **Ironmongery** - Laidlaw Ltd: 01223 212567 - Allgood plc: 020 7387 9951; **Hi -fi and Lutron lighting systems** - CCI Ltd: 01903 507077

FACT FILE

Costs as of Jan 2003
Name: Sarah Gee
Profession: Lecturer
Area: West Sussex
House type: Five bed detached
House size: 480m²
Build route: Building contractor
Construction: Steel frame, blockwork, iroko, flint and stone cladding
Warranty: Zurich Custom Build
Finance: Private
Build time: 16 months
Land cost: £250,000
Build cost: £470,000
Total cost: £720,000
House value: £950,000
Cost/m²: £979

24%
COST SAVING

Cost Breakdown:

Site clearance	£28,300
Foundations and cellar	£75,100
Underground drainage	£17,600
Steel frame	£18,500
Blockwork + brickwork	£23,500
Concrete flooring	£7,200
Iroko cladding	£9,900
Windows, external doors and rooflights	£51,000
Slate roof covering	£23,200
Knapped flintwork and stonework cladding	£16,000
Electrical works	£28,000
Central heating + plumbing	£38,200
Sanitaryware supply	£17,100
Internal doors + joinery	£17,100
Plastering	£14,400
Floor finishes	£22,300
Tiling	£7,600
Lighting + hi-fi system	£29,600
External landscaping	£29,400
TOTAL	**£470,000**

A HOUSE IN THE GARDEN

Julian and Erika Bond have built themselves a house that combines their retirement needs with their love of quality contemporary design.

WORDS: CLIVE FEWINS   PHOTOGRAPHY: NIGEL RIGDEN

WHEN JULIAN AND Erika Bond first moved into a large stone house in their pretty Dorset village, they had no idea that 10 years later they would be living in an ultra-contemporary house sitting on their former garden.

"I have had three orthopaedic operations in the past few years and one day when things began to get too much, we looked at the plot and decided there was room for a small house in the garden," says Erika. The result is the aptly named Half Moon House: a two bedroom 190m^2 property that must surely be one of the most site-specific and carefully tailored retirement houses ever to have been featured in H&R.

The new plot was to prove challenging. It was long and thin — yet the Bonds, who are both interested in the arts, wanted to avoid a long, thin house with a conventional dual-pitched roof in favour of something more interesting. They found architect Phil Easton through the RIBA register, and he was immediately enthusiastic about the project.

When Julian and Erika visited his award-winning Arts Block at Brynaston School near Blandford, they knew they had picked the right man. "We have always liked contemporary architecture," says Erika. "We agreed we liked ➤

The curves of the kitchen were quite a challenge, but the polished concrete worktops and ash units work beautifully together and the kitchen won a design award.

the style of the school's new block, and Phil took it from there."

Half Moon House reflects not only Phil's love of curves, but of roofs that are anything but conventional dual-pitched, of houses in separate sections that are 'tied together' in interesting ways, and of asymmetry. "There is hardly a right angle in the house," observes Erika. "There is even a stone half-moon-shaped seat outside, near the entrance.

"When it came to constructing the kitchen, the curves presented a big challenge to the two builders – Mark Lewis and John Warmley – who had worked on our previous home next door and whom we had known for several years." The kitchen has polished concrete worktops and curved cupboards in ash, and won a design award for Phil's assistants Matthew Haley and Zoe Gibson.

With its gleaming off-white rendered walls, contrasting stonework in the front elevation and four separate mono-pitched roofs, all at different angles,

the house makes quite an impact amongst the stone cottages with thatched roofs that surround it.

You enter under a sharply angled porch, beneath which is a wide oak front door with glazed panels on either side. Inside, nearly all is on one level. "As far as possible we wanted everything on the same floor, with the master bedroom downstairs," says Erika. "We also wanted something that was easy to maintain, light and airy, and largely open plan."

The main living area incorporates a kitchen dining area and main relaxation space, and has an amazing tilted flat roof, which has a curved overhang on the outside to provide shading from the sun. This illuminates the curved walls with their three distinct sets of full-height windows, all with separate doors providing level access.

This roof meets all the others above the long, tapered hall that traverses the house. The hall is the vital link in the building: it connects the main living space to the master bedroom and adjoining study, and also acts as a spine that supports the main drainage channel at the point where all the roofs meet. It is glazed along its entire length and the light diffuses in interesting ➤

Known as the 'drum', this central area of the house has been designed to be home to the enormous 12ft-long burr elm table that Julian and Erika have owned for 30 years.

The hole-in-the-wall gas fireplace in the living room is backed by a glazed panel, giving views through to the garden. Even when the fire is not on, the light from outside animates the fireplace with reflections.

patterns through the timber beams beneath.

Underneath, the hall — known by the architects as the 'drum' — plays an equally vital role. It is the central focus of the house, serving as the area from which the deliberately understated staircase departs for the first floor bedroom. It contains four recessed bookcases that house much of the reference material used by Julian, a screenwriter who still undertakes occasional commissions, but is also home to the enormous 12ft-long burr elm table that they have owned for 30 years. "We have had it in four houses; one way or another Phil had to make room for it in our retirement home," Julian laughs.

The hall is the area of the house with the real 'wow' factor. Eleven European redwood roof trusses radiate out from the central spine of the building and line up with the glazing frames and the solid sections of masonry in between. The trusses are exposed at each end above a suspended ceiling that houses the lights and look almost like the spokes of a wheel.

"People love this space — especially the way the light bounces off the walls and through the three large windows, which are all different and take their shapes from the sloping roof," says Julian. "However, the village is still divided about the exterior. When the parish council, of which I am a member,

decided to oppose our application, I had to stand down. We eventually won on appeal."

Another interesting source of light is the glazed panel in the outer wall of the massive curved chimney, set low down behind the large hole-in-the-wall gas fire. "It was a feature that caused quite a lot of head scratching when we came up with the idea," says Erika. "We had to have specially strengthened glass, but it has proved eye-catching and it creates a very interesting effect even when there is no fire, as it animates the fireplace with shadows and reflections."

The low window at the base of the chimney is not the only surprise as you walk round the outside of the house. The outer window frame of the master bedroom is of chunky reclaimed elm. It is carried through to the inside, where it provides a window seat.

In the hall, 11 European redwood roof trusses radiate out from the central spine of the building and line up with the glazing frames and solid sections of masonry in between.

"IT IS A HOUSE DESIGNED TO SUIT OUR NEEDS. IT SEEMS TO RESPOND EXTREMELY WELL TO THE EVER-CHANGING LIGHT PATTERNS AND BRINGS US DAILY PLEASURE."

The outer window frame of the master bedroom is of chunky reclaimed elm. It is carried through to the inside of the room, where it provides a window seat.

"We have been in here two years now, long enough to appreciate the house's many qualities," says Julian. "I have to say that I do not think it would have come together nearly so well had it not been for our builders. Apart from the windows, the roof, the electrics and the plumbing they did everything, and I think it shows. They had a very craftsman-like approach to the job and they saw problems when they were coming and consulted the architects when in doubt about the next stage. So there was no time wasted on correcting mistakes. It was a very tricky build and I know that the architects, like us, think the finish to be of excellent quality.

"We were also fortunate in that we were able to live next door in our former house for most of the build period and so kept in close touch with the builders. Erika likes to say she acted as clerk of works!"

The couple's only slight complaint is that the en suite guest bedroom is upstairs. Julian and Erika would have preferred the house to be all on one level, but the confines of the site prevented it. However, this gave the chance to introduce interest through the different roof angles.

"As well as being designed to suit the plot and the surroundings, it is a house designed to suit our needs. It seems to respond extremely well to the ever-changing light patterns and brings us daily pleasure." ∎

FACT FILE

Names: Julian and Erika Bond
Professions: Screenwriter and homemaker
Area: Dorset
House type: Two bedroom detached
House size: 190m²
Build route: Self-managed
Construction: Dual-skin blockwork, with render and stone as exterior skin in places
Finance: Private, from sale of previous house
Build time: August '02 – May '03
Land cost: Already owned est. £200,000
Build cost: £277,000

Total cost: £477,000
House value: £600,000
Cost/m²: £1,458

21% COST SAVING

Cost Breakdown:

Connections and fees	£21,000
Groundwork	£27,500
Principal builders	£107,500
Plumbing and heating	£17,000
Electrics	£4,000
Roof	£14,000
Windows	£21,000
Joinery (including kitchen)	£20,500
Flooring	£6,000
Miscellaneous	£28,500
TOTAL	**£277,000**

FLOORPLAN

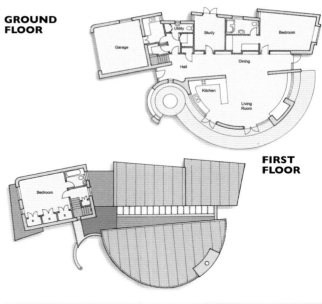

GROUND FLOOR

FIRST FLOOR

USEFUL CONTACTS

Architect: Western Design: 01258 455239; **Principal builders** Lukewarm: 01747 824227; **Roofers** Alwitra: 01202 579208; **Glaziers** Salisbury Glass: 01722 328985; **Kitchen units, hall bookshelves, internal doors, and oak front door** Perry and Son: 01747 811285; **Electrician** Steve Clasby: 01747 851406; **Plumbing and heating** Richard Chatfield: 01747 852179; **Underfloor heating** Nu-Heat: 01404 549770; **Stone flooring** Stone Age: 0117 923 8180; **Reclaimed materials** Semley Reclamation: 01747 850350

SHINING LIGHT

Michael and Lindsay Hird's new home is an extraordinary modern design on a brownfield site in the most ordinary of settings.

WORDS: DEBBIE JEFFERY PHOTOGRAPHY: NIGEL RIGDEN

BUILDING YOUR OWN home is all about fantasy. If you want unusual shapes and features – and they are within your budget – then surely you should go for it? Unfortunately cautious planners and practical constraints frequently result in half-hearted architecture. Michael and Lindsay Hird have been fortunate – and brave – enough to persevere with their dream, however, and are now the proud owners of what has been dubbed 'The Glass House'.

The setting of their home is not ideal: cosying up near brick 1930s semis and next door to a petrol filling station in Doncaster, the market town of South Yorkshire, its surroundings simply serve to further highlight the uncompromising design. Inspired by Gio Ponti's Pirelli Building in Milan, the floor plan has a diamond shape with four free-standing walls rendered with concrete and painted white. These are separated by high ➤

With each pane fitting flush against the other
without the need for conventional frames there
is absolutely no room for error. Such a system is
rarely used for domestic housing. "It's so much
easier for builders to whack up brick walls and put
in tiny little windows," says Colin. ➤

"SUCH INNOVATIVE DESIGNS AND CONTEMPORARY MATERIALS ARE USUALLY RESERVED FOR THE COMMERCIAL SECTOR."

windows, with a thin row of windows running along the top, and end walls made of huge glass sheets.

Lindsay's brother, architect Colin Harwood, literally took a section through the Pirelli tower and developed the idea to create a contemporary, open plan layout with clean, angular lines and a light and spacious feel. Interior features include a spectacular glass staircase whilst, beneath the living area, a large basement with underground parking gave

rise to a 'Batman's cave' comparison.

"The most difficult part of the project was finding a suitable plot, because you are up against developers and dealing with the planners," says Michael of their suburban brownfield site: half an acre of old council land. With the plot bordering a Conservation Area, the council (who have congratulated themselves as being 'one of the most progressive local authorities in the country') initially rejected the white concrete finish of the walls, and the build was greatly delayed whilst the Hirds employed a planning consultant to successfully appeal on their behalf. "Compromising by cladding the house in red brick would have been unthinkable," states Michael. "It was such an integral part of the design that there really was no alternative as far as we were concerned."

The staircase to the basement garage is hidden between stark white walls.

➤

292

A huge blockwork-
and-granite fireplace
takes pride of place
in the sitting room

"IT IS THE USE OF GLASS WHICH STEALS THE SHOW: THAT STAIRCASE, IBSTOCK GLAZED BRICKS AND THE HUGE PANELS…"

The neighbours were not so sure – becoming anxious as the lozenge-shaped blockwork structure rose out of the ground that it could be a car-wash, an art gallery or even a crematorium. Certainly such innovative designs and contemporary materials are usually reserved for the commercial sector.

The Hirds had been living in a village 45 minutes drive from Michael's Doncaster business – recycling railway sleepers and tracks. Moving closer to work would mean more time to spend with Lindsay and their two children, and was one of the main reasons behind building their own home. "Colin had designed and converted a chapel for us where we were able to remain whilst our new house was being built," Lindsay explains.

Having already learnt much from the process of converting, the couple were able to bring firm ideas regarding their requirements to the new build project. Space and light were vital considerations, and

'Bennetthorpe House' certainly has plenty of both. Although Lindsay and Michael were keen to leave as much of the design to Colin as possible, they envisaged that clashes could occur working so closely with a family member and, inevitably for such a complex venture, a number of problems did arise. Colin's previous work revolved around designing interiors and this was his first ever new build. He preferred an 'organic', fluid approach whilst the builders demanded detailed specifications. The resulting confusion ensured that what was initially hoped would be a 12 week build spread over several months. "I had to write a letter to both Colin and Glen, the building contractor, telling them to calm down!" Michael laughs.

Additionally, Colin had encountered difficulties finding structural engineers to work on the project, whilst quotes from various builders had been for more than double the original estimated budget. A suitable building contractor was eventually found, the council tractor shed which had stood on the site was demolished and construction of the basement and underground garage in concrete blocks got underway.

Exact measurements were vital for a building of such strange angles and varying levels but, when the 30 purpose-made concrete beams arrived to make up the ground floor, they fitted precisely. "I was ➤

The master bedroom suite enjoys great views thanks to the wall of glazing and large windows on both sides.

All the glass, including the glass staircase – the first of its kind in the world – came fom an Austrian company Eckelt Glass, which specialises in high-performance glazing and design.

"I WAS SLIGHTLY WORRIED. THE ODD SHAPES, THIRTEEN DEGREE ANGLES AND THE AMOUNT OF GLASS FOR A DOMESTIC BUILDING MADE EVERY CALCULATION COUNT."

slightly worried," admits Colin. "Even though we were using fairly basic construction methods, the odd shapes, thirteen degree angles and the amount of glass for a domestic building made every calculation count."

Even the roof of this house is out of the ordinary: a lightweight aluminium system of double skin insulated construction. This roofing 'sandwich' incorporates an outer 'Kalzip' sheet, mineral fibre insulation, a vapour control layer and liner sheet on structural decking. The insulation depth is accommodated between two skins by selecting from a range of clip heights, with the system proving very permeable — which reduces the build up of moisture and condensation.

With delays occurring at almost every turn the Hirds had no choice but to move into their unfinished home once they had sold the chapel. Michael is philosophical, however, believing that these additional weeks

did not dramatically affect the price of the project and, although unwilling to divulge exact build costs, he does warn other self-builders: "You will always be over budget."

Now completed, however, the finished house is stunning. Transparent walls give glimpses of the chic interiors, with cherry wood floors and a huge open fire in an otherwise minimalist space. Michael says he would be happy to build again whilst Lindsay isn't quite so sure — she loves her new boat-shaped home and, with five bedrooms, the 400m2 property provides more than enough space for the whole family. But it is the use of glass which steals the show: that staircase, Ibstock glazed bricks, and the huge panels of glazing all work together to artfully reflect light and shadow onto the walls and surfaces of this truly amazing home. ■

FACT FILE

Costs as of January 2002
Name: Michael and Lindsay Hird
Professions: Railway contractor
Area: Doncaster
House type: Contemporary
House size: 400m²
Build route: Building contractor

and self-managed subcontractors
Construction: Rendered blockwork and glass
warranty: Architect's certificate
SAP rating: Not known
Finance: Private
Build time: 11 months

USEFUL CONTACTS

Designer - Colin Harwood: 07940 773212; **Glass Installation** - Dean Wheeler: 07989 305348; **Glazing Manufacture** - Eckelt Glass: 0043 7252 894 255; **Structural Engineer** - Darryl Blackwood: 0161 228 2610; **Structural Steelwork** - A&D Fabrications: 01302 341758; **Stainless Steel and decking** - Tilewind: 01302 721205; **Basement Tanking** - Ruberoid: 01707 822 222; **Underfloor Heating** - Thermoboard: 01392 444122; **Timber Floor Insulation** - Aran Joinery: 01302 330231; **Precast concrete floors & stairs** - Tarmac: 01335 360601; **Roof Insulation** - Profile Roofing: 01709 790326; **Specialist Welding** - Armthorpe Gordon: 01302 830202; **Door knobs etc** - Thews: 0151 709 9438; **Stainless Steel Chimney** - Selkirk: 01271 326633; **Precast concrete block chimney** - Isokern: 01202 861650; **Joinery** - Lee Kendrick: 01302 337514; Mick Rowley: 01302 361140; **Stainless Steel Kitchen** - GEC Anderson: 01442 826999

FLOORPLAN

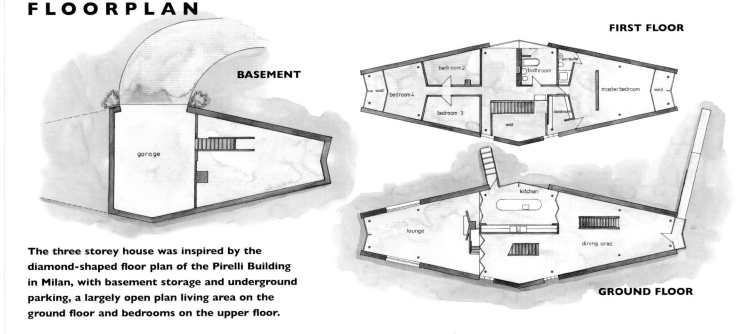

BASEMENT

FIRST FLOOR

GROUND FLOOR

The three storey house was inspired by the diamond-shaped floor plan of the Pirelli Building in Milan, with basement storage and underground parking, a largely open plan living area on the ground floor and bedrooms on the upper floor.

HEAVENLY LOCATION

LOTTE GLOB HAS BUILT A HIGHLY INDIVIDUAL CONTEMPORARY-STYLE HOME IN A SPECTACULAR LOCATION ON AN INCREDIBLY TIGHT BUDGET OF £75,000.

WORDS: CAROLINE EDNIE   PHOTOGRAPHY: ANDREW LEE

LOTTE GLOB KNOWS all about challenges. When the renowned Danish ceramic artist and her family settled in northwest Scotland 36 years ago, home was part of a "vandalised and disused" decommissioned nuclear attack early-warning station, which has since gone on to become the thriving Durness Craft Village. Now, after 30 years of searching and three years of patience and perseverance – as well as a budget of £85,000 – Lotte has helped transform a chunk of wind-lashed wilderness, ten miles south of Durness, into a little Highland Arcadia. Lotte's new house and garden on the banks of Loch Eriboll is a long held dream come true for the artist.

"When I first saw Loch Eriboll, 'I thought this is the place I want to live,'" she says. But it was 30 years later and third-time-lucky for Lotte when it came to actually purchasing a site. Finally, in 1999, and following a tip-off from now near neighbour, Hugh McLellan, Lotte managed to secure, for £10,000, a prime site which led from the main artery road ➤

Lotte's new timber-framed home enjoys spectacular views over Loch Eriboll. Windows have been designed to make the most of the views and to follow the sun around the property.

"PEOPLE HAVE DESCRIBED THE HOUSE AS A BOATHOUSE, A CATHEDRAL AND EVEN A DELUXE CARAVAN – WHICH I LIKE VERY MUCH."

to the banks of Loch Eriboll. It was here that the artist planned to build a permanent home, sculpture garden and studio.

Initially Lotte lived in a caravan and then a bespoke shed on the site, but a defining moment arrived in the shape of an article that Lotte read in a local paper about Aberdeen based architect Gökay Deveci. "I read an article about an energy efficient house that Gökay had built near Aberdeen, so I phoned him, and asked him to come up and visit. Then we went through a few ideas," explains Lotte. Primarily, Lotte's ideas involved an open plan timber house with plenty of light and as many ecologically efficient and sustainable solutions as would be possible within her £75,000 budget. "And luckily," she says, "Gökay understood exactly what I wanted."

This mutual understanding resulted in a 110m², one-and-a-half storey house, comprising a small office, bathroom and compact service space to the north and a spectacular large multi-purpose double-height living, sleeping and eating space orientated towards the south. In terms of construction, the house is essentially a timber post and beam structure,

clad in untreated Scottish oak shiplap boarding designed to silver with age, and with a curved roof of patinated copper. The east and west walls feature narrow linear and pocket windows aligned to the sunrise and sunset, whereas the south elevation is fully glazed with a timber deck – this projects out into the air, and looks directly towards Loch Eriboll and Ben Hope beyond.

The main living space is double-height, with sleeping accommodation based in mezzanine 'shelves'.

Although the house is a recent addition to the Sutherland landscape, it has already caused quite a stir. "It has become a landmark in its own right and that's what I think architecture should do," remarks Gökay Deveci. "People have described the house as a boathouse, a cathedral and even a deluxe caravan – which I like very much. There is even a joke that it once created a traffic jam with people stopping to see it, even though the house is essentially in the middle of nowhere. A traditional building just wouldn't create that kind of debate." But the unusual appearance is not an attempt to stamp some 'iconic' building on the virgin landscape, insists ➤

"THE ENERGY EFFICIENCY IS AMAZING AND IT IS VERY COSY. I'VE ONLY GOT TWO SMALL ELECTRICAL STORAGE HEATERS."

Huge amounts of south-facing glazing in addition to up to 300mm of Rockwool insulation ensure the interiors can withstand the exposed location.

prefabricated in sections and fitted on site. And the bespoke frame arrived from Holland in sections – each leg was a different size, and everything was semi-drilled in order to make no mistake when putting it together. "Dutch engineers did it as I couldn't find any decent engineers here to deal with it – or more to the point they didn't want to take the risk because of the wind load and the terms of their insurance," explains Gökay.

The reluctance to accept risk might seem fairly understandable considering that the structure needed to withstand winds of up to 120kmph. But the house boasts remarkable wind-resistant credentials. A combination of lateral and longitudinal sheathed panels and bolted joints, cross bracing and ties using galvanised steel rods (produced by a blacksmith in Forres) achieve the desired effect. And a rigid roof and floor tie these elements together. Wind uplift is also a serious problem and is counteracted by bolting the structure to steel shoes cast in substantial concrete foundations.

The fruitful collaboration between architect and main contractor is all the more remarkable considering that builders Kenny McRae and Sons of Durness didn't have email or even a fax machine, so communication was difficult. "I was lucky if I got them on the phone!" explains Gökay. "We met once a month or so, but they did respect my drawings and instructions, so actually everything worked out well." The same can be said for arrangements with Highland Council planning and building control, who are described as "wonderful," according to all involved.

The energy efficient performance of this airtight construction has so far been remarkable. This has been achieved via 250-300mm thick Rockwool insulation, which is well above the standard requirements, and the small east and west elevation Nor-Dan windows and huge south-facing glazing means that there is also optimum solar gain. "There are no drafts: the energy efficiency is amazing," enthuses Lotte. "It's so well insulated and with the sunlight coming in, it is very cosy. I've only got two small electrical storage heaters – one in the main living area and one in the ground floor office, and in the winter time I only have the storage heaters on half. Combined with a few logs on the woodburning stove in the winter evenings, and that's me." ➤

Gökay. It is instead a direct and site-specific response to Lotte's brief.

The house is clearly the dream home that Lotte had been hankering after – however it did take quite a Herculean effort to actually get it built. "Although it may look like a small £75,000 house, it's unique in its way so everything had to be designed," explains Gökay. This meant 250 drawings had to be made, and all the sourcing of materials and subcontractors was also painstakingly carried out by the architects in order to get the best deals. The patinated copper roof was manufactured in Germany – then

Underfloor heating has been incorporated into the bathroom, which is located on the ground floor between the north-facing office and main living space. "I made all the tiles in the corridor and bathroom and I also designed the sink," explains Lotte. "The blue colour sort of reminds me of the lochs and sky, and every tile is different — I worked on it like a painting. The mirror reflects the wonderful views. And you have to sit on the toilet! The window is at eye level, and this must be the best view I've ever seen from a toilet!" laughs Lotte.

The main living/kitchen and dining area is the pièce de résistance of the house, and in addition to being a truly spectacular double-height space, an intimacy has been achieved via the subtle palette of natural earthy materials. "The floor is new oak — the joiners didn't like it because they didn't think that it was very good timber. Gökay asked me what I thought, and I didn't know about wood, so we sought a price for a different floor and discovered that it would have cost an additional £2,000, so we used the existing wood. And it turns out that because it has its knots

and variety of colours it has worked out perfectly. I love it and thank goodness I couldn't afford the other stuff."

Lotte also confesses to loving the long timber worktop in the kitchen area. "It's a type of rainforest wood — and the only foreign wood that we've used. My son found it. It's old coupar wood for whisky barrels, and they had stacks of it that they wanted to sell off very cheaply. It's in such thick planks and the young joiner Euan MacRae made this wonderful seamless workbench — he has done a fantastic job.

"Up until I had built the house I hadn't thought about architecture, and now I'm obsessed with it. I can't go into a bookshop without looking at books on the subject. Building this house has given me this obsession," smiles Lotte. "I was thinking at the time that in terms of my own work I hadn't been creating a lot, but then I thought, 'what a creation this place is!'" ■

The house is essentially a timber post and beam structure, clad in untreated Scottish oak shiplap boarding designed to silver with age, and with a curved roof of patinated copper.

BUILT FOR £75,000 – AND THE PLOT COST £10K!

FLOORPLAN

An open plan double height living/ dining/kitchen space forms the bulk of the ground floor living accommodation, with a mezzanine level providing sleeping space.

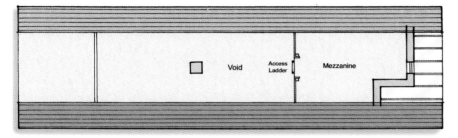

FIRST FLOOR

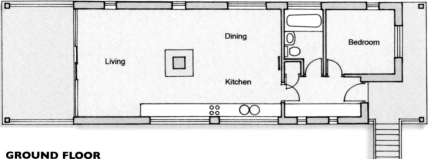

GROUND FLOOR

CONTEMPORARY HOMES ON A BUDGET

Building on a budget doesn't have to mean that you compromise style and architectural interest. While £10,000 building plots are impossible to come by across most of the UK, with an innovative approach to sourcing materials and, crucially, a modest footprint, architecturally bold new homes can be built for sums below £100,000. Visit www.homebuilding.co.uk and search on 'low cost'.

FACT FILE

Name: Lotte Glob
Profession: Artist
Area: Highlands
House size: 110m²
Build route: Main contractor
Construction: Timber frame
Warranty: Architect's Certificate
SAP rating: 103
Finance: Private
Build time: Feb '03 – Nov '03
Land cost: £10,000
Build cost: £75,000
Total cost: £85,000
House value: est. £130,000
Cost/m²: £680

35%
COST SAVING

Cost Breakdown:

Enabling work	£1,000
Substructure/basement	£2,000
Frame	£15,000
External walls/joinery	£15,000
Windows/blind/doors	£6,000
Roofing	£13,000
Internal walls	£1,500
Internal doors	£500
Wall/ceiling/floor finishes	£5,000
Sanitary/kitchen/built-in fittings	£5,000
M&E/plumbing/electrics	£8,000
Landscape/external words	£3,000
TOTAL	**£75,000**

USEFUL CONTACTS

Lotte Glob: www.lotteglob.co.uk; **Architects** – Gökay Deveci & Gary Smollet: 01224 263714; **Structural engineer** – Peter Gallon: 01224 322379; **Cost consultant and land surveyor** – Philip Hunt: 01224 263714; **Main contractor** – Kenny MacRae & Euan MacRae: 01971 511379; **Post and beams** – Douglas Mursell & Jos Kempten: 01489 575073; **External and internal Timbers** – Nor-Build: 01309 676865; **Bracing** – Rennie Fabrication: 01309 676874; **Roofing** – Patinated Copper Roofing WB Watson Ltd: 01560 482588; **Windows** – Nor-Dan Windows from Aberdeen Window & Door Company: 01224 633174; **Heating** – David Bowes Heating & Plumbing Thurso: 01641 521833; **Tiles** – Lotte Glob Far North Ceramics: 01971 511354; **Flooring** – Nor-Build: 01309 676865; **Doors** – Hovland Doors from Aberdeen Window & Door Company: 01224 633174; **Electrics** – Tongue Electrics: 01847 611250; **Finishes** – Scott Coghill: 01847 611293

Small square windows light the timber and glass staircase, and are the only windows on the north side of the house.

LOW ENERGY LIVING

John and Joan Barnes have built a new home for their retirement with the intention of reducing energy bills and providing a comfortable lifestyle.

WORDS: DEBBIE JEFFERY   PHOTOGRAPHY: NIGEL RIGDEN

HOMEBUILDING & RENOVATING MAGAZINE
AWARDS 2004
SHORTLISTED ECO HOUSE

"IN 1965 I had my own building company, and designed and built a stone-clad house for my family," says John Barnes, 75. "We had a village plot overlooking fields, and acquired even more land when a new bypass was built close by and I asked if I could buy some of the wasteland they had used for spoil behind our property. I bought myself a JCB and became quite expert at terracing our 1.5 acres, which Joan landscaped."

Over time, the couple began to find it increasingly difficult to take care of so much land, however, and decided to try and build a more manageable house — something which they had discussed over a number of years. Their son David is an architect, and company director of architectural practice The Genesis Design Studio. John and Joan asked if he would design them a new home in the garden — suitable for their retirement.

The home utilises a partially-dug basement, and makes the most of its south facing elevation with solar panels and a conservatory. ➤

306

The new house has been designed to exploit the slight slope of the ground and the southern aspect. A partial basement was built to maximise and overcome the sloping site, and the mass of the brick and block building helps to control daily and seasonal temperature swings.

Built over three levels, the house appears to be a small single-storey bungalow from the entrance, with only a few small square windows punched into the masonry to avoid directly overlooking the Barnes' previous home.

The rear of the house faces south, and has extensive glazing to make the most of the views and passive solar gain from the sun. Patio doors open onto a balcony at ground floor level, with all habitable rooms arranged on the south and fully glazed.

A two-storey-high conservatory is also incorporated on the southern side of the house, and door openings into this space allow warmth from the sun to work its way up into each level of the main building, with automatic temperature- and rain-sensitive opening vents in the conservatory to prevent overheating. A Velux window above

the back staircase also draws warm air up and out of the building to cool it when necessary.

Ground floor living rooms benefit from the wall of glass and a full-length balcony, part of which is external, with a central section contained inside the conservatory.

Ceramic tiles and beech laminate flooring help to reduce dust mites which could trigger Joan's asthma. Right: Patio doors open onto a balcony at ground floor level overlooking the basement sun lounge in the conservatory below.

John and Joan use the basement conservatory as a sun lounge, which is overlooked by an internal balcony where they can sit and eat breakfast.

"On the whole we managed to agree about most things, although David would have liked us to keep the ground floor living space totally open plan," says John, "but we decided to separate the sitting room from the kitchen and dining areas to allow us to use the rooms independently."

The three bedrooms and two bathrooms utilise the full shape of the roof, and have high sloping ceilings and exposed glulam beams, with a strip of Velux windows which reach down to the floor – affording views south across the Wiltshire Downs. ➤

"WE STARTED OUT WANTING A SMALLER, MORE MANAGEABLE PROPERTY FOR OUR RETIREMENT, BUT HAVE ACTUALLY ENDED UP WITH A LARGER HOUSE THAN BEFORE."

When the Barnes had built their previous house, they had lived on site in a caravan, and John had undertaken all of the building work – even making the doors and windows in his workshop. This time, however, he and Joan were able to stay in their own home while the build progressed.

"We intended to employ builders and subcontractors to build the house for us, but it didn't quite turn out as planned," says John Barnes. "Our son-in-law did most of the brickwork, but by the time we got up to roof level, the builders were scratching their heads over how to bolt glulam beams together. We were getting frustrated by the lack of progress and, as I'm a qualified joiner, I decided to help them out. From there on I became more and more involved, and ended up doing quite a lot of the internal carpentry myself as well."

The Barnes' house is highly insulated and has a solar panel to assist with heating the hot water, which is expected to reduce costs by around 50 per cent. Zoned underfloor heating is used throughout, which allows lower water temperatures in some of the heating circuits and suits the highly energy efficient condensing boiler. Rainwater is collected from the roof in an underground garden chamber to be filtered and recycled for toilets, the washing machine and garden watering, saving the couple a significant amount on their bills.

A continuous ventilation system with heat recovery prevents heat loss, but also substantially reduces draughts and moisture content. This improves air quality which, coupled with the use of tiled and laminate flooring, reduces the occurrence of house dust mites which could trigger Joan's asthma.

"We started out wanting a smaller, more manageable property for our retirement, but have actually ended up with a larger house than before," he says. "The layout allows us a certain amount of flexibility, and although we currently use the basement level as an office and workshop with a conservatory sunroom, this could easily become bedrooms or a self-contained unit, depending on our needs in the future. I'm no spring chicken – although I do still feel like one occasionally – but our self-build project was certainly an interesting challenge at my time of life." ■

Patio doors open onto the balcony at ground floor level overlooking the basement sun lounge in the conservatory below. John ended up doing quite a lot of the internal joinery.

FLOORPLAN

The lower ground floor is currently a workshop and store, with a conservatory seating area, but has been fitted with a shower and could be used for bedrooms in the future. On the ground floor, the kitchen is open plan to the dining room and balcony beyond, with a separate sitting room and a WC and utility. Three bedrooms and two bathrooms have been accommodated in the roof space.

FIRST FLOOR

GROUND FLOOR

BASEMENT

DESIGNING FOR ENERGY EFFICIENCY

High levels of insulation, low-e glazing and an airtight structure ventilated by a mechanical system with heat recovery are a good starting point for an energy efficient home, but the building's design and orientation also have a major impact on energy consumption. The north-facing elevation of the Barnes' home has minimal window openings, while to the south, a large double-height conservatory acts as a passive heat collector, with the energy stored in the mass of the masonry structure. Solar panels on the roof provide much of the household's hot water requirement, further reducing consumption of fossil fuels.

FACT FILE

Names: John and Joan Barnes
Professions: Retired
Area: Dorset
House type: Three storey, three bedroom house
House size: 184m² + 14m² garage
Build route: Subcontractors and DIY
Construction: Brick and block walls, clay pantiles
Warranty: NHBC Solo for Self Build
Finance: Private
Build time: July '00 – July '02
Land cost: Already owned, approx. cost £90,000
Build cost: £219,000
Total cost: £309,000
House value: £380,000
Cost/m²: £1,106

19% COST SAVING

Cost Breakdown:

Building regs	£1,000
Structural engineer	£750
Site set-up & preliminaries	£3,050
Services	£4,250
Substructures	£18,000
Masonry walls and lintels	£20,000
Precast floors and screeds	£3,300
Structural timber	£5,000
Roof structure and covering	£20,600
Ceilings	£2,000
Windows, glazing, rooflights	£11,500
Doors and ironmongery	£8,800
Internal partitions	£3,500
Internal joinery and stairs	£4,500
Flooring	£6,000
Kitchen fittings	£7,500
Underfloor heating	£6,500
Ventilation	£2,000
Sanitaryware	£2,000
Plumbing and heating	£9,500
Solar panels	£1,800
Water recycling	£3,100
Electrical	£7,300
Rainwater goods and soil pipes	£2,500
Plastering and decoration	£14,200
Conservatory	£8,800
Balconies	£2,000
Wall tiling	£500
Insulation	£3,000
External works, landscaping	£35,300
NHBC	£1,000
TOTAL	**£219,250**

USEFUL CONTACTS

Architect – The Genesis Design Studio: 01794 519333; **Structural engineer** – Andrew Waring Associates: 01794 524447; **Windows** – Swedish H-Windows Ltd: 029 2052 2246; **Rooflights** – The Velux Company Ltd: 01592 772211; **External doors** – Allan Brothers Ltd: 01289 334600; **Internal joinery** – Granton Joinery: 01202 841963; **Ventilation system** – Baxi Ltd: 01772 693700; **Underfloor heating** – Pipe 2000: 01268 759567, Enviraflor Ltd: 01268 759567; **Rainwater harvesting** – The Green Shop: 01452 770629; **Solar panels** – Solar Sense: 01792 371690; **Kitchen** – Trade Kitchens (Dorset): 01747 850990; **Guttering** – Dales Nordal System: 0115 930 1521; **Glulam beams** – Structural Timbers Ltd: 01275 832724; **precast concrete cills** – Forticrete: 0870 903 4015; **Bricks** – Taylor Maxwell: 01962 835800; **General materials** – Bradfords: 01935 813254; **Groundworks** – Tercon Construction Ltd: 01202 676940; **Electrical** – BF Keane Electrical Contractors Ltd: 01794 301481; **Mechanical** – R Shepherd and Partner: 01794 512445; **Roofing** – Shire Roofing Salisbury Ltd: 01722 329462

BUILDING AN INNOVATIVE MODERN HOUSE ON A BUDGET

CONTEMPORARY
COUNTRY

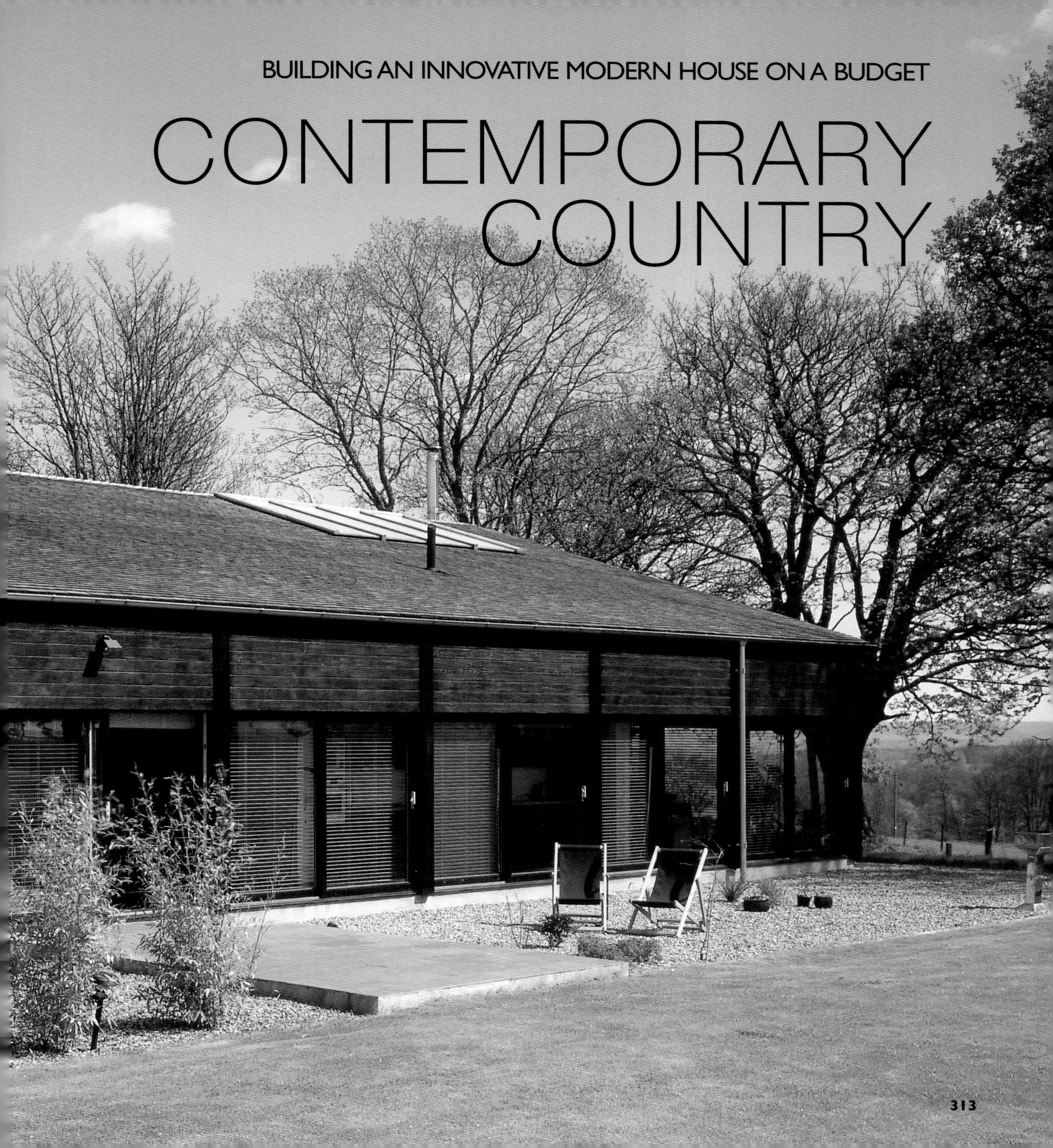

313

■ CONTEMPORARY COUNTRY

An award-winning new home in Perthshire shows how high architecture doesn't necessarily have to mean high build costs.

WORDS: CAROLINE EDNIE   PHOTOGRAPHY: ANDREW LEE

AS IF WINNING the RIBA award for best First Building by a New Practice at the 2001 Stirling Prize wasn't enough, Mark Walker's self-designed home, Cedar House, also features as an exemplar of rural housing in the new Scottish Executive's Policy on Architecture. All of which isn't bad at all considering the total build cost of this landscape hugging, contemporary style family home was little over £127,000, or just over £500/m^2.

Mark and Chloe Walker and family moved up to rural Perthshire from London ten years ago. Architect Mark, who currently teaches architecture at the Edinburgh College of Art, had been keen to build in Scotland as well as teach but the opportunity hadn't quite presented itself. That is, until Chloe was left a legacy of £150,000 which the couple promptly set aside to buy a plot of land and design and build a new family home.

Finding a suitable plot proved difficult. The Walkers had a bit of a break however, as Mark explains. "Planning permission generally doesn't encourage individual houses in Scotland. We were lucky, however, as we managed to hear from a friend of ours that a prime site from the Scone Estate was being put on the market."

So, snapping up this half acre chunk of rolling Glenalmond, it only remained for the planning process to kick in, which according to Mark "has a tendency in Scotland to favour copies of older traditional forms than more contemporary buildings." However the rigorous environmental and ecological design presented by Walker Architecture won a great deal of support from the planning officer who was dealing with the site, and to Mark's relief the challenging stylistic proposals were also embraced. In fact, the precedent set by this particularly enlightened planner has, says Mark, precipitated a response from the Scottish Executive to encourage local authorities in rural areas to be less conservative in their approach to planning.

Now that the obstacles were cleared Walker Architecture could then get on with the "challenge of building something that is not pastiche traditional

The internal layout is based around one open plan living space which has loosely-defined functions. ➤

CUTTING AWAY FRILLY DETAILS AND EMBELLISHMENTS, SUCH AS PROJECTING ROOFS, MEANT THERE WAS MORE MONEY TO SPEND ON HIGH-QUALITY MATERIALS.

asymmetrical roof. This affords the home its unmistakably rural feel, which appears almost like a Modernist barn.

The corridor kitchen has cupboard doors supplied by Swan Robes (01259 762669) and worktops by flooring specialists Junckers.

Mark's decision to create a simple monolithic shell by "cutting away frilly details and embellishments such as projecting roofs and porches," also meant that there would be more money to spend on high quality materials. So, in addition to the red cedar cladding and roof shingles, which Mark claims will only improve with age and weathering, interior walls are lined with birch faced plywood, and floors are finished in reclaimed oak and Brazilian Rio Ferrada slate.

To complete the picture of opulence, custom made Woodslat blinds line the glazed walls, and when closed at night "simulate the effect of a very warm and glowing box," according to Mark.

The quality of interior space is as top notch as the materials. Mark defines these spaces in terms of 'day' and 'night' areas. The 'day' areas, which are arranged along a cruciform layout, begin via a roomy entrance hall on the short axis, which opens up into a light and airy open plan living and dining area occupying the central axis. Following the line of the main south facing glazed wall leads to a long and luxuriously fitted kitchen complete with combination oven and halogen hobs. All services are contained within a semi-transparent polycarbonate 'wall,' which backs on to the double bathroom. The 'day' area culminates in a compact office annex, which Mark claims he would have extended if the site had allowed.

A series of internal 'night' spaces are enclosed within the north face of the house. Four bedrooms facing two identical bathrooms are connected by a top lit corridor and, being contained underneath the lowest trajectory of the sloping roof, the bedrooms especially have a cosiness and intimacy which contrasts effectively with the open plan 'day' areas.

According to Mark, "economical planning and not having any redundant spaces" was pivotal in keeping the budget costs in check. "The actual economy of the building is that I absolutely reduced the circulation space. For example, although there is a corridor linking the bedrooms ➤

architecture or a nostalgia for country living," but an elegant contemporary response to the glorious Perthshire setting.

In terms of design this single storey, four bedroom family home is simplicity itself. Planned on a grid and on top of a foundation of concrete poured in trenches, a timber box was constructed using double sections of 6 inch by 2 inch timber. On to this the roof trusses were positioned. Walls were filled with insulation and then clad externally. The overall effect is like a "packing crate" as Mark calls it.

With the exception of the north facing bedrooms and internal double garage, the exterior walls are timber framed sliding doors, glazed with low-emissivity glass. The crisp transparency of these glass walls is balanced by the warm cedar cladding of the gables and boards above the patio doors as well as the western red cedar shingles of the low pitch

"THE IMPORTANT THING IS THAT GOOD ARCHITECTURE NEEDN'T BE REALLY EXPENSIVE AND THE CEDAR HOUSE PROTOTYPE DOES GIVE PEOPLE SOME CONFIDENCE THAT IT CAN BE DONE…"

The patio doors and windows, supplied by Allan Brothers (01289 334600), help to bring the outside into the house.

and bathrooms, it's as straight and small as it could be. It's also 1500mm wide so it feels like a room, and could potentially be a library.

"There is also a virtual economy in the house, in that it feels a lot bigger than it is. For example, the device of the big mirror on the living area wall doubles the space, and the south east wall of the entrance hall is clad in 16mm triple walled polycarbonate, which creates a translucent internal screen rather than a solid wall."

Cedar House's energy efficient approach also makes economic sense. A steady temperature is achieved by an underfloor heating system in the form of water pipes embedded into the concrete floor. This is fired by an oil fueled boiler which sits in a cupboard next to the master bedroom. Mark admits this would have been better located in the garage as it makes a noise "a bit like a jet engine." Then there is the solar gain, which in this

case is considerable, due to the predominance of glazed facades. As if all this weren't enough a Scan wood burning stove is also on hand if an extra boost is needed.

It's hardly surprising then that the house has become something of a prototype for rural housing. And although Mark clearly "didn't have this intention when I built it originally," the simple modular and economical model made so much sense that a number of prospective clients throughout the UK and Ireland began to beat a path to Cedar House, to see what they could achieve in terms of affordable cutting edge design.

So, with the benefit of hindsight, will Mark be approaching the Cedar House progeny any differently? Well, for one thing he is determined that the construction process won't be the same next time round. "With Cedar House," he explains, "I did a set of drawings, and sourced and priced

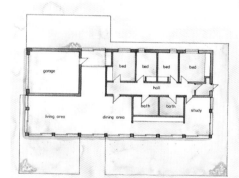

The bedrooms and bathrooms are connected by an enclosed corridor which is lit from above via the glazed roof.

much of the materials (patio doors, slate floor, stove, kitchen, blinds), but didn't want to manage the project myself. I was trying to find a contractor who would do everything and I did eventually find someone but they had only been used to producing the same house over and over again and were not really geared up for this new challenge. I think perhaps I got into bed with the wrong people.

"I would now tackle the project acting as an architect, and would stipulate a more closely written contract. In Cedar House it was just an exchange of letters."

Consequently, the Cedar House project took around a year, when it should have taken around 12 to 16 weeks, which is what Mark is aiming for with the Cedar House prototype he is building for clients in Peebles in the Scottish Borders. "They're taking the same external envelope and wall of glass whilst making a few modifications outside. Internally, however, they've requested a separate garage and a big utility room and three instead of four bedrooms. There are many options in the modular system. The scale, structure and the idea however, are all the same.

"The important thing," Mark says, "is the fact that good architecture needn't necessarily be really expensive and the Cedar House prototype does give people some confidence that it can be done." ∎

FACT FILE

Build time: Jan '99 — Jan '00
Land cost: £43,000
Build cost: £127,000
Total cost: £170,000
House value: £315,000
Cost/m²: £558

47%
COST SAVING

Costs as of Sept 2002
Names: Mark & Chloe Walker
Professions: Architects
Area: Perthshire
House type: Four bed detached
House size: 228m²
Build route: Main Contractor
Construction: Timber frame
Warranty: NHBC
SAP rating: 83
Finance: Private

Cost Breakdown:

Main contract	£110,855
UFH	£5,060
Blinds	£5,553
TV Aerial	£189
Fencing and gates	£555
Floor mats	£179
Tarmac Drive	£1,996
Floor seal	£244
TOTAL	**£127,300**

FLOORPLAN

For economy circulation space is kept to an absolute minimum. The only corridor, linking the bedrooms and bathrooms, is 1500mm wide and could be used as a library.

USEFUL CONTACTS

Architect — Walker Architecture: 01738 880419; **UFH** — Invisible Heating Systems: 01854 613161; **Contractor** — B & B Tealing Woodslat; **Blinds** — Chris Craft: 01356 625111; **Western red cedar shingles** — Loft Shop: 0870 6040404; **Rio Ferrada slate floor** — Kirkstone Quarries: 01539 433296; **Wood burning stove** — LHA: 0151 625 0504; **Patio doors and windows** — Allan Brothers: 01289 334600; **Sanitaryware** — Ideal Standard: 01482 346461; **Garage doors** — Hormann garage door company: 01467 632178; **Boiler** — Delta F45 HR by ACV: 01383 820100; **Kitchen worktop** — Junkers: 01376 534700; **Cupboard doors** — Swan Robes 01259 762669; **Coir mat** — Mat Services: 01568 616642; **Worktops** — Junckers: 01376 534700

HARBOUR LIGHTS

BUILDING A CONTEMPORARY-STYLE HOME ON THE SEA

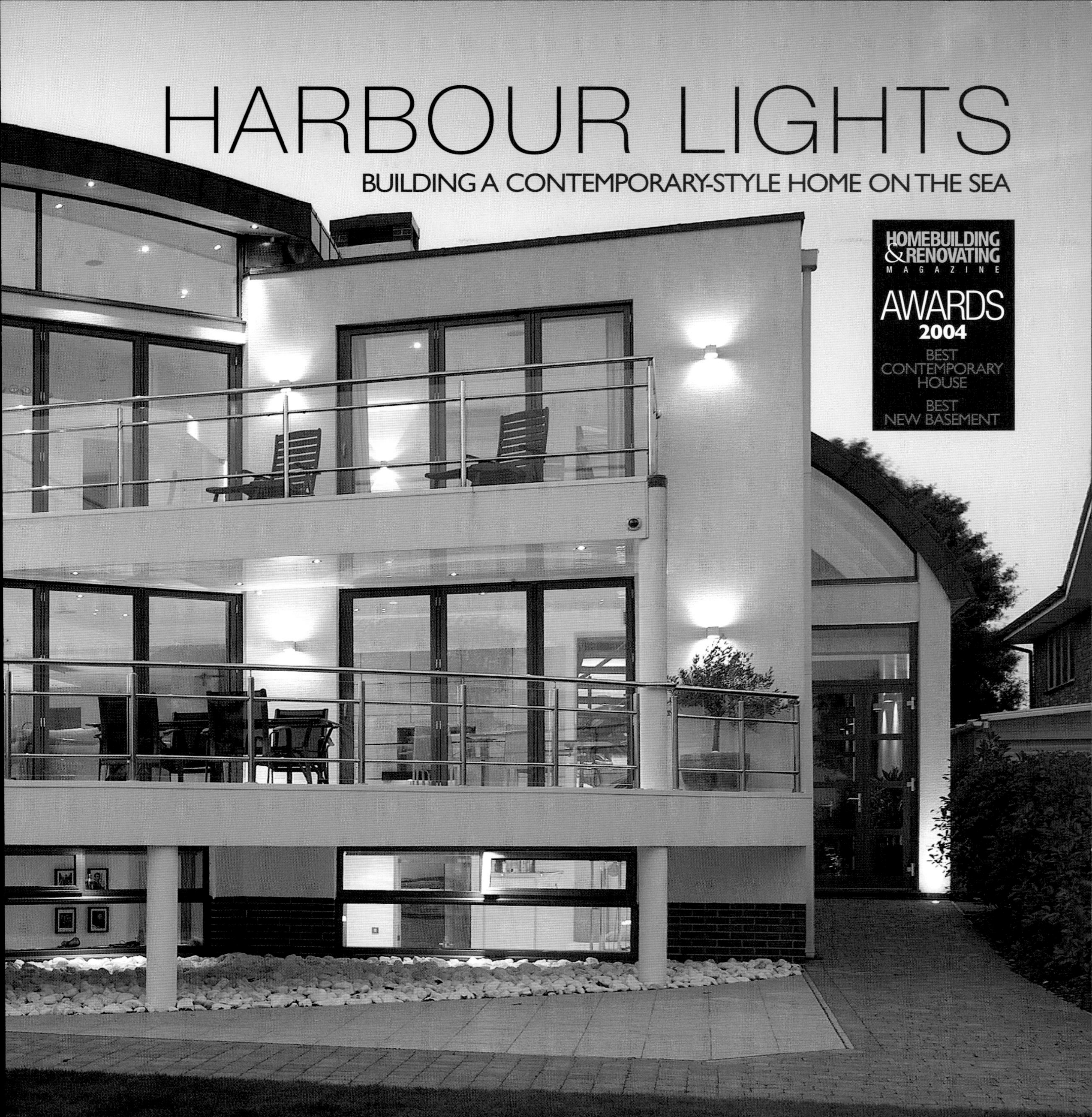

Steve and Sally Gorvin have built a new home on the Dorset coast that perfectly mixes contemporary design with 21st century hi-tech luxury.

WORDS: DEBBIE JEFFERY PHOTOGRAPHY: NIGEL RIGDEN

SALLY AND I took a bit of a gamble when we designed this house," admits Steve Gorvin, "but we wanted to build something adventurous and unique rather than copying an existing period style just to play safe. It does stand out from the neighbouring properties on Poole Harbour, but I think it's an appropriate design for the 21st century. Luckily the planners agreed!"

Twenty four years ago Steve and Sally had built a traditional three bedroom bungalow in an idyllic woodland setting in Dorset, later adding another floor to create a two storey, five bedroom house which was unrecognisable from the original building. Steve, a roofing ➤

Sons Matt
and Edd were
instrumental
in suggesting
and installing
many of the
hi-tech gadgets
which feature
throughout the
house.

"WE WANTED TO BUILD SOMETHING ADVENTUROUS AND UNIQUE RATHER THAN COPYING AN EXISTING PERIOD STYLE JUST TO PLAY SAFE."

contractor by profession, undertook most of the building work himself while the family remained living in the property – but concluded that it would have been cheaper to have demolished the bungalow and have started again from scratch. He decided that, if he ever built for himself again, the house would be constructed using modern materials and incorporate up-to-the-minute technology.

The Gorvins began looking for a suitable site in Poole and, as boat owners, were particularly keen to live close to the water. When a friend mentioned that she had seen a waterfront house for sale while walking her dog, they discovered a tired dormer bungalow overlooking Poole Harbour, which fulfilled their ultimate dream. They realised that they would need to act quickly to secure land in such a sought after location, and hoped to be able to demolish the existing building and redevelop the relatively narrow site to maximise the stunning views.

The open plan interior layout has been designed around being able to enjoy a sea view from the main living spaces downstairs. ➤

"STEVE AND THE BOYS DID AN AWFUL LOT THEMSELVES, INCLUDING CARPENTRY, TILING AND DECORATING."

After confirming with the local planners that they would be able to replace the house with another dwelling on a similar sized footprint, Steve and Sally began to design their new home. They took their sketches to David Wright, a local architect who had been recommended to them, and who merged their ideas into a workable design. Their intention was that every room would have a view of the sea, which dictated a relatively open plan layout at entrance level, where the study, kitchen, utility room, lounge and dining room are positioned around an imposing glass and steel staircase overlooked by a glazed atrium.

"My biggest wishes were for a basement and an atrium, and in the end we achieved both – although our first planning application was refused because of the basement," Steve recalls. "The Environment Agency was concerned that we wanted patio doors leading out into a sunken garden, so we amended the design to include high level windows instead, which give the required tidal threshold protection, and were eventually granted permission. We only wanted four bedrooms, so adding this extra level has enabled us to include luxuries such as the gym, home cinema and pool room, as well as a bedroom and en suite for our son, Edd. The land was expensive, but the basement has allowed us to use it to full advantage."

Steve planned to employ local subcontractors to undertake the build, but was let down on so many occasions that he changed his mind and constructed the shell with the help of his sons Matt, 26 and Edd, 24. "We excavated the hole, but the bottom of the basement was below the water table, which meant running pumps permanently for a month until it was finally double tanked and the reinforced concrete raft foundation was poured," says Steve, who spent his 50th birthday working on site. "I must admit that, at that stage, I was beginning to wonder why I'd ever started it."

In keeping with the hi-tech theme an EIB telecoupler enables the underfloor heating and lighting to be controlled from a mobile phone from anywhere in the world and, for security, this device will also issue an alarm to a mobile if, for instance, the whole-house sprinkler or alarm systems are activated. ➤

The Gorvins were determined that the house would be over-engineered, and the structure is a combination of a steel frame infilled with concrete blocks laid flat, and finished with external insulation applied by a specialist firm. The curved, oversailing flat roof is a particularly impressive feature, designed by Steve and detailed by the architect and structural engineer using computer-bent steel beams. Initially, the family considered a standing-seam metal roof, but decided that – as it would be impossible to see – they would save £30,000 by using a conventional built-up felt roofing system instead.

When it came to fitting out the interiors Steve was, once again, let down by a number of subcontractors, which held things up for several months. "A new house was being built opposite our previous home, and we approached the various tradesmen working there," says Sally. "I even drove around building sites looking for an electrical contractor, because everyone in the area seemed so busy. In the end Steve and the boys did an awful lot themselves, including carpentry, tiling and decorating."

The curved steel and glass staircase has a maple handrail and treads, which have been carpeted for comfort.

➤

WE CAN PUSH BACK THE FOLDING
GLASS DOORS WHEN ITS HOT AND
WALK OUT ONTO THE BALCONIES. IT'S
LIKE BEING ON HOLIDAY AT HOME."

"WE EXCAVATED THE HOLE, BUT THE BOTTOM OF THE BASEMENT WAS BELOW THE WATER TABLE, WHICH MEANT RUNNING PUMPS PERMANENTLY FOR A MONTH."

Each heating zone is fitted with a smart temperature controller and zone valve, with individual rooms controlled to the set temperature with occupied, unoccupied and night modes.

In addition to a new triple garage the Gorvins have built a boat house, and find that living by the water has allowed them to be far more spontaneous. "If the weather is nice we don't have to plan ahead, we can decide to go out on the water to sail or wakeboard," Steve explains. "We can push back the folding glass doors when its hot and walk out onto the balconies. It's like being on holiday at home." ■

The basement houses the leisure areas, including a pool room and home cinema.

FLOORPLAN

GROUND FLOOR

FIRST FLOOR

BASEMENT

Practically every room in the open plan ground floor has a sea view, while the basement contains many of the entertaining areas, including home cinema.

USEFUL CONTACTS

Architect – David Wright: 01202 315595; **Consulting, civil and geotechnical engineers** – Graham Garner and Partners: 01202 697341; **Staircase and steel balustrades** – Fine Line Fabrications: 01202 669026; **Home automation** – Andromeda Telematics Ltd: 01932 870920; **Kitchen and utility rooms** – Wigmore Kitchens: 0207 2241986; **Duravit sanitaryware, Axor taps and showers** – Kitchen and Bathroom Collection of Salisbury: 01722 334800; **Bathroom cupboards, maple and glass doors in hall and study** – Halstock Cabinet Makers: 01935 891762; **Internal and external light fittings** – Deltalight: 01428 651919; **Electrics** – RIS Electrical: 01202 733984; **Air conditioning system** – Rainier Cooling Systems: 07050 199480; **Limestone flooring and granite worktops** – Eaton Stone Masons: 01258 858550; **Artwork** – Harris Interiors: 01202 744081; **Whole house sprinkler system** – Domestic sprinklers: 01305 765763; **Linn music system and flat screen TVs** – Sevenoaks Sound and Vision: 01202 671677; **Supply and fit of carpeting** – Bainton Flooring: 01202 513985; **Supply of all blinds, Wintergarden system and curtain tracks** – Silent Gliss: 01843 863571; **Curtains** – Poppy Designs: 01202 740779; **Furniture** – Viaduct Furniture: 0207 2788456; **Supply and planting of atrium plants and planters** – Parkwood Style Ltd: 01202 717700

JUDGES' SUMMARY

Steve and Sally's new house combines updated Modernist and Art Deco influences to create a home that suits their 21st century lifestyle. The internal layout and light, open spaces – where all the major living areas have a sea view – means that while the home is very stylish, it places the lifestyle needs of an evolving family at its heart. The addition of a basement ensures that the design makes the most of the splendid site, while a range of home automation features make this a fine example of a contemporary home built for modern living.

FACT FILE

Names: Steve and Sally Gorvin
Professions: Builder and retailer
Area: Dorset
House type: Three storey, four bedroom house
House size: 600m², 45m² garage and 60m² boat house
Build route: Selves and subcontractors
Construction: Steel frame, blockwork, high performance built-up roof membranes
Finance: Private
Build time: Feb '02 – Feb '04
Land cost: £605,000
Build cost: £670,000
Total cost: £1,275,000
House value: £2,500,000
Cost/m²: £950

49%
COST SAVING

Cost Breakdown:

Erection and roofing of shell	£150,000
Aluminium framed doors and windows	£40,000
External insulation and rendering	£20,000
Dry-lining, plastering and screeds	£30,000
Kitchen and utility rooms	£50,000
Stainless steel and glass balcony rails and staircase	£30,000
Landscaping	£23,000
Jetty	£20,000
Sanitaryware (7 bathrooms/WCs)	£22,000
Glass doors and partitioning	£20,000
Electronic blinds	£32,000
Multi-room sound and vision	£40,000
Home automation system	£25,000
Domestic wiring	£10,000
Light fittings	£20,000
Underfloor heating and plumbing	£21,000
Air conditioning	£9,000
Domestic fire protection sprinkler system	£6,000
Flooring and carpets	£40,000
Miscellaneous	£62,000
TOTAL	**£670,000**

Your dream fireplace made affordable

birchdale glass ltd
specialists in glazing solutions

Spanning new horizons in quality glazing

Birchdale Glass is a leading glass processor offering an extensive range of products and solutions. Our expertise spans a full range of glazing services covering innovative design, manufacture and installation. To find out about the real difference we could make to your home please contact us on **01895 259 111** alternatively send an e-mail to: **info@birchdaleglass.co.uk** or visit our website at **www.birchdaleglass.com** for more information about Birchdale Glass Limited.

Structural Glazing • Aluminium Windows and Doors • Bi-Folding Doors • Glass Balustrades • Glass Walls • Glass Doors

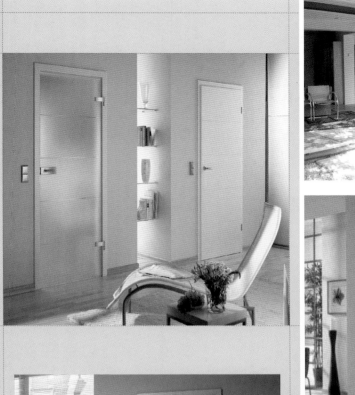

Everything you need for your Underfloor Heating system...

uponor

- A range of flexible, time saving Underfloor Heating products.
- The largest, dedicated, fully trained technical department.
- A market leading training facility
- Full design support
- Complete peace of mind

Underfloor Heating Small Area Packs

The Uponor Small Area Pack is a complete off the shelf Underfloor Heating kit* for small areas, such as one-room extensions and conservatories.

*Packs do not include floor insulation.

...water not included

⫸Rayotec Electric Underfloor Heating

Suitable for Tiles, Carpet, Wooden & Laminate Floors

The innovative ribbon heating mats allows greater choice of floor coverings, lower running costs & makes installation as easy as rolling out a carpet! Unlike other systems these mats can provide primary heating, not just floor warming. They are easy to install and very cost effective heating for home builders or renovators. Please send your floor plans for a *FREE* quotation.

Enjoy the benefits in just 3 easy steps!

1. ROLL OUT INSULATION

2. LAYOUT MATS ACCORDING TO PLAN

3. LAY FLOORING & ENJOY!

Systems start from just £85 (inc. VAT & Delivery)
15 years manufacturer's warranty

(UL) (N) CE

UNDERFLOOR HEATING

Advanced Underfloor Heating and Solar Systems

Our triple tube underfloor heating system offers outstanding performance and a low overall installation cost.

It's 'Contra-flow' action provides rapid heat transfer and even heat with no cold spots.

The increased surface area means that expensive diffusion plates are not required.

Exceptional value for a quality product.

Ask us about including Solar Power to your heating and hot water requirement.

⫸Rayotec

CONTACT US FOR A BROCHURE AND FREE QUOTATION

Rayotec Limited Sunbury Business Centre, Unit 3 Brooklands Close Sunbury-on-Thames TW16 7DX

tel : (01932) 78 48 48   **web** : www.rayotec.com

Strip Bath

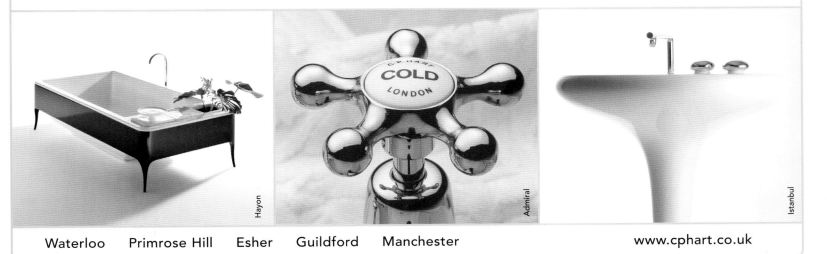

MAKE YOUR SELF-BUILD OR RENOVATION PROJECT A SUCCESS

Thinking about, or in the middle of converting, renovating or building your own home, turn to Britain's best selling self-build and renovation magazine, Homebuilding & Renovating.

Full of inspiration and ideas from readers' homes to practical features about building or renovating plus a complete beginner's with advice on raising finance to getting planning permission or estimating build costs and much more...

GET YOUR COPY TODAY...

Homebuilding & Renovating magazine is available from WHSmiths, Tesco, Sainsburys, Borders, Menzies and all other good newsagents. For up to date subscription prices visit our website or call us:

Visit www.homebuilding.co.uk
Call 01527 834435